Praise for
(not quite) Mastering the Art of French Living

"A bicontinental life with more pratfalls than a Jerry Lewis movie."

—Christine Muhlke, *The New York Times*

"Failure to speak French has never been so funny! Greenside may never master the gender of French nouns, but he sees straight through the French. A smart, delicious memoir of life off the beaten track in France."

—Julie Barlow, author of *The Bonjour Effect*

"Learning how to shop, drive, and eat in France have their own sets of rules, and *(not quite) Mastering the Art of French Living* tackles them with a soupçon of humor. From buying a lamp to mastering mollusks (oysters), and learning the right—and wrong ways—things are done in France, Mark Greenside perseveres . . . and succeeds."

—David Lebovitz, author of *My Paris Kitchen*

"Mark Greenside recounts hilarious experiences only a foreigner can have in France, for they're the ordinary things of French life that go unnoticed by the locals yet are the funniest of things for someone from the 'outside!'"

—Susan Herrmann Loomis, author of *On Rue Tatin*

"With self-effacing humor, Mark Greenside shows us how to adjust to life *à la française* with plenty of perseverance and little personal pride so that you lucky readers don't have to have learn these lessons the hard way."

—Ann Mah, bestselling author of *The Lost Vintage*,
from her foreword

"Mark Greenside does an exceptional job of describing the many fish-out-of-water moments of life abroad. He also writes movingly about how his experiences in a new land have changed him. This is a book not to be missed!"

—*myfrenchlife.org*

"Surely the funniest American to land in France since Jerry Lewis, Greenside 'masters' the baffling rules of French life in principle, while mangling them—to hilarious effect—in practice. A delightful pas de deux of humor and wisdom."

—William Alexander, author of *Flirting with French*

"You cannot read this book, without thinking about spending a delicious slice of life in France."

—Aileen Bordman, author of *Monet's Palate Cookbook*

"A hilarious look at trying to navigate life in France, literally and figuratively."

—Michelle Richmond, author of *The Year of Fog*, *The Marriage Pact*, and *Golden State*

"Thoughtful, heartfelt, and really, really funny."

—Keith Van Sickle, author of *One Sip at a Time: Learning to Live in Provence*

"I recommend this book to anyone looking to read a funny living-abroad memoir!"

—Darlene, *Bonjour: A Francophile Blog*

"Jam-packed with essential information for anyone visiting France or living there."

—Janine Marsh, *The Good Life France*

(not quite)
MASTERING
the ART of
FRENCH
LIVING

Also by Mark Greenside

I'll Never Be French (no matter what I do)

I Saw a Man Hit His Wife (stories)

The Night at the End of the Tunnel, or Isaiah Can You See?

(not quite)
MASTERING
the ART of
FRENCH
LIVING

Mark Greenside

Foreword by Ann Mah

Skyhorse Publishing

First Paperback Edition 2021

Skyhorse Publishing books may be purchased in bulk at special discounts for sales promotion, corporate gifts, fund-raising, or educational purposes. Special editions can also be created to specifications. For details, contact the Special Sales Department, Skyhorse Publishing, 307 West 36th Street, 11th Floor, New York, NY 10018 or info@skyhorsepublishing.com.

Skyhorse® and Skyhorse Publishing® are registered trademarks of Skyhorse Publishing, Inc.®, a Delaware corporation.

Visit our website at www.skyhorsepublishing.com.
Visit the author's website at markgreenside.com.

10 9 8 7 6 5 4

Library of Congress Cataloging-in-Publication Data is available on file.

Cover illustrations and design by Jessie Kanelos Weiner

Print ISBN: 978-1-5107-6547-4
Ebook ISBN: 978-1-5107-3111-0

Printed in the United States of America

To Donna Umeki, my wwwwife

Contents

Note to the Reader

If you're lucky, some of the things that happened to me will happen to you. If you're luckier, some of them won't.

Several names of people and places have been changed to protect them and me from everyone.

Foreword

If you've picked up this book, I'm guessing you dream about being in France. Me, too. Especially during this era of COVID, which has limited most European travel and made exiles of those of us who consider it our spiritual home, the allure of France has never seemed more alluring—or distant.

Mark Greenside gets it. As an American who spends his summers in Brittany, Mark knows the exquisite agony of waiting all year to return to the small Breton town that first enchanted him thirty years ago. Mark knows what it's like to dream of buckwheat galettes while spooning up a mundane bowl of oatmeal. He, too, has fallen under northern France's spell of liquid light and moody sea. And while pitfalls may lurk at every turn—arcane traffic rules, bizarre food, impossible shopping—Mark knows that it's perfectly possible to be thoroughly vexed by a country's culture and customs and hopelessly in love with it, all at the same time. In the pages of this book, Mark proves himself an astute guide, sharing with us readers the knowledge that he has paid a (hilarious) price to attain.

I wish I had read this book before renting my first car in France. For then, I would have felt less mortified by my first French car accident, which occurred approximately eight minutes after I picked up the vehicle, at a roundabout—an incident that Mark assures us is practically considered a rite of passage in France. I have been terrified of *rond-points* ever since—this too, Mark says, is common in France. I wish I had read this book before hosting my first French dinner party, for I would have known that corn is considered animal feed. And I wish I had read this book before the first fifteen times I went grocery shopping at the *supermarché*, for I would have known how on earth to unlock the carts from their chained imprisonment.

Thankfully, Mark reveals all these secrets and more in this witty and worthy book. With self-effacing humor, he shows us how to adjust to life *à la française* with plenty of perseverance and little personal pride so that you lucky readers don't have to learn these lessons the hard way.

There are many people who adore France; some of them also have an intimate knowledge of French culture. It is rare, however, to find a person who loves France and can share his hard-won wisdom with such humor and generosity of spirit. As my time away from France stretches from weeks and months to a year, it has been a joy to visit Brittany with Mark on my armchair travels. I hope that you may find a similar pleasure within these pages. And if you learn one thing from Mark, may it be this: "Under no circumstances forget the word for 'cone' when buying ice cream and ask for 'un con.' Don't ask why, just don't do it."

ANN MAH
JANUARY 2021
HANOI, VIETNAM

Preface to the Paperback Edition

Thirty years ago, I bought my house in Plobien and promised myself three things:

First, I'd pay all my bills on time, no questions asked, because there's nothing worse between friends and neighbors than bad money. And I did. I paid all my bills, no questions asked.

Second, I wouldn't sleep with any of the women in my village—I was single at the time—because the only thing worse than bad money between friends and neighbors is good sex. To my surprise and chagrin, this proved easier than I thought, as none of the local women seemed interested in sleeping with me.

Third, I wouldn't write about my experiences. I was writing my first book at the time, a collection of short stories, but I vowed not to write about my life in France. To write about it meant observing, evaluating, separating myself, taking notes, journals, keeping documents, none of which I wanted to do. I wanted to live the life, not observe it. I wanted immersion, not distance. And for the first fifteen years, I kept my promise and didn't write anything about my life in Brittany except letters to friends.

I did tell stories, though, and people liked them and asked for more—even French people. So after fifteen years, I began writing them, and those stories became the basis of my first book about living in France, *I'll Never Be French (no matter what I do)*. It's about my not wanting to go to France and going; meeting Madame P and her family, Sharon and Jean and their family, Martin and Louise, the insurance guy, floor guy, and oil guy; seeing and experiencing Brittany's light, land, sea, sky, culture, and food; buying a house and fixing it up; arguing with my neighbor about my trees; my fiftieth birthday party.

The book was well received, and I was happy with it until the day my friend Marshall said, "There's nothing in it about day-to-day life," and I realized he was right. Everything I wrote about was a one–off: going to Brittany for the first time, meeting people for the first time, buying a house, fixing it up, my fiftieth birthday. They're all one-time, special events . . . and that led me to write this book, my second book about living in France.

(not quite) Mastering the Art of French Living is about regular, day-to-day life in France—my regular life, which is not exactly like other people's regular life, but close enough: chapters on driving, shopping, banking, cooking, eating, healing, and speaking. The book explores mysteries and conundrums I've never read about in the zillions of books I've read by Americans living in France. Things like:

- What happens when you have a car accident *and* it's your fault
- How to pay a parking ticket
- Getting money out of your bank and post office
- Shopping when you can't find the item you want, don't know what it's called, can't pronounce its name to ask for it, and can't read the label if you find it
- And most importantly, when you can and can't touch the tomatoes at the market and in stores, and what to cook for French people you've invited to dinner

When I bought the house, I thought my three biggest problems would be replacing the roof, the furnace, and the septic tank, but I was wrong. The big things are easy. The roof leaks, I call Bruno, Gilles, or Rick—I like to spread the burden—ask whom I should hire to repair it, hire them, write a check, and hope that everything turns out OK—and it usually does.

It's the small stuff that beats me every time. I can't call friends *every* day for *every* dilemma, though I'd like to. If I did, I wouldn't have any friends. Instead, I lunge and plunge my way through my French life, trying to learn the French ropes— the whos, whats, whens, wheres, whys, hows, and how nots of French life—incident by incident, two steps forward, one step back, sometimes vice versa.

If you like the small stuff, this book is for you, and if you like the big stuff, this book is also for you, because every tiny something looms large.

Looking back, I see some things have changed since I wrote about them, especially in areas like medicine, food, and banking. Individual medical costs are going up, services are diminishing, fewer and fewer doctors will make house calls—but the system is still French and one of the best and most generous and effective in the world. Food is more commercial, frozen, and less artisanal, but French-commercial and American-commercial are as different as Brillat-Savarin and Velveeta. Banking is more computerized, and last summer, for the first time, a clerk asked to see my ID before accepting my check. I showed her my California driver's license, which looks nothing like a French driver's license, and she turned it every which way looking for the verification data she couldn't find, shrugged, and cashed my check, verifying the new France is like the old France, difficult, complicated, contradictory, and confusing—at least for me.

Looking forward, I wonder how long this book will be a guide, and when and where it will become a history, which things I've written about will change and which will remain the same, assured that no matter what, where, and how much they change, however they work, whatever they become, they will be French.

MAY 2021

Preface

In the spring of 1991, against my wishes and all my judgments, my girlfriend persuaded me to spend the summer in Brittany, Finistère: "The end of the world." I wanted to go to Saskatchewan where people speak English, where I could get to by driving instead of flying, and where Americans, if not actually liked, weren't actually hated. This isn't the last time I was wrong.

We rented a house in Plobien, a village of about six hundred people, from an English lady named Sally, and within days, I fell under Brittany's spell: its shimmering light, white cotton candy clouds, and blue-green sea; its granite viaducts and dolmen; ambling rivers, heathered hills, huge skies, beaches, and tides.

I met Monsieur and Madame P and their two sons, Henri and Philippe. Madame was the keeper of the keys to Chez Sally and the knower of everything I needed to know, my first friend, and future Aladdin and guardian angel.

I also met Jean and Sharon and their boys, Yann and Noé. Jean is Breton, a filmmaker, Sharon is Canadian, Quebecois, a painter, and teacher. They are *soixante-huitards*, sixties folks like me, and unlike Monsieur and Madame P, fluent in English: she from birth, he from her.

As it turned out, eight weeks were four weeks too many for my girlfriend and me. By the end of the summer I was out of love with her, in love with Brittany, and ready to return to California—then I bought a house in France.

I, who don't speak French, don't like to fly, who owned nothing at the time but the clothes in my closet and an eighteen-year-old Volvo, borrowed money from my mom and bought a 120-year-old stone house six thousand miles and twenty-one hours (door-to-door) from California. That was twenty-plus years ago, and I've never regretted it—which I can't say about a lot of things I've done.

Over the years, I've met and become friends with many people: Bruno, Françoise, Gilles, Tatjana, Hugo, Nadine, Jean-Pierre, Joëlle, Ella, Rick, Martin, Louise, Sally, and Monsieur Charles. These people, along with Monsieur and Madame P and Sharon and Jean, have become my family and have served as a combination Red Cross and Salvation Army, as they have repeatedly saved and rescued me—mostly from myself—more than they can believe and I want to remember.

All of them are in this book, along with my American friends Peggy, LeRoy, Jerry, Sheryl, Bob, Loni, and Donna—who entered my life and changed it forever, for better, and who unbelievably speaks French, likes France, and agreed to marry me and live part of every summer in Plobien.

This is my world, the Old World that is constantly new to me. I've been coming to France—Brittany—for more than twenty years now, and I'm still trying to master the art of French living. For a guy who likes to think he knows what he's doing, it's been an unexpectedly bumpy ride.

Driving (Me Nuts)

I started driving when I was seventeen and had my first accident when I was seventeen and a half. I'd successfully completed driver's education in high school and was convinced I knew what I was doing, which is often the first and best sign that I don't. In those days, driving was a sign of adulthood—manhood—even more than sexual experience, probably because it was easier to get a car than a girl, and definitely easier than getting a girl into a car, which was my chief aim at the time.

My driver's ed teacher was Mr. F, a pleasant man who was also a history teacher and tennis coach. He liked teaching driver's ed most because it was where he could pay the least attention. I passed the class easily (we all did) but I didn't learn anything about driving or safety or sanity or adulthood (no one did), which is why I had the accident.

It was one thirty in the morning. I had just dropped Shelly Grebin at her house after summoning the courage of Jeanne d'Arc, Socrates, Galileo, and Shackleton to kiss her under the strobe lamp her parents left on to dissuade her, or me, or us. I was elated, having accomplished my two chief goals in life: getting a girl into my car and kissing her. I was also slightly drunk from partying all night. I sped through a red light, hitting another car and totaling mine. Amazingly, no one was hurt.

I had my second accident twenty years later. A woman named Bea Bee, a name I will never forget, dead-stopped her car at an all-clear, open-all-the-way freeway entrance, and I nicked her impetigoed Volkswagen. I gave her a check for five hundred dollars for invisible, caused-by-her damages, and that was that.

Since then, I've had my share of speeding and parking tickets. Nothing unusual, really—until I started driving in France. Driving in France, especially before GPS and Mapquest (but even after), is more complicated and difficult than Magellan's sailing and *navigating the seven seas: he had the stars and a guy in the crow's nest to guide him; I have myself and French signage, and more often than not, that's not enough.*

Getting My Car

Every summer begins with a telephone call to reserve my car, and even though there's never been a problem, and I know I'm going to get my car, it's always a surprise when I do. Surprise is my new routine.

I start in January, when I'm feeling most optimistic (about the Giants and a new year) and most pessimistic (about the Giants and a new year), and call Rob. He has his own agency—Liddiard Travel—and always manages a discount greater than everyone else's. Plus, he's friendly and thorough, and answers all of my questions no matter how many times I ask them. I tell him my pick-up and return dates and locations, and he goes into action, searching for the cheapest combination possible: Renault or Peugeot, gas or diesel, rent or lease. I do this even though we both know the outcome: Renault (sans GPS), gas, and lease.

This year isn't any different: it's Renault (sans GPS), gas, and lease. What is different is I'm getting my car at Aéroport Charles de Gaulle and driving to Brittany, something I haven't done in more than a decade. When I made the reservations six months and six thousand miles ago, it seemed like a good idea—the way invading Iraq must have seemed to W.

My plane lands on time, two o'clock in the afternoon, five o'clock in the morning California time. Thanks to a mileage award, I'm flying United. Except for the food, less legroom, and smaller and harder seats that barely recline, it's just like flying Air France. This is what I'm thinking as we taxi to the docking area and the pilot announces, "Welcome to Paris, Charles de Gaulle Airport, Terminal One."

This is how I learn that Terminal Two, the newest terminal, the one I've been landing at for years, with its spacious, airy, light-filled, air-conditioned, glass and wood interior; many free, comfortable chairs and benches to sit on; clear signage; helpful personnel; easy access to a newly automated, quick and efficient baggage claim; lots and lots of bathrooms—and elevators and escalators that work—is where Air France lands. United and the other U.S. airlines have to share Terminal One, the oldest terminal and the worst, as I recall from the last time I was here, ten years ago.

I pull my briefcase with laptop, three-hundred-page manuscript, and several notebooks filled with notes from the overhead bin and lug it to the baggage area, a trek that makes Mao's long march seem like a lark. My back aches, my shoulders, my hands. I arrive looking and feeling like Quasimodo. I've been traveling fifteen and a half hours, door to de Gaulle. All I want is to get my luggage and car and drive to Senlis, where I'm spending the night, so I can wake refreshed in the morning and drive to Plobien.

Ninety minutes later—after the death march to the baggage area, a forty-minute wait for baggage, plus the additional wait for customs, which goes smoothly, but not quickly, because only three of the sixteen booths are open, and one of those is closed for a worker's break—I'm ready to go.

I wheel my baggage cart through the doors, into the terminal, and realize the games haven't even begun. People are everywhere, moving every which way. I know there's a protocol, there has to be a protocol—there's *always* a protocol—but I don't see it.

I push my two-bags-plus-briefcase-laden cart into the crowd like a bumper car, saying, "Pardon-moi, excusez-moi," with every hit. I'm looking for the elevator to the ground floor. I know I want the ground floor, because Rob at Liddiard told me, in English, "Take the elevator to the ground floor and look for Renault."

I search and search and can't find an elevator. I wheel the cart back and forth and in circles. The entire terminal is a circle. I make a complete loop. I want to sit down, but the few free, uncomfortable, non-restaurant, non-shoe-shine, non-toilet places to sit are taken. An apple-cheeked boy of about fourteen walks up to me and says, "Monsieur?"

I think he's going to ask *me* for directions. "Oui..."

"May I help you?"

I could kiss him. This is France, I *could* kiss him, maybe I should, I don't know. I tell him I'm looking for the elevator. His face turns grave. He looks serious. He takes my cart and leads me in another series of circles to a dark corner under the stairs and points to a wedge fifteen people deep, each person commandeering one or two overflowing baggage carts, waiting for the elevator. In the U.S., this would drive me nuts, but in France, a nation whose people lack the chromosome for line-formation, this is the way it is. Wedges of people are everywhere: movie theaters, supermarkets, post offices, banks, bathrooms.

I thank the lad, get in the wedge, and wait, relaxing until I see in front of me, along with everyone else, an old lady in a wheelchair, pushing a cart, and once again I'm reminded there's no coddling of the weak, needy, or infirm in France, which doesn't bode well for me.

I get behind the old lady and wait. There's no pushing, grumbling, anger, or rage. Everyone accepts this as normal. *C'est normal*. I accept it, too—even when I see two of the three elevators aren't working, and the one that is is barely large enough for three or four people with carts, meaning the wedge never gets smaller. Three people enter the elevator; three people join the wedge. It's like some immutable law of French physics.

Thirty minutes later, I push myself and my cart into the elevator along with the lady in the wheelchair and an African family of four. The African man pushes the button. The elevator goes up. I didn't even know there was an up. It stops. The doors open. No one gets on or off. He pushes the button again. It goes down, back to the floor where we started. The doors open. The people in front move forward, then scowl when they see it's us and there's no room for them. The African man quickly pushes the button, and we go down.

The wheelchair lady and African family push off in opposite directions, knowing where they are and where they're going, probably in both the geographical and ontological sense. Not me. I stand there, lost, frozen, mesmerized, surrounded by every car rental agency in the world except Renault. I'm looking for a sign that says Renault. I ask four people, "Où est Renault?" and get pointed in four different directions. I follow each one and get nowhere. An old man who has been watching me stands and lumbers over to me, takes my hand—to balance himself, I tell myself—and leads me to a telephone on the wall under a sign that says TT. He points with his other hand and says, "Renault." I thank him and marvel at how anyone finds anything. Then I shudder as I realize I've already been lost twice in the last forty minutes and I haven't even left the airport. What's going to happen when I hit the road?

I pick up the phone, and before I can speak, the person on the other end says, "Oui."

"Parlez vous anglais?" I ask.

"Non."

"Bon. Je suis Greenside. Vous êtes Renault?"

"Oui. Votre nom?"

"*Greenside,*" I repeat, and realize I'm going to have to spell it. G is *zheh*; R is *ehr*; *euh* is E; *enn; ess; ee* is I; D is *day;. euh.* "Zheh-ehr-euh-euh-enn-ess-ee-day-euh."

"Cinq minutes," he says and hangs up.

Five minutes what! Walk? Drive? Crawl? I go to them? They come to me? Merde. Double merde. I wait five minutes, ten, fifteen, convinced I'm supposed to be somewhere else when a young man of eighteen or nineteen arrives, calling, "Monsieur Greenseed, Monsieur Greenseed!"

"Oui," I call back.

"Monsieur Greenseed?"

"Oui."

"Anglais? Ing-lish?"

"Américaine," I say. An American girl.

He shakes my hand and smiles. I smile, too, happy to be found even if he thinks I'm a transvestite.

He leads me to the van, puts my bags in the back, and races to the car rental location, chatting all the way in rapid-fire French and heavily accented broken English, not caring in the least that I don't understand a word he says in either language. He stops at a tiny shack with the sign TT on it: the Renault office. It looks to me like a shed for a lawn mower.

I walk in. There are no chairs or benches to sit on, and

no music to comfort or distract. It's worse than the Department of Motor Vehicles in Oakland, and the woman behind the counter looks just as forbidding, jabbing the air with a pen when she speaks, her hair *and* face pulled tight in a bun. I get in line and wait. When it's finally my turn, I say, "Bonjour," and resignedly ask, "Parlez vous anglais?"

"Yes," she says, "bien sûr, of course," and transforms into a freckle-faced fairie, speaking flawless English with an Irish lilt. She hands me a sheaf of papers, all in French, and tells me where to sign. I do, not knowing or caring if I'm making her my heir. She tells me the insurance covers everything except flat tires, how to get road service, and, most importantly, where to get gas.

I already know leased cars in France come with an empty gas tank. Basically, what I'll get is fumes. I'll have five minutes to find a gas station, and God help me if I don't. So when the lady says, "Take the first right after you exit to the left and you'll find the Total station," I write it down: *take first right after the exit.* I fold the paper in half and put it in my shirt pocket. She hands me a map of Paris and its environs, says, "Bon voyage," and points out the window to my car, a Twingo.

It looks like a stubbed toe, a windup toy, something designed by LEGO. The only distinguishing features are the red license plates that tell everyone I'm a foreigner and that they should stay far, far away from me and this car.

I place my bags and briefcase in the back, which surprisingly has a lot of space, open the driver's door, and sit down. I feel like I'm on a ride at Disneyland. The car's so basic, I'm glad it has seats. The fellow who met me at the airport walks over and explains how to operate the car—in French. I nod whenever he pauses, and say, "Bon. Bon. Oui," not having a clue what he's saying. When he finishes, he gives me the keys, shakes my hand, and says, "Bonne chance."

I adjust the mirrors and the seat, start the car, and look at the gas gauge: sure enough, a milliliter above empty. I back up and exit left, feeling confident until I get to the first right and see it's a service road. The *next* right is the A-1 freeway entrance to Paris. There are no cars behind me, so I stop. I definitely do not want to go to Paris, and will never get there anyhow, given the amount of gas I have. But a service road? That doesn't seem right either. I take out the Mapquest directions I smartly printed a week ago—who needs a GPS when there's Mapquest?—and look at them for the first time.

Step One says, "Start out going south." I open the window and look for the sun. It's Paris, June, there is no sun. Step Two says, "Take the first right." I take the note out of my pocket. The Renault lady also said, "Take the first right." I remind myself of the pride French people take in their use of precise language and logic—and how first means *first*, not second . . .

I follow Mapquest, the Irish lass, and French logic and turn right, onto the service road, and immediately realize they're all wrong. I take the next right, hoping to loop back, and begin driving in circle after concentric circle around the service areas of Aéroport Charles de Gaulle, watching the fuel gauge dip, drop, slip, slide closer to E, then beyond to the red, flashing panic light . . .

I have no phone, no language, no AAA card—and no idea where I am or where I'm going—and I'm about to run out of gas. My hands are so sweaty I can barely hold onto the wheel. I turn right again and again and again and drive down another service road winding up back where I started. I take the *next* right, the *second* right—so much for French logic!—and see the Total station up ahead. I coast to the pump.

My legs are shaking when I get out of the car. I wait several seconds and carefully remove the green unleaded gas hose, making sure not to use the yellow diesel hose, because I made that mistake once before, and start filling the tank, amazed as always that I pay *after* it's filled. In the U.S., I'd have to leave a body part or a family member as a down payment.

I go inside to pay—it costs sixty dollars to fill the tank of the economiest of cars—then return to the car and look at the Mapquest directions. I've already driven the first thirteen steps—from Renault to the Total station. There are fifteen more to Senlis. I'm going to Senlis because it's twenty miles away, less than three miles from the highway exit, and avoids—at least for today—the Périphérique, the thirty-six kilometer bypass loop that allows you to circle Paris forever and is the best representation of the eight circles of hell on Earth.

I start the car and enter the A-1, following the signs for Lille, where I don't want to go—a common occurrence when driving in France. Forty minutes later, I park in front of a hotel. I enter and make my usual request for a room. "Je voudrais une chambre pour un noir avec un lait." I would like a room for a black with a milk, (instead of "Je voudrais une chambre pour une nuit avec un lit," I'd like a room for a night with one bed). Unbelievably, the man hands me a key to room 303, the third floor.

I drag my two heavy bags and briefcase, one by one, up the forty, dark, progressively narrower, winding stairs to the *fourth* floor, because as I always forget, the ground floor isn't counted in France. I lie down on the bed and crash. It's 6:30. I've been in France four and a half hours, and I've managed to travel twenty miles from the airport. There's a lesson here, but I don't know what it is.

I wake up early, refreshed, and eat breakfast. It's a six-hour drive from Paris to Plobien. I should be there by early afternoon. I put my bags in the car, start the engine, and look at Mapquest, then put it away and look at the map. Senlis and Aéroport Charles de Gaulle are northeast of Paris. I'm going northwest. There ought to be a way to drive due west, but I don't see it. I put the car in gear, reluctantly enter the A-1 and follow the signs to Paris, where I don't want to go, swearing, as I do every year, that next year I'm getting the GPS.

I pass the airport, take a huge breath, and brace myself. I'm about to commit one of the bravest, most dangerous, blood-chilling acts in my life: I'm going to enter the Périphérique.

My heart's pounding. I'm sweating. I'm more afraid of this than a bungee jump off the Brooklyn Bridge. I'm looking for signs to Lyon, where I don't want to go, gripping the wheel, staying in my lane, letting the traffic lead me. Signs whiz past me, appearing from nowhere, without regularity or warning. I'm hugging a middle lane in case I suddenly have to veer right for an exit or left for a fork in the road, trying not to hit or get hit by the trucks, buses, taxis, vans, motorcycles, and cars switching lanes and passing me on both sides at 120 kilometers per hour, 40 km/h over the speed limit of 80 that I'm driving. It's worse than the "MTA song," where you want to get off and you can't. Here I don't want to get off, and I'm afraid I will, and it will be the wrong exit, and I'll never get back. It's the harrowing ride around Charles de Gaulle airport, running out of gas, driving in circles, feeling completely lost and confused, logarithmically multiplied. It's Fantasyland meets panic room.

After fifteen minutes, I feel like I'm going into anaphylactic shock. Blindly, I follow a van with a picture of a chicken on it—a metaphor if I ever saw one. I pass exits for Strasbourg, Metz, Lille, Rouen, and aim toward Bordeaux, where I don't want to go. Bordeaux is *south*west. I want to go *north*west—but it's the only *western* destination I see, so I head there. I'm looking for the A-6, which connects to the A-10, which converges with the A-11 in the direction of Orléans and Rambouillet, two other places I don't want to go, but which are closer to Brittany than Bordeaux.

Miraculously, I see the sign for the A-6, take it, and success-fully connect with the A-10, but miss the A-11, and wind up in Orly Airport. The good news is I've been here before, I have a full tank of gas, and Orly is smaller than de Gaulle. The bad news is it takes me an hour and an eighth of a tank of gas to get out and back on the A-10, looking for the A-11, once again following the signs toward Bordeaux, because my other choices are worse.

Thirty kilometers before Orléans, I stop at an *aire,* a rest stop. My whole body is shaking—from fear, frustration, and the vibrations of the nearby idling trucks. I have to go to the bathroom, but I've stopped at the only *aire* in France that doesn't have a toilet, and I'm not French enough to pee on a tree. I unfold the map and see I've gone wrong again. I drive to the next exit, which by another immutable French law is never less than twenty-five kilometers in the direction you don't want to go, turn around, and drive sixty-five kilometers back to connect with the A-11 to Le Mans, the A-81 to Laval, and the N-157 to Rennes, where I miss the bypass because it's not called a bypass, but a *rocade*—what the hell is a *rocade?* It's not even in my dictionary—and drive straight into the center of town (*centre ville*) of the capital city of Brittany at two o'clock in the afternoon when everyone is getting into their car to go back to work after their two-hour lunch, complete with wine. It's almost enough to make me wistful about the Périphérique.

I drive around and around *centre ville*, avoiding pedestrians, bikes, cars, prams, and buses, searching for signs to Brest. There are none, no signs for anything west. Clearly, there's no "Go west, young man" in France. I can go north to Mont-Saint-Michel, east, back to Paris, or south to Nantes.

For no reason at all, I choose south, which turns out by the law of averages to be right. As soon as I'm out of the city I see a sign to Quimper and follow it all the way to Plobien. I arrive at the house at five thirty, ten hours after I left Senlis, me and my Twingo intact, and to my great surprise I've already forgotten about Aéroport Charles de Gaulle and the ten-hour drive, and I'm happy. . . . "Happy" being one of the operative words for my life in France.

My First Accident

My friend Peggy, who's fluent in French, has come to Plobien to help me. She's been here before with her husband, Larry. This time she's alone, and she's stayed a week, adding to the questions, lore, and consternation my neighbors have about me. As in, who is this guy, anyhow?

French people marry young, have children young, and are grandparents by their late forties. And here I am, of grandparent age and living alone. I'm married, but Donna's self-employed and doesn't have summer-long teacher vacations, which means most of the time I'm in France I'm solo. To the people in my *petite ville*, this makes me an oddity and a challenge: what to do with me?

Mostly, I think, they pity me. After observing French men, I understand why.

Every French man I know is much more capable than I am with things mechanical, electrical, and physical. Something breaks, they fix it. They change electric sockets, rewire lamps, repair lawnmowers, insert fireplaces, fix leaky faucets, replace roofs, rebuild houses, but hardly anyone from my generation knows how to wash his clothes or fry an egg. When it comes to the domestic, they are helpless. Without fail, once a week, when I hang my laundry on the clothesline, couples of all ages walk past the house, holding hands, and take note. The women smile and nod at me in silent appreciation, perhaps collusion, maybe even hope, and the men grumble, a sound so familiar, universal, and disparaging I understand it immediately: 'Nuh-uh. No way, baby. Not me. Not a chance.'

The result is women visit me at the house. Men visit, too, but less often. Mostly, I think, because whenever they do, I ask for their help. Can you fix this? Look at that? Tell me what to do here? The women visit because I'm an anomaly, and because I have something to give to them. They arrive at different times of the day, late morning, afternoon, early evening—never at lunch, *midi*, or dinnertime. They always bring something; flowers or vegetables from their gardens, something they've cooked, or an invitation to dinner at their home, as if they, themselves, aren't enough. They take their favorite kitchen chair and sit at the table, some facing the window, looking at the geraniums, the river, and trees; others facing the dining-living room and the granite walls, terracotta floor, and fireplace. They sip tea or coffee I prepare for them and they talk,

sometimes smoking, telling me things they know I can't understand, suspecting I do, knowing also I couldn't tell anyone what
I heard if I wanted to.

My American friends visit me because it's France, and I'm
here, and they know I need all the help I can get. Hence
Peggy.

I'm driving her to the airport outside of Quimper so she can
fly to Paris to meet Larry, who doesn't speak French, and is
arriving at Aéroport Charles de Gaulle with his luggage and
two bikes. His greatest fear, which I fully understand, is that
she won't be there, and he'll have to get to the car rental place
by himself, which, he made perfectly clear before she left,
would be grounds for dismembering or divorce, whichever
hurt most. She left a week before he did because she's a dear
friend, loves France, and I hired her thirty years ago for a job
she still has and likes. She volunteered to help me with things
I don't have a prayer of doing myself—like understanding my
insurance policy and paying my water bill over the phone. She
volunteered the evening she heard me practicing my French.
"Je voudrais un verre du vent." I would like a glass of wind. But
it was, "Je voudrais une chambre pour une noir avec une lait,"
that cinched it.

I'm taking the old route through Quimper because it's the route
I took the only other time I drove to this airport. Luckily, over
the years, I've learned a few things about driving in France:
navigating the fantasy of speed limits; gauging the safest distance between vehicles in centimeters; parking anywhere I can.

I've also learned about relations with other drivers (no guns, horns, yelling, or digital finger waving), pedestrians (never have the right of way; crossing the street—*any* street—is a life-threatening, nearer-to-God experience), and police (speak Franglish). But the most basic rule of driving in France is this: there is no grid. There is no straight line to anything.

France discovered roundabouts, *ronds-points*, somewhere in the recent past, and driving has never been the same. Maybe it's a nationalistic thing, the desire to replicate the Place de l'Etoile on every ten to fifteen kilometers of non-highway roadway, or maybe someone went to England in the 1950s, saw what the English did with their roads, and returned with an idea and a plan to better them. In any event, *ronds-points* are everywhere and determine the geography of French driving. To go west, you drive east. To go north, you drive south. The good news is you can circle a *rond-point* for eternity trying to decide which way to go. The bad news is the odds are you'll choose wrong. But the best news is up the road, not more than ten or fifteen kilometers away, there will be another *rond-point*, and you'll have another chance to try your luck, and luck is what it takes, believe me, because greeting you at every entrance to every *rond-point* in France is the sign *cédez le passage*: you don't have the right of way. It's France's mantra from Caesar to the Maginot Line, direct, confusing, and ineffective—like much of the road signage in France.

It's eight forty-five in the morning, and we're approaching Quimper. There's not much traffic, and it's a beautiful, cloudless, blue-sky sunny day. I'm carefully following the signs with the name of the airport—Pluguffan—and a picture of a plane beneath it, knowing at any time the signs could disappear, or I'll misread an arrow and go left instead of straight—something you'd think would be impossible, but I've done numerous times. Still, I'm confident. The airport is a forty-minute drive from the house, and I've given myself an hour and a half to get there. And Peggy is here, and she speaks French. *She* can ask for and understand the directions—if worse comes to worse comes to worse . . .

I'm moving with the traffic, maintaining five times more space between my Twingo and the car in front of me—about half a car's length—than any other driver on the road. We're almost at the cutoff to the airport, when I see Quimper's mother-of-all *ronds-points* up ahead . . . *Merde.*

Roundabouts in the United States are single lane, occasionally double, because Americans hate driving in circles. In Paris and other large cities, I've seen seven, eight, and ten lanes of cars circling around and around like hawks. This one is three lanes. I slow down, knowing I don't have the right of way: *Cédez le passage.* Every entrance to this *rond-point*, all six of them, has this sign, meaning everyone is confused, worried, anxious, and waiting for someone else to gun their motor and make the right move, so they won't make the wrong move and feel bad. Or worse, do bad. Understand this, and you'll understand French people. As immoral as they appear, they're moral. (The reverse of the U.S.: the more moral we appear, the more immoral. Think Rush Limbaugh, Newt Gingrich, and John Edwards.)

I stop—*cédez le passage*—and wait for my opportunity to enter the *rond-point*. Looking left into the oncoming traffic, I see an opening, hit the gas pedal, and plow broadside into a car that just zigged across three lanes of moving traffic to reach the exit that was carefully, scientifically, rationally, *logically* planned and placed eighteen inches to the right of my entrance. Boom! I hit him broadside, smashing in the passenger's side door. I look at Peggy. She's whiter than usual.

"You OK?" I ask.

She nods.

I leap out of the car to apologize and see how the other person is, though given that I'm driving a toy car and went from a dead stop to five kilometers an hour, how bad could he be? Still, I want to do what I can to not completely destroy Franco-American relations and not give them one more reason— McDonald's, global warming, peanut butter—to hate us.

"Vous allez bien?" I call.

He looks at me, blank.

I think it's my accent. So I say it again, louder and slower. "Vous . . . allez . . . bien . . . monsieur?"

He's walking toward me slowly, giving no recognition of hearing, seeing, knowing anything. I figure it's either *Night of the Living Dead* or I hit a narcoleptic. That's when I realize he's in shock. Shock! What is with these people? This was a nothing, a tap. No big deal. I look back at Peggy. She's sitting in the front seat, crying. Why? Because I hit the guy? Because she's going to miss her flight and her husband, my friend Larry, is going to divorce her and dismember me for making his worst nightmare come true? I'm torn between my friend, who's in a panic, and this stranger I just put in shock. This all happens in less than five seconds: (1) I'm out of the car; (2) I call to the guy once; (3) twice; (4) I look at Peggy and see she's in worse shape than the guy; (5) I stand there helpless.

This is where French people are at their best: in a crisis. In the U.S., everything is OK—I'm OK, you're OK, we're all OK—so when a crisis comes, we're like Peggy and me, lost, confused, and helpless. Not the French. They're often in crisis, so when a real one comes, they're ready.

Four young men, singly, on their own, stop their cars, and without saying a word to one another, go to work. Number One steps into the busy, now backed-up traffic and begins to direct the cars around us. It's almost nine o'clock, commuter time, and not a single horn has sounded. No one jumps out of his car screaming—or worse, shooting. No one throws anyone's dog into traffic—and there are plenty of them to throw. People just wait patiently, as they do in stores, airports, post offices, banks—unlike Americans, who like me, grumble, grouse, moan, curse, want to kill. It must be the difference between a two-thousand-year-old culture and a three-hundred-year-old culture. Time has a different meaning. When I say now, I mean yesterday. When they say now, they mean tomorrow. So the drivers, knowing they will now be late, patiently sit and wait for direction. Young man Number One provides it, as one by one, he waves cars safely around us.

Young man Number Two is on his cell phone. He calls his wife, his boss, the police, an ambulance—in that order. He's absolutely calm and buoyantly animated. He retells the story each time.

Number Three has joined the victim, who's in his late forties, looks in the prime of health, and is lying on the grass with his hands folded over his chest like a corpse. Number Three takes the guy's hand and holds it. He strokes his hair, his forehead, his cheek, like a lover or nurse or family member, speaking so gently, so comfortingly, reassuringly, so sweetly I think he's going to break into song. I don't get it. Unless the guy has some dread disease or the accident has triggered a bile or adrenaline so potent it's drowning him, the guy ought to be OK. Then it hits me: it's an insurance scam, the French version of whiplash, back pain, and stress. If this were New York, the guy would already be a millionaire: they'd pay him right here, on the spot.

Number Four, thanks to the unluck of the draw, gets Peggy and me. She's useless, sitting in the car, fretting and worried, probably having visions of divorce and dismembering. Number Four looks at me and steps backward. It's early morning—who's going to see me?—I'm wearing flip-flops, black socks, frayed and paint-stained cutoff jeans, a Curly of the Three Stooges T-shirt, and a green and yellow A's hat worn backward: this, in a country where women wear heels to go grocery shopping, and where only old men, young boys, and crazy people wear hats. Number Four quickly eliminates two of the three hat-wearing types and slowly steps forward, arms outstretched in either a welcome or self-defense, saying something I don't understand.

"Comment?" I say, pronouncing it *como*, as in "lake." What? He says it again.

I repeat it again. "Como?"

A look of fear streaks across his face. It's a look I've seen before—that look of sheer helplessness, a feeling I know French people abhor. Number Four looks at Numbers One, Two, and Three in envy. All is normal, natural, as to be expected. They are doing what should be done. Number Four also knows what should be done—knows his job is to take care of me—but he can't do it, because unlike Numbers One, Two, and Three, Number Four has to deal with a moron, an idiot, an ET, someone clearly not from around these parts. He begins to panic because *he* doesn't know what to do.

It's now my job to put *him* at ease. "C'est bien," I say. "C'est bon. Ça va?" He looks around—traffic is backed up, two cars are smashed, one lady is crying, one guy is lying on the grass holding his heart, and I'm repeating, "It's good. It's good. How you doing?"

Number Four begins to walk away from me. He walks over to Number Three, says something, and all of them—Numbers One, Two, Three, Four, and the victim, who, as in a miracle, manages to raise his head from the ground like the Ascension and stare, which in France is a very odd and disparaging thing to do. I understand and don't hold it against them. Like that, a *tableau vivant*, we wait.

The police arrive, sirens blaring—right out of the *Diary of Anne Frank* movie. It scares the bejesus out of me, and I know I'm going to one of those secret, deep-underground, Jean Genet prisons, rotten with mold, rats, cold, and spiders. Two cars stop. Five gendarmes get out. They park in the *rond-point*, causing even more of a traffic jam, and still no one in the surrounding cars objects or hits his horn, yells, grabs a gun, a knife, or a dog.

Immediately, the police fan out. Two go into the street, to the scene of the accident, and begin measuring who knows what. There are no brake marks, but one guy holds the tape measure and begins walking back and forth, left to right, right to left, in circles, around my car, the other car, measuring everything and writing it all down in a little black book, looking more and more certain with every notation he makes. The whole time he's doing this, the other guy watches.

Gendarme Number Three goes to the victim, bends over to look at his face, and says something to the four young men, who say something back to him, and now, all five are staring at me.

Gendarme Number Four is talking to Peggy, who suddenly comes alive, remembers her French, and begins to laugh. In five minutes, they've exchanged addresses and phone numbers and are on their way to becoming buddies for life.

Number Five is the captain, and he, unfortunately, gets me. He speaks as much English as I do French. He's asking me questions about what happened. I know he's asking me questions, because after he says something he stops, looks at me, and waits. The only word I understand is "passeport," which I don't have with me, so I hand him my California driver's license with a picture of me that's ten years old. After two or three additional attempts, the captain gives up and fills out the police report himself. He walks all around, looking about, jotting things down, talking to the guys who did the measurements, then heads over to the victim to get his story. I figure I'm going to jail for life—at the very least I'll be sued and lose my house and everything in it. I pull Peggy away from her new best buddy so she can explain I wasn't speeding, I had stopped—*cédez le passage*—and *monsieur* cut across three lanes of traffic, from inside to out, and *that's* why I hit him.

None of it makes a difference: I *should* have stopped. *Monsieur* has the right of way. What does make a difference, I later discover, is the accident happened at a *rond-point*, where most French accidents happen—and French drivers are as terrified of *ronds-points* as I am. Any accident at a *rond-point* is viewed with great understanding and commiseration, because all French drivers know someday it will happen to them. But I didn't know any of that then. I saw myself as the ugly American—more so than usual given my attire—about to become a hostage for U.S. foreign policy: They saw their opportunity and they took it . . .

That's when the ambulance arrives. The victim is still lying on his back, holding his chest, his face the color of ash, with five people hovering over him like a deathwatch. The ambulance, with the same Anne Frank siren, stops, blocks even more traffic, and three guys leap out as if on springs—like Jacques in a box—and race over to everyone, the four young men, the five gendarmes, Peggy and me and shake our hands, shouting, "Bonjour," "ça va," "salut," *before* they go to the victim. Hellos and *ça va*s in order, they go to the victim, take one look, put him on a stretcher and leave, siren blaring, waving and calling, "Bonne journée." They're there and gone in less than five minutes.

It's 9:20. Peggy's flight leaves in forty-five minutes, and she's supposed to be at the airport now. I'm thinking about this and how Larry is going to hate me when gendarme Number Four, Peggy's buddy-for-life, says something to the captain. The captain walks over and says something to me.

"Como."

He looks at me, wishing I was dead.

Number Four walks over and says something that sounds like, "allée."

I figure he's telling me to get off the road, stop blocking traffic, pull over to an alley, where they're going to grill and barbecue me. I'm about to protest when Peggy grabs my arm and says, "Let's go."

"Go where? To jail?"

"The airport."

"Oui," says the captain, "aéroport," waving us away like flies.

Peggy, it seems, explained to Number Four that we were on the way to the airport so she could take the flight to Paris to meet her husband and save her marriage. Number Four told the captain, and the captain, either in the spirit of marital fidelity, romance, or frustration, tells us to leave, go, *"Allez."* He'll finish writing the report. He hands me a phone number and tells Peggy to tell me to take her to the airport, then go to the hospital to meet the victim and fill out the required accident report for the insurance.

I'm flabbergasted. Here I am, a foreigner—a U.S. citizen—with no passport and a ten-year-old photo on my driver's license, looking like a Betty Ford dropout or a Jerry Lewis grad, not speaking French, having just hit a French citizen, sending him to the hospital, and the police are telling me to leave the scene, drive off, and call them when I get back. I'm supposed to find the guy I just hit to fill out the papers that prove I was wrong. If this was California, I'd be in jail. But this isn't California, it's France, and after gendarme Number Four bends the fender away from the tire, I say, "Bonne journée," and drive, very, very carefully, to the airport.

I follow the signs with the picture of the little plane, and we arrive just in time for Peggy's flight. We say our goodbyes, *au revoirs,* and à bientôts, and she kisses me French style, three times on my cheeks, telling me not to worry. "This is France," she says, "everything goes wrong and turns out right."

I hope that's true, because five minutes out of the airport, I'm lost.

There are many, many signs leading to the airport, all with a picture of a little plane on them. There are just as many signs leading away, but I have no idea which ones will take me to the hospital. Local road signs in France are good at telling you what's there, where you are, what road you are on, the name of the house across the street, the farm down the road, how to find the *supermarché*, industrial zone, or garbage dump. They're also very good at telling you how to get to Paris or one of the other ten major cities, like you're in St. Louis and the sign tells you how to get to New York. What they don't tell you is how to get from where you are to where you want to be if it's *not* the farm down the road or Paris. And since the signs do not direct you to other road numbers—as in, "this is the way to highway D-785"—and the same city avenue often changes its name ten times in ten blocks, it's impossible to figure out how to get where you want to go from where you are. Even a GPS wouldn't help: I don't know the address where I'm going or the name of the hospital, and even if I did, I couldn't spell it or pronounce it. No wonder the French invented existentialism; Sartre probably came up with it while driving on the Périphérique.

I'm in the suburbs of Quimper, searching for two signs, *Centre Ville* and *Toutes Directions*. *Toutes Directions* always takes you to a *rond-point* with a spur coming off it that will take you where you want to go (if you know), back to where you started, or to *Centre Ville*. *Centre Ville* is the most congested, difficult, time-consuming route into and out of a city. *Vieille Ville*, old city, is the only sign that's worse. Better to leave your car on the sidewalk and walk.

I'm driving around, looking for *Toutes Directions* or *Centre Ville*, hoping to avoid *Vieille Ville*, circling and recircling *ronds-points*, reading signs with Breton names, looking for the hospital or signs with tiny red crosses. I say *the* hospital, but Quimper actually has four. I know this because I follow the Red Cross signs to three other hospitals before I find Laënnec. Not that I care.

The truth is I'm not too keen on getting there. For all I know, the victim died of shock, a heart attack, or virulent anti-Americanism, and the police are waiting to take me off to jail. I don't even know if I'm entitled to make a phone call. And who would I call? Madame P? Jean? Sharon? Bruno? Gilles? And tell them what? I hit a French man, help *me*.

I drive around the parking lot looking for a place to park. Nothing is clearly marked, so I brave a place right in front of the hospital, hoping the red plates on my car signifying I'm a foreigner will scare the sane and reasonable away, and I won't get ticketed or towed.

I leave the car, half-expecting to never see it again, fully expecting to find the police or a corpse or a very incapacitated person in a full-body brace, suffering from backache, whiplash, nerve damage, impotency, necrophilia, Tourette's, Alzheimer's, something terribly, horribly, permanently triggered by the accident and me.

I walk around looking for Admitting and see a sign that says *Admission*—and hope it isn't referring to guilt—and there, in the lobby, sitting up and reading a magazine, is the victim. I recognize him by his green and yellow plaid pants and blue and green striped shirt, which as bad as it sounds, looks okay. He's calm, has color in his face, and is alive. He's not on a gurney, wearing a neck brace, or in a plastic bag. There's no walker in front of him, no cane, no IV, or priest in sight. It's a miracle, better than the Second Coming. This guy, on the verge of death from panic, is fine, reading a food magazine, eating a chocolate bar, and waiting for me. And that's the most amazing thing. He's absolutely sure I will be there. Why? Because the police captain said so, and because this is France. *C'est normal.* And here I am. I'm more surprised than he is.

"Bonjour," I say, and offer my hand.

He hesitates, but is French, so he takes it. "Bonjour."

"Ça va?"

"Oui, oui, bien."

I'm delighted and start to tell him how sorry I am—"Je suis désolé"—and how it was all my fault, and as I'm saying this I can't believe it. I just broke Dad's legal rule Number Two: Never admit to anything. I've already broken #1: Don't sign anything. In the U.S,. I'd be saying, "Why didn't you signal? Why didn't you swerve? Why did you cut across three lanes of traffic to exit?" I'd be looking for complicatory fault or negligence. But here, in France, I'm repeating, "I'm sorry, I'm sorry, I'm sorry," because I am, and because it's all I know how to say.

The fellow looks at me blankly, then speaks for five straight minutes, none of which I understand.

I look at him blankly. "Parlez-vous anglais?"

"Non. Parlez-vous français?"

"No."

Like magic, a young man, who looks to be about twenty years old and is a surgeon, offers his assistance. His English is better than my French, but not much. Still, it's all we have, and Jacques—the victim—and I stick to him like cheese to a *croque monsieur.*

What we—Jacques and I—are supposed to do is complete the insurance form and mail it in. That's why we're meeting, only neither of us has the form, speaks the other's language, or knows what to do. Then I remember the phone number the police captain gave me. I give it to Jacques and the twenty-year-old surgeon, and they go off together to call. Again, I think, am I nuts? These two guys are going to go off, work it all out, get their story straight, and screw me, the getting-uglier-by-the-second American. I'm just about ready to bolt when they return holding two pieces of paper with our names—mine and Jacques's—license plate and driver's license numbers, arrows, circles, and all kinds of information written in French. I know I'm going to be deported.

The surgeon explains the two pieces of paper contain information from the police report and that Jacques and I are to fill out the insurance claim and file it. He also explains that Jacques' car has been towed away, and he has no way to get home.

I figure the least I can do is drive him. Maybe I'll even win him over and we'll both accept blame and the report won't be so harsh. "I'll take him," I say to the surgeon.

He tells Jacques, who immediately turns white again, as if he's in shock. There's no way he's getting into a car with me. The surgeon says something innocuous and kind, trying not to hurt my feelings, while Jacques walks away and uses his cell phone to call a taxi.

I think he's being extravagant. He lives in a village forty-five minutes from the hospital, which means the taxi will cost between seventy-five and a hundred dollars, and *I'm* probably going to have to pay! I didn't know then that everything—the ambulance, his treatment and care, and the taxi—is all reimbursed by national health. When I find out, I want it, too.

I follow Jacques out of the hospital and stand next to him waiting for the taxi. "C'est joli." It's pretty. I point to the hospital. "C'est bon . . . Beau?" I nod to the sky. "C'est chaud, it's hot, je suis désolé." Jacques looks at me as if I'm nuts. Then he removes his cell phone from his purse and calls his wife, telling her about the accident, the car wreck, that everything is okay, he's okay, "d'accord, d'accord, d'accord, bien," and he'll be home soon with "l'américain."

The taxi arrives—quicker than any taxi I've ever called in the U.S. The driver leaps out of the car and the two of them,

Jacques and the driver, who may or may not be buddies—who can tell when everyone shakes hands and kisses like they're family—shake hands and get into the taxi, Jacques in the front seat, talking nonstop. Simultaneously, they turn to look at me. Through a series of hand motions, lots of pointing, yelling, and arm waving, I understand I'm supposed to follow them. I get into my car, and they take off: down narrow streets, congested avenues, through alleys, over speed bumps, and around *ronds-points*. I stay close enough to not lose them, and far enough away so I don't rear-end them when they jump the curb, pull onto the grass, and stop. I'm concentrating so much on not losing or hitting them I don't see we're back at the scene of the accident.

Jacques and the driver leap out of the taxi. I get out of my car. The two of them walk around, looking up, down, pointing, waving the papers with all those numbers, circles, and arrows, Jacques muttering, "Merde, merde, merde." He shows me. Everything in the police report is wrong: the name and location of the *rond-point*; the road I was on; the road he was exiting to. "Merde!" He's waving the papers, getting more and more excited. I take two steps backward to get out of his way. He takes three steps forward. He's in my face, and I think he's going to flip, but he only wants to show me again, make sure I understand, that the gendarmes, like police everywhere in the world, screwed up.

Cursing together—in French, Breton, and more English than I thought they knew—Jacques and the taxi driver get back in the taxi, and with hand, arm, and finger motions I'm becoming familiar with, tell me to follow.

Forty minutes later the taxi stops in front of a sad-looking apartment building. Jacques gets out of the car, walks around it, and shakes the driver's hand as if he's known him all his life.

The driver pulls away, leaving Jacques and me alone on a dark deserted street, facing an apartment building that looks like public housing in Chicago, circa 1960 . . . Our Lady of Cabrini Village. My first thought is to gun the motor and run. My next thought is Jacques is smaller than I am, I can take him if I have to—assuming he doesn't have a black belt in karate or a knife: proof once again, if needed, you can take the boy out of New York, but not New York out of the man.

He points to a place across the street, telling me where to park. I pull in and take the Renault booklet with me—the one the lady at the airport gave me when I rented the car, telling me to use it "if you need service or have an accident." I'm hoping it'll work for both.

I follow Jacques through cracked glass doors into a barren foyer, up narrow, more barren stairs that get darker and more claustrophobic with every step. In the U.S., I would never follow a man I didn't know (whose car I just wrecked) up dark stairs in a dingy building in a neighborhood I've never been with no one knowing where I am or whom I'm with, but this is France, and I do what's expected. I follow the rules even if I don't understand them, *especially* if I don't understand them.

Jacques unlocks the door, opens it wide, and lets me in. His wife is standing in the hallway, waiting, expectant, terrified. She's three times the volume of Jacques, about five-foot-five square, and she's palpably shaking. I don't know if it's because of the accident and she's worried about Jacques and the car, or she's scared I'll butcher her and her husband on the spot. We stand there staring at each other: she trembling like late Parkinson's, me squirming because I left the house at 8:15, and it's almost noon, and I have to pee. I blurt, "Madame toilette," which is like calling her "Mrs. Bathroom."

She points to a door, and I go in and pee like a horse.

When I exit, I see she's stopped shaking and has relaxed. Somehow, I've put her at ease by letting her know I'm more frightened and confused than she. I stand there, smiling like a jerk, then point to my Renault booklet and make a writing motion with my hand.

The next thing I know I'm sitting in their living room, which is tiny and crammed with more furniture than a Public Storage warehouse, drinking a Kir Royal. Ten minutes ago Madame was incapacitated by fear, but now, assured I'm neither seriously dangerous nor crazy, she moves into action. She sets a bowl of chips and a platter of *crudités* in front of me and adds one more setting to the table. Jacques is nowhere in sight. She refills my Kir Royal, and he suddenly appears. She leads me to the table and she sits me at the head, the guest of honor, me, who two hours earlier almost killed her husband and wrecked their car. In the U.S., I'd insist on a food taster. Here, I just dig in.

We start with a fresh, sweet, juicy melon, like a cantaloupe, but not like any cantaloupe I've ever eaten. The melon is followed by *cabillaud*—fresh cod—potatoes, green beans, red lettuce vinaigrette, and three kinds of cheese—Port Salut, a chèvre, and Camembert. Throughout, we're drinking rosé. We finish with fresh fruit, cookies—galettes of pure butter—coffee and brandy. I'm beat.

It's 2:00. I've spent more than four hours with Jacques, two with his wife, whose name I still don't know, and we haven't even begun to fill out the insurance form, and I'm drunk. All I want to do is nap, and I vow then and there never to allow a French worker to work on me or my house or car or anything after lunch, though the truth is *they* seem perfectly fine.

Jacques opens a huge bureau in the living room and rifles through papers. I stand and try to help Madame with the plates, silverware, and leftovers. They both sit me down with more force and direction than I've seen either of them exert so far. Jacques finally finds what he's looking for—the accident form—and sets it on the table and studies it as Madame clears the table around him.

I assume he knows what he's doing, and we'll be done in ten minutes and I'll be out the door and on my way to bed. But no, neither Jacques nor Madame has ever filled out such a form before, and I see a reticence developing, a reticence I've seen in France before when it comes to putting things on paper and filling out forms. Jacques studies the paper. Madame stands over his shoulder and reads it out loud. They look at each other—nervous, scared, wanting more than anything to do the right thing and not sure how. They look at me, and I perceive the incredible: they want *me* to tell them what to do. Me, who can't read or understand a thing. Clearly, they have to know this—in the two hours we've been together, I've said, "C'est joli," "C'est beau," "Bon," "Bien mangé," "Magnifique," "Merci, merci beaucoup," and "Je suis désolé," ten to twenty times. How can they possibly expect me to know this? But they do. They sit there looking at me hopefully, as if I'm a doctor and they're the patients, and soon I'll make everything OK.

I don't want to disappoint them any more than I have, so I open my Renault booklet to look for the accident form, and miracle of miracles I find it, and beneath the French, in tiny letters, everything is explained in English. I thank God and Renault's insurance company. "Ah, bon," I say. "Oui." Jacques and Madame look as if they've witnessed the resurrection: their faith has been tested, and they've been proven correct; this moron, this idiot, this child who can speak only a few words, mostly nonsense, has arrived to help them fill out this government form—thankfully forgetting or ignoring or forgiving the fact that they wouldn't need to fill out the form if I hadn't clobbered their car.

I take the pen from Jacques and boldly print my surname and "Christian" name (I'm Jewish, but why get into *that?*), address, insurance policy number, and the date, then stop. I can read the form, but beyond what I've written I can't write the answers in French. I turn the paper around and hand the pen to Jacques.

"Votre nom." I point.

He fills his name in carefully and never stops writing. At the space for location of accident, *lieu de l'accident*, he and Madame disagree about whether to use the correct location or the one the police wrongly identified in their report. Jacques wants to use the correct location. Madame wants to use the wrong one from the police report. I understand the issue perfectly, clarity versus accuracy, maintaining the simple white lie or presenting the more complicated, confusing truth. I opt for simple and clear and point to the location identified on the police report. Madame smiles at me. Jacques scowls, but he's outvoted, so he writes the name of the wrong location on the form. Beneath it, as required by the form, he draws a picture of the *rond-point*, its entrances and exits, and my car plowing into his. It's true, of course, so I don't object, though the American in me resists enough to move the point of impact a millimeter back to minimize whatever damage he might claim. Under the drawing Jacques writes several sentences, none of which I can read. I sit there smiling and nodding, certain when the insurance form is read my rates will double, and I'll never be able to lease a car again. Last, is *blessé*—injury, bruise—and remembering his shock, the hospital, and ambulance, I expect the worst.

Jacques looks at me and shrugs. "Vous?" he points.

I say, "No."

"Vous?" I ask.

He says, "Non."

"Bon," Madame says, and we both sign it. That, I think, is that—but not quite. It's four o'clock, *goûter* time, and Madame has coffee, cookies and *Far Breton*, a pudding cake that would be banned by the American Heart Association if it knew it existed. Finally, I say, "Merci. Au revoir. Je suis désolé," and stand as best I can. Madame kisses me four times. Jacques shakes my hand, and I suddenly remember, thanks to me, he has no car. This sets me off on a string of "Je suis désolé," but he and Madame wave it off.

"Ce n'est pas grave, no problem. Ce n'est pas grave," and Jacques tells me his car will be fixed in three days. "Trois jours." He holds up three fingers, and to be sure I understand, shows me on the calendar that today is *lundi,* and he'll have his car on *jeudi.* I look at him in disbelief. He's French, for God's sake, how could he possibly think this? Nothing happens quickly in France. Even in the U.S., land of efficiency and the clock, it would be two to three weeks before he saw his car again. Jacques is humoring me, I know, so I won't feel bad about wrecking his car and his life. "Je suis dés—"

"No problem, no problem," Madame cuts me off and hands me a peach. And then the strangest of all the strange things that day happens: Jacques hands me an envelope and the accident form we just filled out—the only copy!—and asks me to mail it because he doesn't have a car or a stamp.

Madame kisses me on the cheek again, and Jacques shakes my hand, the way he did with the taxi driver, and walks me out to my car, probably to make sure I really leave, wishing me "Bonne journée," and "Bonnes vacances," as if he means it and wouldn't mind spending another lovely afternoon with me sometime soon.

I drive home, astonished. Jacques and Madame don't know me from Cain. They don't know my last name, where I live, or how to reach me. The official police report is inaccurate, and I have the only copy of the insurance report that blames me for causing the accident. In the U.S., I'd think about dumping it in the trash and blaming the post office. All the way to Plobien, I'm thinking about this and wondering why in the world they trust me?

I learn later it wasn't trust. French people are as suspicious and doubting and provincial about human behavior as Americans, maybe even more, given their Catholic belief in fate and fatalism. It was simply expected of me, the way in the U.S. we don't *trust* other drivers, but we expect them to stay on their side of the road. Without that expectation, we could not/would not drive. The same is true in France, but over a much wider range of behavior. It's expected of me, because it's what you do when you have an accident. *C'est normal.* It's another of those rules by which rational, reasonable, no-fault, nonlitigious people live. I stop at the post office, buy a stamp, make a copy of the form for me, because *I* don't trust the mail, the police, or the insurance company, mail it, and go home to take a nap.

The next day, using my dictionary, I write a postcard—more for my sake than for theirs—to Jacques and Madame telling them I mailed the insurance form. I thank them again for lunch and *goûter* and apologize again for wrecking their car. Then I mail the card and drive to the local Renault dealer. When I leased the car at the airport the lady told me the insurance was "complete," implying the fees included everything, with no additional costs to me. I wouldn't have believed it in the U.S. I believe it even less in France, and now, less than one month later, I'm going to find out. I'm about to enter my worst nightmare: the French bureaucracy. Kafka and the Gulag couldn't scare me more.

I drive into the Renault garage as slowly as I can, making certain I don't hit anything else. I have my confident American look—I know what I'm doing, don't even think of taking advantage of me—but I'm scared, wondering how much this is going to cost me, and feeling sheepish, like I've let these people down. They gave me a new car, trusted me with it, and look what I did. I park far away from everyone else, get out of my car, and stand by the passenger's side, the *good* side, waiting.

I'm hoping for someone who speaks English, or at least will be helpful, or kind. I wait about fifteen minutes, and when no one speaks with me I walk into the shop. With each step, I'm more and more surprised. In the U.S., every garage I've been in is filled with greasy men with bloody knuckles and torn fingers and banging, whirring, and slamming things. The worst calendars are on the walls and talk radio stations are blaring; parts are on the floor, hanging from the walls and ceiling, with barely an unoccupied space; the smell of oil and gas and antifreeze is pervasive—and in summer, as now, the added smell of sweat. But not here. Here, the garage is like a research lab: wide-open, clean aisles; workers dressed like hospital lab technicians, in white, not a grease or blood stain on them. There's no banging, sawing, cutting, whirring—no loud noises at all.

The radio plays *Daphnis and Chloë*. If cars weren't in the air, I wouldn't know I was in a garage.

A fellow in a pristine white lab coat walks over to me and shakes my hand. His hands are an ad for hand cream. They're baby-skin soft, moist, almost feminine, except he's six feet tall, two hundred pounds—a giant in Brittany—and has a voice like Pavarotti. "What can I do for you?" he asks. At least I think that's what he asks, because it's the question I answer.

I walk him around the car to the driver's side and point at my bent, mangled, deformed little Twingo. The fender, hood, lights, and bumper are all smashed, making the car look less like a toy and more like advanced arthritis.

He puffs up his cheeks, expels air like a five-year-old, and begins talking and asking me questions. I know he's asking me questions, because every few minutes he stops. He continues doing this, speaking and stopping, until he realizes my shrugs and multiple "Bons," and "Ah, ouis," don't mean a thing. He walks away and returns with a tablet and begins to write. He walks all around the car, touching it, rubbing it, probing, putting his face and nose to the metal, periodically sucking in a mouthful of air and expelling it, making a noise that sounds to me like expensive. He spends twenty minutes doing this and hands me the papers to sign. I give him my insurance papers, which, as I feared and expected, he waves away. Now what? He gives me *his* papers and a pen. I hold the pen and look at the paper. Who knows what I'm signing? Maybe I'm agreeing to pay the first ten thousand dollars. Maybe I'm buying the Eiffel Tower. In the U.S., I'd never sign. I look at the guy. He looks like a nice man, so I write my name.

"Combien jours?" I ask him. How many days? I walk to the car and point at the fender, then myself, the ground, and turn my hands as if turning a steering wheel.

"Ah," he says, and holds up three fingers.

Three weeks. "Trois semaines!" Holy cow.

He laughs.

"*Trois mois!*" I won't even be here.

"Vendredi," he says. "Vendredi matin." Friday morning.

Three days! That's what Jacques told me when I "désoléed" him a zillion times. "Pas grave," not serious, "no problem." He'd have his car back in three days.

Wow. I start to walk away.

"Monsieur."

"Oui."

He gives me another sheaf of papers to sign. Now what? Probably a promise to never lease a Renault again. I sign, hand it back, and thank him again, saying, "Merci, merci beaucoup. Vendredi matin," and start to back out the door.

"Monsieur." He takes me by the hand like a three-year-old, the same way my dad did when he was taking me to my room to be spanked. We walk through the garage, out the back door, and stop in front of a new, cherry-red Twingo. I think he's going to lecture me, tell me, "See, this is how you're supposed to treat a car." He hands me the keys.

"Pour moi?"

"Oui."

I love this country. I wreck a new car because I'm foolishly driving without knowing the rules, and instead of punishing or inconveniencing me—or at least ridiculing me—they're handing me the keys to another new car. All I can think is God, I hope I can afford all this. The man shakes my hand as if I'm a relative, and says, "Vendredi, vendredi matin," the one thing we seem to understand and agree on. Then he does something I know he doesn't do for anyone else. He steps into the road—into traffic, on a highway!—and stops five cars and a huge truck carrying pigs to slaughter, halting them so I can back out and get away and do whatever it is I'm going to do to this new car far away and out of his sight. And the most remarkable thing: no one screams, beeps, flashes lights, or gives me or the garage man the finger. I drive home more carefully than I've ever driven anywhere in my life.

Three days later, *vendredi matin*, I return to the garage. I've managed not to dent, scratch, or in any way mangle the new Twingo, mostly by not driving it. In the three days I have it, I drive to the *supermarché* twice, a trip of about three kilometers each way. I feel proud, pleased I've upheld my part of the deal—bringing the car back safe and sound—and righteous, because I know they'll fail in theirs. There's no way the car will be ready.

I drive into the garage and stop. There, inside, waiting for me—I can tell by the red license plates—is my car. I park next to it, get out, walk around it, and marvel. It's finished and looks great, cleaner and shinier than when I got it at the airport. I walk into the garage looking for Monsieur, again feeling like I'm in a research lab or a hospital waiting room: white coats, quiet, no dirt or grease, Ravel on the radio, and not a single customer arguing about service, price, their bill, or the work.

I walk into the office and a girl no more than eighteen shyly smiles at me and sings, "Bon-jour."

"Bonjour," I say, and hand her the keys to my second Twingo, adding, "Bon. C'est joli. Merci." Good. It's pretty. Thanks.

The girl smiles wider. She's thinking about saying something to me, thinks better of it, and hands me a pile of papers to sign along with the keys to my first Twingo. I sign the papers and stand there, waiting. She looks at me, like, "Oh merde, now what?" I look at her the same way. I'm waiting for the bill, the deductible, the cost of the loaner, the gas. They never even asked for my credit card. "C'est tout?" I ask. That's all?

"Oui. C'est tout."

I see the fellow who helped me when I brought the car to the garage. "Au revoir," I say to the girl, "à bientôt, à tout à l'heure," goodbye, see you soon, in a moment, and run over to thank the man.

"Merci beaucoup, Monsieur, merci, merci beaucoup," as if he'd just delivered my firstborn or removed a brain tumor and a bit too much brain along the way. He looks at me like I'm *un peu spécial* and shakes my hand again like I'm family. Then he walks out to the highway and stops the traffic again so I can get away safely and quickly, and he can resume his work.

My First Ticket

The wonderful thing about French parking meters is they do not operate from twelve o'clock noon to two, during *midi*. Lunchtime parking is free! Even better, if you park at a meter at 11:45 and pay for two hours, the meter credits you the time after 2:00. Your two hours start at 11:45, stop at 12:00, begin again at 2:00 and go to 3:45. Still, I manage to overstay and get ticketed.

I have no idea what to do. I ask my guardian angel, Madame P, who tells me I have to buy a stamp. "Achetez un timbre."

"Une timbre?"

"Oui."

And mail it to the address on the ticket.

Madame explains all of this to me by taking an envelope from her kitchen cabinet drawer and becoming Marcel Marceau. She mimes putting something in it, sealing it, stamping it, dropping it into the mailbox, and waving bye-bye.

The next day I go to the *Poste* and *demande*—this is a question in French, not a demand—"une timbre pour la parking." A stamp for the parking.

I get that all too familiar blank look.

"Une timbre pour le parking." I take the ticket out of my pocket and show it to the lady behind the counter. "Le timbre pour la parking."

"Ah, un timbre pour la parking . . . Au bar-tabac."

"Le bar-tabac?"

"Oui, bien sûr. Le bar-tabac."

This makes no sense to me. I get a ticket for a driving or parking violation, and the government sends me to a bar to pay the fine.

I walk along the quai to the *bar-tabac* farthest from the center of town, knowing, once again, I'm about to make a fool of myself. I walk in, thankful it isn't crowded.

"Bonjour, Madame." The woman I'm calling Madame looks to be about sixteen years old.

"Bonjour."

I don't even bother trying to explain about the ticket, the stamp, the lady at the *Poste*, who I know doesn't like me anyhow. I just hand her the ticket saying, *"Ici,"* trying to make it sound like a question, "Here?"—as opposed to a gift, "Here."

She takes it, looks, and tells me to come back tomorrow. "Demain."

I don't know why. Maybe it's against the law to sell stamps on Tuesday afternoons at 3:00, 15 hundred hours.

I return the next morning. This time I don't have to say a word. The same girl smiles, says "Bonjour," and shakes my hand as if I'm her favorite uncle. Then she hands me a stamp—sees I haven't a clue, which you'd think she would have figured out by now—licks it, sticks it to the ticket, puts it in the envelope, addresses it for me, and charges me twenty euros, about $25.00.

"Merci, merci, merci," I say and walk back to the *Poste* to buy a postage stamp. I wait in the wedge and get the same lady as yesterday. "Bonjour," I say, and hand her the letter. She looks at me bewildered. I look at her more bewildered. She hands the letter back to me and says, "Non."

"No?"

"Non."

"Pourquoi?"

"Ce n'est pas le bar."

I'm dumbfounded. She bursts out laughing. "Ce n'est pas le bar." This isn't the bar. It's a joke, she's making a joke. I put my elbows on the counter, lean down, and demand, "Un bière, s'il vous plaît." We laugh together, both of us pleased that I got it, then she takes the letter, puts a stamp on it—certain I wouldn't do it correctly—and charges me seventy-five cents. "Au revoir," I say, "À bientôt." I can't tell if she's happy about that or not.

The Police

I'm driving home, still thrilled about my success with the *Poste* lady, when two gendarmes standing on the side of the road point to my Twingo and order me to stop. I've been through this before and know what to do. I park and get out of the car like John Wayne.

"Qua," I say, "qua?"—which isn't a word. "C'est une problem? Qu'est-ce que c'est." What? What? What is it? I walk toward them, talking, asking questions, in English and French. As expected, one cop walks away. The other shudders and begins backing up, realizing he's dealing with a loon. He's short, square, solid, a Breton who could handle anything—guns, knives, bombs, terrorists, wild pigs—except what I have: English and bad French. He's out of control, and both of us know it. Desperately, he looks around for his partner, who is now in the *pâtisserie*, and out of sight. I put out my hand to shake, and say, "Bonjour, Monsieur Gendarme." Hello, Mr. Policeman. I'm over fifty years old, and I'm addressing him like a three-year-old. He looks at me with hatred, but he's French and won't be rude, so he shakes my hand as if I have Ebola or the plague and walks me back to my car. He opens the door, ushers me in, and locks the door before he shuts it and walks away.

I wave and call out, "Merci, merci, au revoir, Monsieur Gendarme." It's the last time I'm stopped by the police in Plobien.

My Second Accident

Throughout June and early July I've been invited to friends' homes for dinner, but when Donna arrives the invitations increase: she speaks French and has *savoir-faire*.

It's one of those long French dinner nights at Sharon and Jean's, an evening that starts at eight thirty and ends early at two in the morning, where I drink too much: Ricard for apéritifs; rosé with the chips and *crudités*; red with the meal; and a homemade Breton moonshine that makes *calvados* taste like apple juice—a drink strong enough to souse a pig, embalm a brain, and receive open-heart surgery without anesthetic—as the *digestif*. No question about it, I'm semi-looped, not an uncommon experience for me in France.

"Can you drive?" Donna asks.

"Shore," I laugh, "and you can't." The Twingo is a stick shift, and she only drives an automatic.

We say our *au revoirs* and *à bientôts*, kiss cheeks four times, and manage to leave by two thirty. The drive home is short, less than three kilometers, on a one-lane back-country road, a road guaranteed to have no traffic or gendarmes at this time of night, a road I drive every day and know as well as the road to our home in California. *Pas de problème*. And there isn't, until we get to the house.

The driveway is gated—like every detached house in the village—and the gate is held in place by two five-foot-high cement posts. I turn into the driveway, and one or both of the gateposts leap in front of me, causing me to destroy the passenger-side mirror and scratch the car from the right front fender to the rear. Compared with the earlier accident, it's nothing. Added to my earlier accident, I figure next year I'll be driving a bicycle.

Donna says nothing, having long ago adopted the Japanese (which she is) strategy of silence and waiting. I don't say anything either. What's to say? The screech of cement ripping metal says it all, and hearing what I heard, I don't have the heart to look. I park the car, and we go to bed.

The next day, before Donna wakes, I go outside to see what I heard, and it's every bit as bad I feared. The mirror's hanging out of its casing like guts, the scratch is a full-body gash. I know I'm supposed to report it, but I don't have the nerve to return to the Renault garage and see the look of disapproval on the nice man's face when he sees what I did to his car. Besides, Donna and I are returning to the U.S. in five days. My plan is to drop the car at the airport and hope they don't see the damage until we're over Greenland or Prudhoe Bay. Donna thinks I'm nuts and breaks her code of silence (she's Japanese-*American*, after all) to say so.

"You're nuts," she says, "Of course they'll see it. Why wouldn't they, it's their job?"

What she doesn't know is I have a plan: I'm going to tell them a story that will make sense *and* break their hearts—*if* anyone asks.

Five days later we return to Aéroport Charles de Gaulle to dump the Twingo and fly home. My plan is to park in the farthest corner of the lot and get out of there as quickly as possible. I turn into the TT car rental area, and a young man who's lurking near the gate points me to an empty place right next to the office. Donna looks at me, then slides down in her seat. The young man sees the damage, runs to the office, and returns with the papers I've already become too familiar with.

To save time, something I've never known the French to care about, the lad—Monsieur Felix—completes the papers. He fills them out without saying a word until he gets to the place where he has to explain what happened and show it with a diagram. "Monsieur," he says, and turns the papers around and hands me the pen. I draw two posts and a gate with the car and three stars turning into the driveway.

Monsieur Felix looks at me, at the drawing, back at me. He's eighteen years old, and already he's a critic. No wonder

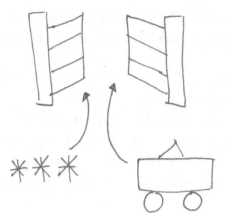

Foucault and Levi-Strauss are French. What the hell do they teach these people in school? I inhale slowly, deeply, and exhale. "Une chien," I say.

He says nothing.

"Oui," I say, nodding vigorously. "C'est vrai," and I point to the three little stars. With much waving of arms and hands and pointing of fingers accompanied by screeching sounds and a bark, I show Mr. Felix how I was driving home very slowly, carefully, about to turn into my driveway when a dog, a baby dog, "*un chien bébé*," jumped in front of my car, and I had to turn the wheel into the post to avoid "morte le chien . . . C'est vrai."

Monsieur Felix looks at me with sorrow and concern. He's young, serious, sympathetic, responsible, trusting. I don't want to lie to him or Renault or France. I cross out the three-star *chien*, sign the paper, and hand it to him, once again honest *and* guilty at the same time.

He signs the papers, accepts my damaged car, and drives us to the terminal, making sure I get out of the country without getting behind the wheel of another Renault. At the terminal, he shakes my hand and Donna's hand and wishes us, "Bon voyage."

The next year I lease another Twingo without a hitch. Since then everything on the road has been fine—*c'est normal*—probably because I now drive like a Frenchman, which means *all* of us are uncertain about what to do when entering a *rond-point*. *Cédez le passage.* It's a difficult rule for driving and a daunting rule for life—especially for an American.

10 Things I've Learned about Driving in France

1. The car to the right has the right-of-way at all intersections except at *ronds-points*, where the car to the left has the right-of-way, and at entrances to *ronds-points*, where no car has the right-of-way: *cédez le passage,* except on the Périphérique, where cars entering have the right-of-way, except for cars exiting.

2. Posted speed limits are a fabrication, except where there's a sign that looks like a warning for a nuclear disaster: a black dot with three expanding semicircles radiating outward toward a picture of a driverless car and motorcycle. This sign means I'm about to enter a speed trap—and if I'm traveling five kilometers (three miles) over the speed limit, a radar gun will clock me, a camera will photograph me, and I'll get a very expensive ticket in the mail. It's like if we tell you there's a speed trap up ahead, and you are stupid enough to speed through it, you're going to pay through the nose. Note: the ticket is *not* for speeding, which everyone does, but for stupidity, which French people abhor.

3. Any open space, no matter how tiny or where it's located, is a possible picnic area or parking place. If there are trees, bushes, or a wall nearby, it's also a possible toilet.

4. Along with *ronds-points*, France has discovered speed bumps. Unfortunately, they are not uniform in height, length, width, or color—*and* they are moveable. Sometimes it's a mock bump, red or white wavy lines on the road telling me this is where a speed bump would be if they bothered to put a speed bump here. As soon as I discover it's not real, I race over it. Most times, though, it is real. I'm driving along and see a sign that looks like a picture

of a World War I English doughboy helmet, and before it registers, I've cracked my skull on the roof of the car. For some reason only French urban planners understand, the bump is always *immediately* after the warning sign, and the steeper and sharper the bump, the closer it is to the sign. It's taken me several head-shots, but I now remember the speed bump on the road under the viaduct near my house. I slow down, ready for it every time, until the time it's not there—then I speed up. This particular speed bump has come and gone three times, returning to a different place on the road, higher, lower, wider, longer, sometimes made of rubber, and sometimes macadam, surprising me each time with a bump on my head. The last time I was there, it was gone, and I happily raced down the road only to discover it newly placed a few kilometers later when I smashed my head on the roof of the car as I raced down the road to the freeway.

5. Brittany has no toll roads, but the rest of France does— they're called autoroutes, and they're expensive, which means I need to carry lots of money when I'm traveling because U.S. credit cards aren't always accepted. That's the easy problem. The harder one is which line to get in to pay the toll? My normal American reaction is to race to the booth with the shortest line and smirk—but not in France! In France, the booth with the shortest line has a flashing yellow *t* over it, and that *t* means trouble for me. It means an automatic, electronic deduction will be taken from the prepaid card French people have and I don't. And *that's* not the biggest problem. The biggest problem is *no one* is in that booth. It's empty—so if through ignorance or mistake, I get in that line, as unfortunately I have, ten, twenty, or

three hundred cars will have to back up (as three hundred new cars move forward) to give me enough space to get out of that line and into the line with the flashing green arrow on top, or the picture of a man with a cap, or a picture of something that looks like a ticket. *That* is the line to be in. For an American, it is diabolical. I've composed a mantra so I remember: "the longer the line, the more likely it's mine."

6. France illuminates everything except its roads. It's some of the darkest driving I've ever done. Plus, for some reason, which certainly cannot be energy conservation, drivers use their fog lights well into the night, instead of their headlights. People *flash* their headlights to tell me *my* lights are on then go back to their fog lights, letting me know (1) they have headlights, and (2) they're not going to use them.

7. Given Derrida, Foucault, and postmodernists, it's not surprising that French people excel at signaling. They use their turn signals to indicate intent to pass, actual passing, pulling over, turning left or right, parking, and parked— and they use their headlights to tell you the gendarmes are lurking up ahead or you're doing something bizarre— like driving in the dark with your headlights on. Once they've given notice, however, they're done. The rest is up to you.

8. I no longer drive on the autoroutes on July 1 (the start of July vacations), July 14 (Bastille Day), July 31 (the end of July vacations), August 1 (the start of August vacations), August 15 (Assumption Day), August 31 (the end of August vacations), or during any period called *la rentrée*, which in English means 'See you in September,' and in French means 'Don't even think about trying to drive anywhere.' For the same reason, I avoid getting stuck behind

deux chevaux, Smart cars, or farm implements. For other reasons, I avoid trucks carrying live animals on their way to slaughter. One whiff will tell you why.

9. There are road signs in France I've never seen before: a white diamond-shaped sign with a yellow diamond inside means I have the right-of-way; the same sign with an orange diamond inside and a black line through it means my right of way just ended. A triangular sign with a black X on it means no one has the right-of-way, which is the new rule of thumb, *or* the car to the right has the right-of-way, which is the old rule of thumb. A circle with a red rim means no vehicular traffic. A tiny white sign with the blue or black drawing of what looks like an old box camera means limited parking, and it's up to me to post the time I arrived on my dashboard. I'm supposed to post it with a free time card (if I can find it) or pay three euros (if I can't), identify the time I arrived, and leave the card on the dashboard for the police to see. The only way to know this is to get a ticket for not posting the time you parked. I know, because when I got a ticket and said to the policeman, "Porquoi?" he pointed to the tiny sign with a drawing of an old box camera and said, "Regardez."

10. France has a Good Samaritan law. Every day, in every way, I try harder and harder to be one, because life is better and easier for all when I am . . . The operative word is "try."

Shopping for . . .

The easiest things to do in the U.S. are often the most complicated in France. Take, for example, showering. For some reason I will never understand, until very recently, most French homes, hotels, B & Bs, gites, and chambre d'hotes had no shower curtains or doors.

In the U.S., I step into the shower (tub or stall), close the curtain or door, turn on the water, adjust the temperature, and enter the cascade, luxuriating in total, wrap-around comfort and warmth. In France, I step into the tub and freeze. In the U.S., showerheads are mounted on the wall above my head—exactly where they ought to be. In France, in an effort to keep the room from soaking because there are no shower doors or curtains, shower heads are set lower and are attached to long, slinky, eel-like hoses that have been unwillingly force-wrapped around the bathtub faucet and temperature knobs. Every time I see one of these contraptions I shiver: literally.

I step into the tub and stand there, knowing what I have to do and not wanting to—and knowing what's going to happen next: no matter how I sit (lotus-style, with my legs outstretched, or on my cracking, breaking knees) or which way I face (toward the faucet or away), I'm going to drench the room. I'm going to uncoil the eel and drop it or lose control of it with my soapy, slippery hands and before I can recapture it it's going to jump around like a lunatic frog and soak the room, or I'm not going to drop or lose control of the eel, and I'll spray water on me, over me, and off me, and soak the room. There is simply no way an American can shower like this and not souse the bathroom.

There's also no way to shower like this and not freeze. I sit or kneel in that moment's least of the least uncomfortable positions and spray my left arm, shoulder, chest, face, head, back, while the rest of me goose-bumps, because it's impossible to wet all of my body at once.

Even today, when more and more places do have shower curtains and doors, for another reason I'll never understand, they do not fully *close. There's a gap. A planned gap, like if they close 80% of the space it will be enough! And, if by some miracle of planning or error the door or curtain does fully close, it leaks.*

That's showering. Then there's shopping. In the U.S., I successfully shop for most things—the more important the item the better shopper I am—and almost never experience buyer's remorse. In the U.S., I'm a shopper par excellence. In France, I'm subpar, and on really bad days, like the first times I shopped for food, I'm sub-subpar. In fairness, though, it's not entirely my fault: there's me, and there's French people, language, customs, and rules.

Food

As I said, the easiest things to do in the U.S. are often the most difficult and confusing in France. Take, for example, shopping. After I verify the balance in my bank account and withdraw money, I drive to Leclerc, a chain of *supermarchés* that are France's answer to Walmart, the French son of Sam, and shop for household items and food.

I know I should shop at the *petit marché*, from the moms and pops and the locals, where the quality is better, and it's more interesting, quaint, and politesse. But to shop at the locals you have to speak French. Besides, the locals, meaning Sharon and Jean and Monsieur and Madame P, tell me they buy everything *moins cher*, cheaper, and *soldes*, on sale at Leclerc, which is why I'm going there, too, opting for low prices and invisibility above all, especially since I shop by geography and pictures: locate the breakfast cereals; look at the picture on the box; and for the first time in my life pray for U.S. hegemony and General Mills. From the start, Leclerc and shopping have been the scene and circumstance of some of my most stupendous humiliations, surprises, and lessons.

The first time I went to Leclerc, I parked in a football-field-size parking lot and walked toward the longest row of shopping carts I've ever seen. Several rows—the straightest rows of anything I've seen in France, except for traffic jams and Le Nôtre's gardens: two rows here, two there, two there, each row with a hundred carts. The good news is the carts are outside, meaning there aren't six hundred people inside, though the fact that they're there means they *expect* six hundred people, and want them, and probably at better times— meaning worse times for me, not one thirty in the afternoon of a beautiful sunny beach day—get them. I make a note of this as I yank a cart and get nowhere. The cart cries out but doesn't budge. I yank harder. It whines and still doesn't budge. I lift the rear end by the handle and shake the cart to release it, expecting the front wheels or the carrier or the kid's seat to come unstuck and discover to my amazement the carts are all chained together—like airport carts or railroad trains or prisoners. No wonder they're in a straight row.

I'm standing there trying to figure out why the carts are locked together—as in why would anyone want to make shopping more difficult and unpleasant than it is—when a middle-aged woman in a flowery skirt and three-inch heels steps out of her new Mercedes, walks to the row of carts, pushes a ten franc coin—now one euro—into a slot on the handle, and wheels off nonchalantly. I'm shocked. They're charging $1.30 to shop here *and* these people are willingly paying. It's an outrage. I will not do it. I will not pay to shop. I'll pay a porter to carry my bags at an airport, to park to go to the movies or shop in downtown Berkeley or San Francisco, even to go to the bathroom in

Paris or Quimper, but I will not pay to shop at a supermarket. This is one of those lines that cannot be crossed. Soon we'll be paying for air as well as water.

I walk to the entrance and stop as the glass doors slide open and two women exit, each pushing a shopping cart overflowing like Mount Vesuvius. If there was anything to eat in the house, I'd leave . . . I wait for them to pass me and enter the store—and see it's worse than I even imagined.

It's a mall in a store, complete with a sit-down restaurant and a three-course dinner menu in case shopping and being around all this food makes me so hungry I can't wait to eat. All around me are bikes, patio furniture, barbecues, and lawnmowers—the big sit-on-and-drive types *and* the hand-pushers. Signs on the walls tell me I can purchase heating oil for a house, have keys made, shoes fixed, locks repaired, and laundry cleaned. I'm overwhelmed, and I haven't even begun to shop.

I push through the turnstile and spot a three-foot-high stack of tiny shopping baskets, hiding as if they're ashamed to be there. I grab one before Monsieur Leclerc decides to charge for these too. Basket in hand, I walk down the aisle, aiming toward the rear of the store, which I know is somewhere out there on the horizon.

I pass TVs, radios, clocks, stereos, watches, lamps, jewelry, magazines, newspapers, post cards, CDs, movies, books, paint, hardware, car parts, batteries, light bulbs, plumbing and electrical supplies, kitchen and car tools, clothes, shoes, bedding, towels, and toiletries. The only thing missing is food. I know it's here someplace. Monsieur and Madame P and Sharon and Jean told me they shop here, and I've seen the Vesuvius ladies' carts.

In the last aisle, far, far away from where I started, I hit pay dirt—literally—frozen foods and corporate meats. This is what I'd expect to find in Texas, not France. I walk away dismayed, continuing my search for essentials—cereal, butter, milk, fresh meats, water, eggs, salt, pepper, fruit, and wine—hoping for better choices.

I find them in the middle of the store: bloody red meats in cuts I've never seen before, beneath signs saying, *Eléve en France*, raised in France, to assure people they aren't buying anything English; cheese, cakes, tarts, pies, baguettes; an entire aisle filled with chocolate bars; fruits and veggies heaped in a rainbow of colors under signs identifying them as Bretagne, Spanish, or Moroccan; and the largest collection of seafood I've seen outside of the ocean. I walk over to look. There are at least two dozen fish, some filleted, most whole, resting on crushed ice, eyes open and mouths agape, looking even more surprised to be here than I am. At the other end of the counter, pink-ish-reddish thingies that look like a cross between a tiny lobster and a scorpion crawl over each other and fall onto the floor, where a three-year-old girl plays with them like they're Lionel trains. The sign says they're "langoustine," a name I intend to remember and avoid.

I step over the girl and her friends, bag three tomatoes, four peaches, a head of garlic, and two oranges, and go to the butcher for meat. I hold up two fingers for two lamb chops, one finger for a thick slice of fillet of pork, and six for slices of ham, then grab a baguette from a rack, where they're lined up and stacked like rifles. I balance the baguette on top of the box of tin foil, which is balanced on top of a twelve-pack of toilet paper that is under the arm of the hand holding the overflowing shopping basket. My other hand holds a six-pack of two-liter bottles of

Volvic water. Under that arm, I'm scrunching an eight-pack of paper towels.

I waddle to the shortest wedge, where everyone looks at me like I'm crazy. I look at them with disdain. I'm balancing everything like one of those guys from Cirque de Soleil, shaking and twitching under the strain, but never dropping a thing. When I get to the front, I place all the items on the counter and wait. The girl says, "Bonjour," and starts ringing me up.

I say, "Bonjour," and take a plastic bag from the bunch on the counter and start to bag, as I've watched others do, then wonder how they do it, as I fumble, searching for the top or an opening—getting ready to rip my own—when the girl behind the counter says something I don't understand. I look at her in a way that says, please, don't ask me anything. She looks at me in a way that says, 'Why me?'

She holds up the bag with three tomatoes in it.

I shrug. "Tomate," I say.

"Oui," she says.

Everyone in line steps back, and we all watch as the girl pushes her stool away from the counter, stands, and walks in the direction of produce. How am I supposed to know it's my job to weigh the tomatoes? I'm to identify them—there are four different types—push the correct button on the electronic scale and stick the label that emerges with the type, weight, and price on the bag so the girl at the register won't have to do what this one is now doing. In the U.S., people—*I*—would be tempted to choose the most expensive tomato and push the least expensive button, say the *grappe* and push the button for the roma, or put three tomatoes in the bag, weigh it, then add two more. Apparently, *that's* not a problem here. Here, the problem is me. The girl returns, taps in a number, and smiles at me. It's a smile that's not going to last. Under the box of cereal is a bag of four peaches, none of which I've identified or weighed. This time when the girl stands, the people behind me make audible sounds. One guy even gestures. To save her a trip, I hand her the bag of oranges hiding under the rubber gloves and say, "Thank you," hoping everyone thinks I'm a Brit.

While she's gone, I continue fumbling with the plastic bag. It's so small and difficult to open, I'm glad I couldn't buy very much. I can't imagine what I'd do with a Vesuvius load.

The girl returns and finishes ringing everything up. I pay her by counting the bills and holding out a handful of coins, indicating she should take what she likes. Then I lumber out of the store lugging eight plastic bags, knowing I haven't dented my list, and at this rate, it will take me all summer.

Three days later I return with a plan.

I stand near a row of carts trying to look busy, or like I've suddenly forgotten something important, something that if remembered could save the world or France or my life. A wobbly, silver-haired woman with short, spindly legs and low black heels walks toward me pushing an empty cart. I run toward her and stop her by putting my hands on the cart, as in "Thanks, don't bother, I'll take it back."

She looks at me wide-eyed and yanks it away. I pull it back.

We're standing in the middle of the parking lot, pulling the cart back and forth, me and this seventy-year-old woman, who I can tell you is stronger than she looks. I finally realize she's not going to let go, so I do, then watch, incredulous, as she rolls the cart away, shoves it back into the row of carts, and chains it. *She chains it!* She'd rather lock the cart up and keep it from me than share it. She paid her lousy dollar-thirty and wants to make sure I pay mine too. I'm astonished, embarrassed and disheartened. What's happened to these people—to Liberty, Equality, *Fraternity,* for God's sake, that they won't even share a shopping cart. I'm outraged.

I'm also without a cart. I could pay my own lousy dollar-thirty and get one, but I've vowed not to pay to shop, and I'm not ready, after only three days, to violate myself, at least not in *that* way.

I enter Leclerc with my list and again buy as much as I can hold, this time carrying two baskets and a large shopping bag I brought from the house, tripling my take from the last time. I fill each basket and the bag to overflowing and slide into the shortest wedge, far, far, away from the wedge I was in before, hoping I never see that checker again. Ingenuity, that's what's lacking here. Clearly, this is the way to go—as opposed to the dollar-thirty cart.

I'm wondering what's wrong with these people that no one has thought of this, as I place everything on the conveyor belt. The girl slides each item over the bar code reader, and I place it back in my bag and the baskets, separating the food from the cleaning supplies. I hand her a bill larger than the amount so she has to count the change, and I don't. When she's finished, she says something I don't understand. I look at her, hoping she's talking to someone else or herself or God—anyone but me. She points to the baskets and says it again.

In the U.S., when I don't understand something, I say no. In France, I say, "oui."

The person behind me says, "You can't take the baskets outside."

No wonder no one else does this. "S'il vous plaît," I say, and point at the floor behind the checkout girl. When she doesn't move, I lift the baskets and place them on the floor behind her.

"Une moment," I say, ignoring the way she's looking at me and two-hand lift my about-to-split, overflowing shopping bag and carry it to the car and unload it . . . It takes me three more trips to unload the baskets, fill the starting-to-split bag, and carry everything back to the car. I figure as of now there's probably a picture of me on every cash register telling the checkers, *beware*. Soon there won't be a checker I can go to . . . I'm going to have to try something else.

A week later, I drive into Loscoat and go to the neighborhood fruit lady. Peaches, apricots, apples, pears, plums, oranges, nectarines, melons, bananas, lemons, limes, strawberries, and cherries are all beautifully arranged and displayed in front of the shop. The woman inside is talking to a customer or friend or family member, I still can't tell. I take a paper bag from the stack of paper bags and pick up a nectarine. It's hard, so I put it back. The woman races out of the store, grabs the bag out of my hand, and scolds me. Luckily, I don't understand a word. Unluckily, I don't know what to do. We stand there staring at each other, dueling eyes. Finally, she shakes the bag, opens it, points to the fruit, herself, and the bag.

I get it! No self-serve. *She* picks the fruit and puts it in the bag. Ha! I know that one—give the American the crap, the moldy strawberries, the rotten peach. *Pas de chance.* The alternative, however, is Leclerc, where I haven't been doing much better. I decide to test her. "Trois pêches," I say, and hope I asked for peaches and not the catch of the day. I don't see any fish around, but this is France, and you never can tell.

"Jaunes?" she asks. Yellow?

Or maybe she said *jeune*—young. I don't know, but I figure the answer to both is yes. "Oui," I say.

"Aujourd'hui?"

Yeah, I want the peaches today. Does she really think I'm coming back for them tomorrow? "Oui. Aujourd'hui."

She picks up a peach, looks at it, turns it in her hand, smells it, and drops it in the bag. She does the same with two more, and says, "Monsieur?"

The melons look beautiful. "Une melon." I use the feminine because what else could it be? Masculine, I find out later.

"Aujourd'hui."

Again with the *aujourd'hui*?

"Vous le mangez aujourd'hui?"

Oh! She's asking if I'm *eating* it today. No wonder it's not self-serve! In France, you buy your fruit and veggies according to the hour and day you want to eat them. "Demain," I tell her, tomorrow. I then buy two apples for Thursday afternoon and four apricots for Friday morning. It's wonderful—and wearying. It means everything has to be planned, not to mention you have to know how to say the days of the week and the time, which isn't easy since it's military time—17:00 *heures*—and I've never been in the Army, Navy, Air Force, or Marines. I leave with ten paper bags of fruit and veggies, trying to remember which day I said I wanted each fruit and veggie so I'll eat them in the proper order. I have a feeling if I eat the wrong thing on the wrong day I'll either get sick from food poisoning or the fruit lady will come and take everything away, and worse, never sell me anything again. It's another French rule I'm learning: the relationship between buyer and seller is personal.

Shopping the moms and pops *is* interesting and the quality *is* better, but it's all I do. I'm spending most of my life shopping and dealing with food. Every day I go to several stores. I buy fruit and veggies from the *fruiterie*; meat from the *boucherie*; fish from the *poissonnerie*; milk, cheese, butter, yogurt, and eggs from the *fromagerie*; toothpaste and shampoo from the *pharmacie*; cleaning supplies from the *droguerie*; cleaning tools from the *quincaillerie*; wine and prepared foods from the *charcuterie*; bread from the *boulangerie*; cakes and tarts from the *pâtisserie*; crêpes from the *crêperie;* books from the *librairie*; nibbles from the épicerie or *snackerie* or *sandwhicherie*; and dinner, if I go out, from the *brasserie*. It's like living in Lilliputian land, a land of a thousand diminutives.

After a week, I'm ready to give in. There's a reason the locals are spending a dollar-thirty to shop at Leclerc—nothing else makes sense. It's either that or revert to hunter-gatherer status, which is nuttier than saving a buck-thirty. Throw in the price of gas, and it's costing me money, not saving me. If time is money, I'm old and late.

I drive to Leclerc, defeated. Sam and his son win again. I park and walk to a row of carts and insert my coin, and voilà! The chain uncouples and frees the cart. On my way in, I see the woman I tried to take the cart from coming out. She sees me and wheels a wide arc around me.

I don't get it. I thought these people were careful with money, yet here she is spending a dollar-thirty to shop, and her cart is practically empty. Not me. If I'm going to spend a dollar-thirty to shop, I'm damned well going to shop. I'm going to fill this cart like the Vesuvius women so I don't have to pay this often—and don't have to shop every day.

I enter the store and go straight to spices. I bought salt and pepper the first time I was here, now I need oregano. I go to the aisle where spices were a week ago, but spices aren't there, breakfast cereal is. I roll away and come back several times, making sure, yes, this is where they were, and they definitely are not here now. They are not where breakfast cereals were either, soups are. I walk up and down, frustrated and beat. There are no spices in sight and no sign telling me where in this huge, super, son of Sam market they are. The same thing happens with evaporated milk. It's not where it was a week ago.

I'm beginning to understand a basic difference between French and American marketing. In Oakland, the theory is to leave a product where it is so the customer will come back and locate it with minimal effort, then move to the next item he or she wishes to purchase, which is also where it was a day, week, month, year, and decade ago. Even if the store changes owner-ship—from Safeway to Albertson's—the location of the prod-ucts do not usually move. Not so in France. In France, they move products like the wind: no notice, no signage. No reason *I* can think of, though I'm sure *they* have one—for why spices are now next to cookies, and not where they were a week ago—and that's not even the worst of it.

I go to the section where Volvic water was and find a gazil-lion types and brands of cider and beer. I'm too tired to search the store, so I do what I fear most—a common experience in France—I ask. I walk up to a sympathetic-looking old guy, hoping for a man-to-man, lost-in-shopping, exchange. "Où est eau?" I ask. It sounds onomatopoeic, something like the Purple People Eater would say, and gets the same response.

I try an older woman. "L'eau est où?"

She says something, gives up, leads me to a part of the store I've never seen, and points to an open door that looks like a cave. I walk in, and sure enough, there are hundreds, maybe thousands of plastic bottles in a dozen sizes and shapes, packaged singly and in twos, fours, sixes, eights, and twelves, a score of brands—not one of them Volvic. How can this be? Volvic is a major brand—like Coke or Pepsi—and it's not here. I look everywhere—behind Isabelle, under Perrier, in the corner next to Evian, above Badoit. It's nowhere. It's not just moved, like spices—it's gone. I, who until recently never heard of Volvic and couldn't tell the difference between Volvic and tap, now want nothing else, can drink nothing else. Anything else would be wrong—poison. Talk about branding! I don't know if it has to do with Volvo, which I drive, or vulva, or some secret addictive ingredient like coke. Whatever it is, I want it.

I ask a teenage girl, "Où est le Volvic?"

It's like I asked the $64,000 question. She concentrates, looks concerned, worried, like she lost her best friend or I lost mine. She walks all around, looks everywhere, and shrugs. "Je ne sais pas," and walks away. I can't believe it. It's vanished like a dream or mirage. Volvic ads are everywhere, on TV, billboards, in newspapers, and magazines, but there's not a liter of it in this store. I buy a bottle of Perrier, deciding to wait for Volvic, certain it will be back when I return, but it doesn't reappear all summer.

I continue filling my Volvic-less cart with everything on the list, and with enough of it—at least the nonperishables like paper and cleaning supplies—to last all summer. The cart is so full and heavy I can hardly steer it. I push and pull it to the nearest counter and begin to unload. The checker, a girl in her early twenties, looks at me like I've never seen a checker look at anyone. People behind me—French people, people who wait patiently for anything—start switching counters.

The girl grabs a handful of plastic bags and tosses them on the counter. I pick up the bundle, rip one from the bunch, and with trepidation, remembering the first time, roll the edge of the shorter side between my fingers, hoping to find the opening. I don't. I turn the bag one hundred eighty degrees, wet my thumb and forefinger, and roll the edge on the other side. A family at the end of the wedge wheels away. I turn the bag again, back to where I started, and more people leave the wedge. If "plastic bag opening" was an event in Special Olympics, I'd score 0. If this were *Survivor*, I'd be dead. I'm frantically, hopelessly, turning the bag and wetting my fingers, rolling, twisting, and squeezing the edges, getting nowhere and starting to panic. Then something happens I've never seen before or since. The checker and the next two people in line help me. All of us are bagging my stuff: me, because it's mine; they, so they can get out of there before the store closes, their food rots, or they die from starvation or old age.

I pay with a check because the guy in front of me did, and I saw they have that cash register that fills everything out for me. I sign the check without looking at the numbers and roll the cart to the car and unpack, filling the trunk, back seat, passenger seat, and floor. Then I wheel the cart back to the row of carts and leave it there. I'm trying to set an example, maybe start a revolt. I paid *my* money, but there's no reason the next person should. Maybe I can start the next French revolution: free shopping. I leave the cart and walk away, righteous.

"Monsieur," a woman calls.

I turn around. I think she's going to thank me. "Oui."

"Votre chariot?"

"Oui." I point, "Pour vous."

"Monsieur," she walks over to me, takes my hand, and together, her hand on mine, we push the cart into the row. I watch, horrified, as she chains it. I can't believe it. Even when you try to help these people, to liberate them, they follow the rules and lock their damned carts so no one else can use them. I'm flabbergasted and disappointed. I walk away, my experiment with consumer rights failed.

"Monsieur."

I turn around. The lady smiles and hands me my coin. It seems when you lock your cart your money is returned to you. There is no cost. It simply guarantees the return of the cart, unlike the U.S., where abandoned shopping carts litter the streets. Oh, these people are smart. Once again, I feel like a jerk.

I now shop Leclerc like a local, though I still get lost and confused when things are moved or disappear. I know to buy what I want when I see it—and to buy it in bulk, because I may never see it again. This apparently is their marketing plan, and I'm here to tell you it works. I spend more than I want and buy more than I need all the time.

Shoes

One day, every summer, signs suddenly appear in shop windows, newspapers, hanging from mannequins, posted on walls, brightly and colorfully proclaiming *soldes*, sale. Two to three weeks later, additional signs announce *deuxième*, *troisième*, and *dernière démarque*: reduced, reduced, reduced.

As an American, I dismiss those signs as part of the normal business of lying, like the Macy's absolutely rock-bottom, last-chance, cheapest ever underwear sale that appears in the newspaper every day, or the going-out-of-business sign that's been in the window of the same furniture store with the same owner for the past twenty years and counting. I see those *soldes* signs and walk past the stores, unbelieving—until Gilles and Tatjana tell me these sales are real, official, regulated, approved by the state, and these are the *only* days in summer (and winter) certain kinds of stores can have them—which is why I'm standing in front of a Mephisto store.

I like good shoes: good fit, construction, and looks. In the U.S., I buy Eccos, but I covet Mephistos, and here I am at *soldes*-time, and there's a *dernière démarque* sign in the window, and a black shoe and a pair of brown sandals I like. In the U.S., I refuse to spend two hundred fifty to three hundred dollars for a pair of shoes, not to mention for sandals. But here, for two hundred fifty dollars I can get the black shoes *and* the sandals. It's a deal too good to pass up, and since I've already learned the basic rule of French shopping—buy what you like when you see it and buy it in bulk—I walk in. The store's tiny, but who cares: it's a Mephisto store, and I've seen what I want at a price I'll pay.

"Bonjour," I say to the saleslady and head toward the side of the store where men's shoes are displayed.

"Bonjour," she says, and thankfully leaves me alone. I look for the shoes and sandals I saw in the window and don't see them anywhere. I walk to the women's side—who knows how they arrange things here? If melons, *les melons*, are masculine, as Jean has told me, how clear can the divisions be? I look and don't see them there either. The saleslady sees me on the women's side, rushes over, and says, "Monsieur," like this isn't *that* kind of store.

"Oui, oui," I say, "je compris," though it's clear I don't understand a thing. I walk her to the window and point to the shoes and sandals I'd like to see.

"Quelle taille?"

I shrug. "Je ne sais pas." I know my size in American—8½ or 9—but I have no idea in French. I sit on a stool and look around for one of those foot-measuring things that shoe sales-people in the U.S. carry and use like stethoscopes. There are none. There's no way to measure the width and length of my feet, to know if the right foot is longer or wider than the left, or vice versa. Somehow everyone in France, maybe in Europe and the world, knows their shoe size, maybe has it imprinted or bar-coded on their driver's license or credit card along with their photos and fingerprints. The saleslady looks at me like I'm a dolt, which isn't actually wrong, but for this? It feels excessive, especially when there's so much more she could find lacking in me.

I remove my left shoe, pleased I'm wearing socks without holes. The saleslady moves and acts like she's ninety, though she can't be more than twenty-five. She sits facing me and sighs. Clearly, she doesn't want to be bothered, and wouldn't be either, except I'm the only customer in the store. She reaches behind her and removes the nearest shoe from the display rack—a huge, maybe size 11 in American, ugly brown loafer with tassels—and holds it against the bottom of my foot. "Quarante-et-un, quarante-deux," she pronounces: 41, 42, two numbers I will never forget.

"Bon," I say.

She stands and walks to the back of the store. It's ten o'clock on a Tuesday morning. The store was closed Sunday and Monday, and she's moving like she's been here for a hundred years without a vacation, holiday, or break. She returns carrying six boxes, not a good sign, since I only want two. She drops the pile down in front of me and removes the cover from the top box.

"Voilà!"

I look and see it's close to the sandal I want, except it's black not brown, has a Velcro strap instead of a buckle, and is size 40. Somehow, I know the other boxes won't fare any better. The second box *is* a 42, but the shoes are tan, not black. The third box has the same shoe in dark brown, the fourth is a white loafer. The fifth has exactly what I want in a size 46. One look and I can see they're too big. The last box has the ugly brown tasseled loafer in my size. I don't want any of them. In the U.S., I'd say, "Thank you," and leave. But this is France, and even though the sales girl seemingly could not care less, *I* don't want to be rude or wasteful of her time, though, as far as I can see, only SNCF trains and Air France seem to acknowledge its existence. I put on the dark brown pair, walk around the shop, stare at my feet in the mirror, take off the left shoe, and replace it with the tan.

A mother-daughter team, maybe sixty and forty years old, enters the shop while I'm doing this. They see me walking around, one foot tan, the other dark brown, and sit down to enjoy the show. As far as they're concerned, this is Paris, and I'm Kate Moss. Meanwhile, the saleslady has gone from ninety to sixteen. I don't know if it's because she senses a sale, likes an audience, or is that much closer to lunch, but she's now actively urging me to get the tan, which to me is the color of caca.

"C'est beau, c'est beau," she keeps repeating, all but jumping up and down.

"Oui," the mother agrees. The daughter prefers the dark brown. All are very emphatic and enthusiastic about my choice. They begin to argue with each other, "Marron, fauve, marron, fauve," like a football cheer.

At least the shoes they like fit. The pair I want, the black, are clown's shoes. Now, instead of getting to disappoint one person, I get to disappoint three. I take the shoes off—I won't even try the ugly tasseled loafer—and say, "Madame, avez vous ce la . . . " and point to the black shoe, " . . . en quarante-deux?" and hold up four fingers on my left hand and two on my right. I say it as if this is a wholly new idea. A *bonne idée.*

"Non," the saleslady says.

The mother says, "Les fauves, les fauves." The daughter says, "Les marrons."

I don't know why, but I persist. "Quand?" When?

They all look at me as if I asked for the shoes for free.

"La semaine prochaine, peut-être?" Maybe next week? I ask.

"Oui. C'est possible."

This is incredible. This is a Mephisto store. It sells nothing but Mephisto shoes, and they don't have the style or color I want in my size, and they don't know when, or apparently *if* they ever will. How do they stay in business? Who shops here? That's what I'm thinking as three more people walk in. I thank the saleslady, mother, and daughter, and say, "Au revoir," pleased at least that I now know my French shoe size, and will never have to go through *that* again.

The rest of the summer I go to Mephisto stores in Quimper, Vannes, Lorient, Morlaix, and Rennes, searching for those shoes and sandals in a size 42. The salesperson always says, "Oui," and goes to the storeroom. God knows why, there's nothing ever there, unless they're going back there to laugh, and returns with the right shoe in the wrong size or color or the wrong shoe in the right size. We then have the conversation that ends like this: "No, we don't have that style." Or, "We have it, but not in your color or size." And, "No, I don't know when," and, "No, I cannot call and order them."

I leave France $250 richer, wondering how these people stay in business. They have little stock or inventory—sometimes all they have is what's on display—and no idea or control over when they'll get more or what they'll get. They get what Mephisto gives them, and the customer gets what they have in stock. If the customer wants something that's not available, the answer is "peut-être demain," but I can tell you after returning many times to many stores, you have a better chance of finding Atlantis. I once went into a shoe store where every shoe in the store was in a pile on the floor. It was the customer's job to find the style, color, size, and mate. I now know why they're named Mephisto, short for Mephistopheles: it's a devil of a shoe to find—and why I'm still wearing Eccos.

A Bookcase

In California, my furniture is old and used, bought at flea markets and antique shops. I prefer honey-colored oak in arts-and-crafts style, creating a Carnegie-library effect of straight lines, good light, and open space. I want the same in Plobien, but it isn't easy.

The wood of choice in rural Brittany is dark, heavy, thick mahogany, which feels to me like grandma furniture and funerals. Finding oak—especially honey-colored oak—is rare. That's the bad news. The good news is when I do find it no one else wants it, and the seller has had it a long time and wants to get rid of it quickly. It also helps that I like lots of open space, so I don't need a lot of furniture.

Space, I've come to learn (like time) is one of those huge cultural divides: take the men's room, for example. I'm at the movies in Quimper, and I have to pee. I head straight to the urinal farthest from the door. A French guy walks in and uses the urinal right next to me. In the U.S., this is not normal behavior. It's a sign of a possible—probable—invitation to a party I don't want to attend. In the U.S., if there's an open urinal between urinals, you leave it. You *never* stand next to someone unless you have to. Not so in France. At this point, I'm surprised the guy doesn't want to share. In France, people congregate. In the U.S., they separate. I see it all the time.

There's a little public park across the street from my house. The village provides a public shower and toilet for overnight campers and boaters. Year after year I watch, amazed. In the U.S., if I arrive at a camping or picnic area where others have already set up, I go as far away from them as possible. In France, the rule seems to be the closer the better—and the closest to the toilet is best. In the U.S., I want to be far away from the noise, lights, smell, and activity. In France, people want to be within sight, smell, and feel. Maybe it's a difference in diet and camp food. In the U.S., when I go camping I get constipated. Maybe it's the reverse in France. Whatever it is, people pile on top of each other. Campgrounds are as densely packed as high-rise apartment buildings, with most people deliberately camping and parking right next to each other. I often see people happily picnicking luxuriously—Champagne, flute glasses, cloth napkins, foie gras—sitting in concrete parking lots surrounded by cars and RVs or on the gravel on the side of a highway.

Americans tend to search for private, out-of-the-way, one-of-a-kind, solitary, secret places. French people like to go where everyone has been and is going, and they want what everyone has. Cars are not customized in France. The exteriors of houses are not different. Day-to-day clothing does not differentiate among people. In France, if it's good enough for everyone else, it's good enough for me. In the U.S., if everyone else has it, who wants it? The more people have it, the less it's worth. Americans tend to open their space. French people tend to close it. French space is internal, American space is external. I think I'm the only person in the village who sleeps with my shutters *and* windows wide open.

Once, when I was with Philippe, Madame and Monsieur P's eldest son, he pointed to a guy walking in the other direction, and said, "He's an American."

"How do you know?" I asked.

"The way he walks—his stride and the way he swings his arms. No one else takes up that much space."

He's right—and it applies to U.S. foreign policy, the footprint of the U.S. on the environment, and also to aesthetic taste: "Give me room, lots of room . . . Don't fence me in . . . " To cross any room in my house in Plobien, you walk a straight line. To cross a room in a traditional Breton home, you walk in arcs and zigzags.

I'm willing to change many things about myself in France, but not my aesthetics. I like what I like: the Carnegie-library effect of honey-oak, arts-and-crafts design, and space. That's my comfort zone, and since everything else in France is so different, I want to keep my aesthetics, which is why week after week after week I've been shopping for the perfect bookcase— to shelve the piles of books and magazines that are accumulating on my floors, tables, and chairs, taking up space.

Twice a week I drive to Emmaüs, France's version of the St. Vincent de Paul charity, in Brest and Quimper, to see if anything new and interesting has arrived. Over the years, I've bought furniture and appliances from them dirt cheap: an oak armoire and bureau, my washing machine, and an animal trough that I use to store tablecloths, seat cushions, CDs, and books. When French people visit and see it, they always ask what it is, knowing full well, but not believing it, or wanting to. It's more proof, if needed, that I'm weird: like, who but an American would bring an animal feeder into a house? And its unstated corollary, how much do you think he paid for it? And *its* unstated corollary, what other weird things do you think he has bought? I've been going to Emmaüs all summer. No bookcases or oak have been found.

I've also been making a weekly circuit of local *vide greniers* (attic sales), *marchés aux puces* (flea markets), *dépôt-ventes* (second-hand stores) and *brocantes* (a mix of antique store and Goodwill), where I've bought furniture in the past. I've seen two oak bookcases I like, but both are priced out of my league. Aesthetics are one thing, price is another—and in my income bracket, the two rarely meet.

My best bet is the once-a-year weekend antiques fair at Plomelin, where a château and its grounds are rented and filled with several hundred booths of antique dealers and *brocantes* from all over France. Most items cost much more than I can afford—like the shards and broken and cracked pieces of Quimperware selling for hundreds of dollars—but the array is endlessly fascinating (think of all the episodes of *Antiques Roadshow* you've ever seen happening in one place). Over the years, I've bought a few things here—a chair, a couple of tables, a lamp. If I have any chance of finding what I want, this is it.

I arrive late in the afternoon on Sunday, the last day of the fair, knowing sellers often let their goods go cheaply rather than pack them up and carry them home. I start at the booths farthest from the large tent and château because their rent is cheapest, and they're most likely to have what I can afford, which I figure is around five hundred dollars.

I go to the farthest stall and start walking in. Stalls are arranged in concentric circles, like a labyrinth or maze, which (like when driving) makes knowing where you are and finding your way back a challenge. Since that's my normal state in France, I'm comfortable. My system, based on years of flea market shopping in California, is to walk an aisle in one direction, then to turn around and walk back, because what I see coming is different from what I see going, even though nothing has changed.

Sure enough, there, in the center of the circle—a bull's eye—I see what I'm looking for: light oak, five-shelf, beveled glass door, about six feet tall, with deco-like Aztec designs carved into the front piece; a beauty. I turn and walk as far away from it as I can and stare at it. It's the same method I used to meet girls at parties in high school. I'd spot one I liked and go to the opposite corner. This system works better, I can tell you, with furniture. By the time I was ready to meet the girl, she was gone. Furniture, thankfully, stays put.

I meander my way slowly toward the bookcase, arcing this way and zigging that, stopping to look at things I couldn't care less about: a chipped ceramic vase, cracked leather chair, monsieur-and-madame matching andirons. The closer I get, the better it looks. I walk past it, continuing to meander through other booths. Then I meander back, ready to begin the *pas de deux* with the seller, and see no one is there. It's the last hours of the last day of the fair, and the salesperson is gone. There's a note pinned to a tablecloth. *Retour à 15h30*, 3:30. It's now 3:00. Anyone could walk away with anything, though I appear to be the only person thinking that. It's the same when the fruit lady closes her shop for lunch. She locks the shop and leaves all the fruit outside. There's a level of trust here that's unnerving.

I circle the bookcase looking for the price. Sometimes items are marked and sometimes not. I'm thinking five hundred to seven hundred dollars would be a bargain, when I see the sticker pasted on the side—250 euros—about three hundred and fifty dollars, a steal. It's rare, and a find, and I want it. I'm burning to buy, but my composure is cooler than ice. I don't want to appear too eager.

I walk around looking at other booths to see if there's anything else I like, or a better deal, and return at 3:45. "15h30" has been crossed out and "16h00" added. Once again, I marvel at how the French expand time the way Americans do space.

The seller returns at 16:15. He's a big, hefty, smiling guy with a beard and suspenders. He walks slowly toward me—and the dance begins.

I turn away to look at a mahogany table and chairs I hate.

He walks past me, to the front of his stall, and peers out as if he's expecting Audrey Tatou or Jesus.

I open the drawers of a bureau I couldn't care less about, then go back to the bookcase and remove a tape measure from my pocket and measure: two meters high, one meter wide, 0.4 meters deep. It's perfect. I shake my head "No," and make a sound like disappointment amplified. I want him to know I'm interested, *but* it may not fit in my house, a conundrum—though I already know I'm buying, as per Rule Number One of shopping: if you see what you want, get it, don't wait, it will be gone.

He walks back toward me, visibly disappointed neither Audrey nor Jesus has appeared.

Now that we're both disappointed, it's time to conclude and make us both happy.

"Monsieur," I ask, as if passing the time, "connez vous le an au cette pièce?" I'm asking the provenance, the year it was made, its history, if it has been involved in any murders or scandals, anything he can tell me about the bookcase. He'll tell me what he knows, nothing more, nothing less; of this I'm certain. I have never been lied to or cheated by a salesperson.

"Je ne sais pas," he shrugs, and tells me he got the bookcase in the north, near Roscoff, which makes sense because there are lots of English people living there, and they, like me, like oak. He also tells me he's had it a "longtemps," letting me know he's ready to move it.

"Bon," I say. "Merci. Je pense," and I point to my head to let him know I'm thinking and don't have a headache, or something worse, like Alzheimer's. He walks away to let me ponder. We both know I'm buying, but it's up to me to make the first move.

Sellers are always willing to deal, but the best deals come when no one else is present, *especially* no other French people— like now. Transactions like this are private. I have one shot at drastically reducing the price. He has to believe I'm serious about my bottom line—and the bottom line has to be fair, not insulting. I'm going to offer him twenty percent less than the asking price. I circle the booth one more time and stop in front of the sales guy, who's standing behind his desk, waiting for me, smiling.

"Monsieur, acceptez-vous deux-cents?" I offer him two hundred euros—about $300—and point to the bookcase.

"Oui."

"Bon—et le livraison?" The delivery?

"Cinquante euros." Fifty euros.

I see where this is going. He's determined to get his two hundred fifty euros, and I'm determined to get my twenty percent discount.

"Monsieur, j'ai d'argent." I have cash.

"Ouiiiii."

The 20 percent sales tax is the fifty-euro difference between us. It's the old under-the-table transaction, which works especially well if you buy the table too—which I do. I pay him 200 euros for the bookcase and 75 for the table, and he delivers them that night, as he said he would, as I fully expected.

The next day I fill the bookcase with books and magazines and luxuriate in my additional space. It's my personal version of western expansion and Manifest Destiny.

Light Fixtures

Thanks to native rural frugality, old houses with old wiring, and the high cost of electricity, people prefer 40- and 60-watt light bulbs to 75s and 100s, even with today's modern lights. I once put a 150-watt bulb in the overhead kitchen light and Madame P went nuts. When I left at the end of the summer, she replaced it—out of deference to me—with a 60-watter, though I know she preferred the 40. When I returned the following year, I replaced her 60-watter—out of deference to her—with a 100, though I preferred the 150—and there we stand in quiet truce, she thinking I'm profligate; I thinking, to hell with the Green Party, she's conserving too much.

This year, I've decided to mount a pair of halogen lamps on the wall behind my bed, so when I read at night before going to sleep I won't have to get out of bed and cross the room to turn off the light, as I've been doing for years. Leaving the warm cozy bed is a pain, banging my toe returning in the dark even more so. I'm finally ready to buy, which means returning to the lamp store—which means trouble with a capital T.

I've been to this store many times and bought several lamps, including two very expensive ones, because I like lots of light, and when the sun's not out, like in the evening or winter or one of the two hundred fifty days a year it rains, I need a little brightness. This store, unlike most—and I've been to many—is huge, has lots of choices, and does not favor those tiny, decorative, 25-watt lamps that wouldn't light a fish tank, not to mention a room at night.

Over the years, I've spent hundreds of dollars in this store, yet each time I enter and call out, "Bonjour," whoever's behind the counter—the *propriétaire*, his wife, daughter, or son, all of whom I've bought from—says, "Bonjour," as if they've never seen me before. I'm used to it now, but for the first thousand dollars it was unsettling.

"Bonjour," I call out as I enter the store.

"Bonjour," comes back from the *propriétaire*, who doesn't bother to look up.

I don't care. I *want* to be left alone to survey, see what's new, what's on sale, check the prices, and ponder my choices. I go straight to the area where halogens, wall lamps, art glass, and sconces were last time I was in the store and am surprised to see they're still there.

Unlike the French, I want something simple and plain. I resist the temptingly beautiful, ultra-modern, stunningly elegant, delicate, intricate, fragile lamps French people seem to prefer: lamps designed and accessorized in ways guaranteed to snap, crackle, and pop—like the one with the ornate snow-flake-like filigree shade that won't survive the first changing of the bulb, or the beauty with the impossibly thin two-inch-long tapering arm for adjusting the direction of light. No way. I learned my lesson from a thermos, teakettle, and vacuum cleaner: the better it looks, the worse it works.

I bought a thermos to keep my coffee hot in the mornings. It's gorgeous, iridescent blue, missile-shaped, curved, metallic, Brancusi-like-cool, but something about the shape of the plug makes it impossible to pour without spilling, and the seal doesn't seal, so liquids don't stay hot *or* cold. In twenty minutes, everything becomes lukewarm. I bought a beautiful, sleek, stainless steel teakettle with a catchy whistle that broke almost immediately and a handle guaranteed not to get hot that scalds. I thought they were flukes, mistakes, one-of-a-kind lemons. Then I bought my first vacuum cleaner—a space-age, indus-trial, cyclotron-inspired model that looks like it could suck the gold out of fillings, only the thing wouldn't even eat spider webs. I swear, spiders laughed when they saw it coming. So I now forego the sexy and buy the simple, sturdy, easy to install and maintain, which is usually German, English, or Dutch.

I find what I want hidden behind the gleam and the junk. It's brushed bronze, not glittering chrome or brass, with a simple 50- and 100-watt switch, a two-screw mount, and easy access to change the bulb. It doesn't stand out, it fits in, which is why I didn't see it right away—and it's the most expensive lamp on the shelf: two hundred dollars for one, and I want two.

I look everywhere and don't see another—not a good sign. Inventory must be a dirty word in France, because if it's not on the shelf or counter or rack, it usually doesn't exist. This is where the trouble begins—when I need help.

In the U.S., I indicate my need by standing in front of the desired or contemplated object and stare at it, or touch it, or pick it up and put it down several times, at which point someone usually says, "May I help you?" If no one does, I pace back and forth in front of the object, widening my route until I'm standing in front of the cash register. By then, unless it's service I want, or I'm in a store where only fifteen-year-olds are working, someone will usually help me. If everything fails, I ask, "Hey, can I have some help here?" which is what I'm about to do now.

I've been in the store twenty minutes, found the lamp I want, stared at it, walked in front of it, picked it up and put it down several times, paced the aisle, then the area, and have been standing in front of the cash register for a full two minutes. Finally, I ask. "L'assistance, s'il vous plaît."

"Un moment," Monsieur answers without raising his eyes and continues adding receipts. If this were the U.S., I'd leave. But this is France, Brittany, Finistère—"the end of the world"— and I've seen the lamp I want, and I know no one else within fifty miles, if that, will have it. And I know from experience to buy what I want when I see it, because odds are I'll never see it again. So when Monsieur says, "Un moment," I wait.

He finishes adding his receipts, which as far as I can figure are fewer than twelve, though he's spent at least ten minutes doing it, looks up, and says, "Oui," as if he didn't know I was there and had never seen me before.

"S'il vous plaît," I say, and lead him to the display. I'm the only customer in the store, but he follows me reluctantly, as if there are a zillion other places he'd rather be. I understand— but he's here and so am I, and I need his help. I point to the lamp I'm interested in and say, "Une."

"Oui," he says, clearly not impressed with my math or vision.

"Je voudrais achete deux." I hold up two fingers.

"Oui."

"Avez vous deux?"

"Non."

"C'est possible?"

He shrugs.

"Quand possible?"

"Peut-être le fin de semaine." Maybe by the end of the week.

It's déjà vu all over again, only now I'm in a quandary. Do I buy the one I really like and want, understanding I'll never see the other and won't have a matched set—which suddenly seems to matter more than anything—or do I wait till the end of the week, which could easily be the end of the month or eternity, and have the other one arrive and this one sold? Shit. Once again, the shopper's dilemma in France: buy now and don't get what I want, or buy later and don't get what I want. How soon do I want to be disappointed? How long do I want to live with false hope?

I opt for the latter and tell Monsieur I'll return "fin de semaine." It's a forty-five-minute, fifty-kilometer journey. They have a phone and an answering machine, but I have to return to find out if the lamp's sister has arrived because they rarely answer the phone and never return messages. On the rare occasion when someone does answer the phone, they are always too busy to look for anything or answer any questions even if they understand what I am asking. It's no use asking them to call me when the lamp arrives. They'll agree and never do it. No, if I want that lamp—*really* want it, and the harder it is to get, the more I do want it—the burden is mine. "À bientôt," I say and leave, hoping it sounds like a threat.

At the end of the week, I return to the store, say, "Bonjour," and go straight to the display. The good news is the one lamp is still there. I'm hoping there's even better news and number two has arrived and they're holding it for me. I walk up to the counter and wait. Madame is arranging light bulbs—by size, wattage, price, shape, color, screw-in or bayonet—who can tell? All I know is, it's more important than talking to me, the only customer in the shop. Finally, I say, "Madame." She lifts her head and looks at me as if she's never seen me before, though she said "bonjour" to me less than ten minutes ago and sold me a four-hundred-dollar lamp last year, acting as if I were a relative. Now I see how relative I am.

"S'il vous plaît," I say, and lead her to the display and pick up the lamp I want. "Vous avez une."

"Oui."

"Je voudrais deux."

"Oui."

"Avez-vous une autre?"

"Non."

"Quand arrive?"

"Je ne sais pas. Peut-être deux semaines." Now it's a two-week wait.

Again, my quandary: buy now and be disappointed or buy later and be disappointed. Again, I opt for the latter. Living here has made me Edwardian: I require symmetry and a matched set, two one-of-a-kinds will not do. It's mid-June, I'm leaving in eight weeks, and would like to complete this transaction by then—but just in case, I have a plan.

I write down the name and number of the lamp model and

the name of the manufacturer. I go to lamp stores in Brest, Quimper, Morlaix, Rennes, and Vannes. No one has it. No one has seen it. No one can order it. Plus, the shop owners act as if I've asked them to buy AK-47s or Mirage Jets and launder money—and perhaps I have. For all I know, the lamps are made in Pakistan or North Korea and the money is going to some Iran-Contra-type intelligence scam for lamps. I don't care. I want that lamp. I look for other matched pairs while I'm in these stores, but nothing is as nice as the *one* I've been looking at, which makes me want the second one more. Besides, if I bought one of those, I'd be back to the *sine qua non* of French shopping: disappointment. You'd think since I'll be disappointed buying one, disappointed buying two that don't match, and disappointed buying a matched set I like, but not as much as this *one*, I'd settle for the least disappointment and move on. No way.

I return to the store in two weeks, say, "Bonjour," though I don't really mean it, and have the same conversation with the daughter, which ends the same way: "Peut-être la semaine prochaine."

On my way out, as a throwaway, just to get the last word, I ask, "Madame, avez-vous un autre magasin en autre ville?'"

"Oui."

Holy shit! I'm speechless. They have another store in another village and they've never called to see if *they* have the lamp. It truly is unbelievable. Still, I try to contain my joy, though I feel like I've hit the mother lode. As nonchalantly and as servile as I can, I say, "Pardon moi, Madame, s'il vous plaît, c'est possible vous telephone le autre magasin et demande si avez le même lamp?" Can you call the other shop and ask if they have the lamp?

"Non."

"No?"

"Non. Ce n'est pas possible."

That's it. Over and out. She lifts the lamp from the display and walks toward the register as if I've agreed to buy this *one*.

"Madame, je voudrais *deux*!"

She waves the lamp in front of me and says, "C'est tout," and brings me back to my quandary and my quest, which is now becoming my own little "Impossible Dream."

"Quand arrive le autre?" I ask, trying not to sound desperate.

"Ça dépend."

"C'est depende a qua!"

"Je ne sais pas . . . Peut-être . . . "

I give up on the daughter—the whole damned family. This is war, and I intend to win.

I begin showing up at the store at different times over the next few weeks, each time checking to make sure the one lamp is still there, then demanding of the father, mother, son, daughter, nephew, niece, whoever is behind the counter, would they please call the other store? The answer is always the same: "Non."

I'd call the other store myself, but French telephone books and information directories are arranged by village. If you don't know the village, you can't find the number, and I don't know the village—there are thousands of them—and these people aren't telling. Besides, even if I had the number, they wouldn't answer the phone, return my message, or help me if I reached them. The only comforting thing is they treat French people the same way they treat me. They must be independently wealthy, or the store is a front. Nowhere else in the world could they survive. The thought is comforting, but of little solace, since this is where I am and I need them.

This continues for seven weeks. I go to the store, affirm the one lamp is still there, and inquire about purchasing a second. Each time, though, I'm a little less resolute. It's in that mood that I return to the store one last time before returning to the U.S.

"Bonjour," I say to Monsieur and go to the display and see the *one* lamp I've been eyeing all summer. It looks more and more perfect the farther away it gets. I pick it up, resigned now to have only one—or worse, a nonmatching set. I carry it to the counter and put it down, a gesture of surrender—Lee at Appomattox, Cornwallis at Yorktown—and take out my checkbook. Monsieur picks up the lamp, enters the model number and price into the computer and bags it. While I'm writing the check, he says to me, "Voudriez-vous que je téléphone au magasin de St. Brieuc?"

He's asking *me* if I'd like *him* to telephone the store in St. Brieuc? Is he kidding or perverse? I've been in this store a dozen times, spoken to anyone breathing behind the counter, have begged, pleaded, entreated everyone to make this call, but only now when I've completely lost, surrendered, accepted defeat, does he offer. In the U.S., I rarely acknowledge defeat: the best offense is offense. In France, the best offense is defense. It's a lesson I learn over and over and over again. The surest way to win is to acknowledge you haven't. So I do. "Oui," I say, duly vanquished. "S'il vous plaît."

Monsieur goes into action. He picks up the phone and punches in the numbers he knows by heart. He makes the requisite small talk, then picks up the lamp I just bought and reads the model number and manufacturer's name and waits.

"Oui, oui, oui," he says, covers the mouthpiece and says to me, "Ils l'ont . . . Elle sera ici dans deux semaines." Two weeks.

I'm leaving in five days. In the U.S., I'd explain this and the lamp would be here in twenty-four hours. Here, two weeks is fast. For all I know they're saving shipping costs and walking it over. "Oui, oui," I say, hoping Martin will pick it up in two weeks and install it. "Oui!"

And here's the kicker—I leave the store happy, a satisfied customer, with one lamp in hand, the other on promise, both of them paid for, *merci*-ing, *merci*-ing away, and meaning it.

The one thing I am sure about is not being cheated. French businesses and salespeople may not be customer-attentive, but they are scrupulously honest. The previous winter I bought Christmas gifts for French friends through a French mail-order house. I sent a check for five hundred dollars, feeling smart and happy because I was saving the cost of U.S. postage, which is formidable. I continued to feel that way until I received a letter telling me the company was out of business. I bought replacement gifts, paid the postage, and sent them, lesson learned—capitalism is capitalism—and kissed those five hundred dollars bye-bye. Six months later, when I arrived at the house in June, my check was waiting for me in the mail, uncashed.

After eight frustrating and humbling weeks, I leave the store not disappointed, but not content. I have the promise of a lamp I paid for, but until Martin has it mounted and glowing from the wall, there are many, many things to go wrong. In this case, they don't, but disappointment is never far away. In that way, the exceptions don't undermine the rule—*cédez le passage*, as once again I'm reminded that in the U.S. the preferred motion is full steam ahead, and in France, it is often better to yield.

Shampoo and a Mattress Cover

One of the most difficult things about shopping in France is not being able to read the labels. Mostly it involves words I don't know, and also those I do.

I just bought a shampoo that proclaims itself *antipelliculaire*. I don't have dandruff, so why did I buy it? I bought it because I didn't see the word *antipelliculaire*, which was translated into every language except English, written in the lightest, tiniest script on the back of the bottle. What I saw was "SHAMPOO," written in big, bold letters in front (not *bain moussant*—bubble bath—which I've already bought and don't need, or *douche soin*, skin care gel, which I've also bought and don't need) and the company name, L'Oréal, a name I recognize and can find in the U.S. and sue if I become bald.

This is how I shop in France: preventively. I once bought a shampoo that said, *cheveux secs*—dry hair—and after using it a few times became convinced it wasn't to treat dry hair but to give you dry hair, because my hair looked and felt like wheat, though this being France, it smelled like lavender, and also because it's France, I wasn't completely unhappy with the wrong purchase, because it could have been worse, like the *dépilatoire* I once bought and thankfully didn't use. This too, I think, is part of French marketing strategy. In the U.S., if I'm dissatisfied with my purchase, I bring it back or go to a different store. In France, I return to the same store again and again and again, making more and more wrong purchases, and once again buying—and spending—twice as much as I need. For example, bedding.

Because of my language skills, I shop by picture. That's how I bought the wrong mattress cover, and also why I'm back in the store, determined to get it right.

I'm holding the plastic package, being *very* careful and deliberate. I check the size: 190 x 140 centimeters. I look at the picture: it's an aerial view of a mattress cover pulled Beyoncé's-pants-tight over a double bed, not a pimple, crease or fold in sight. It's *exactly* what I want. It's also what I thought I bought a week ago.

Somehow, I bought a mattress cover *without* fitted corners—why would they even make them like that? Who would knowingly buy them?—the kind that wrinkles and bunches like rhino skin when touched, making sure, (1) you can't sleep on it, and (2) you have to return to the store and buy another version of what you just bought and thought you were done with. What's particularly galling—"Gauling"?—I see, is there's absolutely no way to know by looking at the picture that the sides are not fitted. You have to open the package to see that, but once you open it, you can't return it. French law or store policy or management caprice, one of them, is very clear about that.

Still, I'm not too upset. I usually allow myself one mistake when shopping by picture, but *another* mistake would confirm a level of failure even I could not accept, which is why I'm stealthily bending, twisting, mangling the package, searching for those fitted corners. I see the cushioned flannel top, but not the sides. I twist the package harder, further, and barely visible, under a fold, almost hidden, I see a millimeter of the curved elastic corner that will fit over the edge of the mattress and allow me to sleep the sleep of the fulfilled. Voilà!

I buy it, bring it home, rip open the packaging with a knife, because the "New, open here" doesn't work, and see, yes indeedy, I've finally got the fitted mattress cover I want—only it's rubberized. I pick up the plastic packaging and see in tiny print the word *imperméable*.

I've now spent over one hundred and fifty-dollars for two mattress covers I can't return, so I decide to try it. I unwrap it, stretch it over the bed, and fit the ends over the corners. It *is* Beyoncé's-pants-taut. I'm counting on the tautness and cushioned flannel top to hide the feel of the rubber. Ha! It's horrible, like sleeping on plastic. Safe sex is one thing, safe sleep another. I take it off, store it with the nonfitted mattress cover, and go back to sleeping on the disgusting, old, stained mattress cover that fits and is comfortable.

The following year, I decide I need a new mattress cover. It's one of the things I like about being in France. Every year I'm filled with new hope, a tabula rasa. In the U.S., this feeling is limited to baseball. In France, the tabula rasa applies to everything. *Every* part of my life seems new, which can make life exciting, but also a perpetual *Groundhog Day.*

I'm back in the store holding the plastic-wrapped package, pondering the word *imperméable.* I know it's important, vital for the success of this purchase, but I cannot for the life of me remember if I want it to be *imperméable* or not. It's like *embarquement* and *débarquement.* Every year, on the flight to France, the airline distributes a green card to be filled out and given to the gendarme at customs. The last question on the form is "What airport did you disembark from?" Every year, I ponder my answer. Did I disembark at San Francisco International Airport or Paris? Every year, I write Paris, because I *embarked* at San Francisco. Every year, the gendarme crosses out Paris and writes San Francisco, and I tell myself next year I'll remember and get it right, and the next year I forget, and ponder, and reason it out, and reach the same conclusion: I disembarked at Paris. So I buy the *imperméable* and bring it home.

This time, though—fool me once, shame on you; fool me twice, shame on me—I look for the seam, which is so cleverly hidden I can't find it. I give up—another *sine qua non* of French shopping—and snip a tiny piece from a corner of the package and slide my pinky in to feel if there's rubber. That's when I remember what *imperméable* means. Shame on me.

Clearly, I need to do something different. I decide I'm going to return the package I've opened. Receipt in hand and package in the bag, I go to the smiling lady who's sitting in a booth under a huge *Accueil*—welcome—sign and say, "Bonjour."

She looks at me suspiciously.

I hand her the receipt and the package and say, "Ce n'est pas nécessaire," meaning, I don't need rubber sheets.

She looks at me like, "Yeah, right."

I stand my ground and say nothing, mostly because that's all I can do.

She opens the bag, sees the package has been opened and starts talking. She's probably accusing me of having wild sex on the mattress cover or using it as a toilet and now trying to return it, and she, the store, all of France will not be taken in or fooled by this ploy.

I stand there and don't say anything, which is guaranteed to drive French people nuts. I know it, but there's nothing else I can do—or say. All I know is I'm not leaving without a refund. I've already got two mattress covers I can't use—one rubberized, the other without fitted corners, and I do not want a third. It's a matter of principle. *En principe . . .*

People are waiting behind me, curious about what's going to happen, ready, if I win, to return hundreds of their own open packages bought by mistake. I stand there for all customers and shoppers, unwilling to move or relinquish my place.

The now not-so-smiling *accueil*-lady buzzes her supervisor, a guy about twenty, who takes one look at me, a middle-aged guy wearing cutoff shorts and a Mr. Bean T-shirt, and the wedge behind me, which must look to him like the Paris Commune or May 1968, and approves the refund: in cash, not credit, probably so I won't return to the store.

As I leave the store, cash in hand, my fellow shoppers pat me on the back and wave their receipts, acknowledging a victory for the people against the system. French people love the idea of the winning underdog (unless *they* are the overdog) and they hate the system, all systems, systematically: 98 percent of the time they follow the rules, and the other 2 percent they go Robespierre. It's an interesting paradox.

So is this. I have my refund, but I'm still sleeping on the old, stained mattress cover. The following year, I decide to buy a new one—and here is where it gets truly pitiful. I go to the same store and pick up the sealed package, bending, twisting, and mangling it until I'm sure it has fitted sides. I read the small, smaller, and smallest print in every font and European language and don't see the word "impermeable" anywhere. Satisfied and confident, I buy it, bring it home, rip the package open with impunity, and immediately see I bought the wrong size: I have a double bed, and I bought a mattress cover for a twin. Even I don't have the nerve to try and return it. So much for the people's victory.

Like most of history, I'm back to the Restoration. It's my own little Tiananmen squared.

10 Things I've Learned about Shopping in France

1. Avoid anything that says "easy to open" or "new packaging," because it's never easy, and if it's new, it's worse than it was before.

2. Form follows form, not function—especially for products made in France. There's an inverse ratio of looks to works: the prettier it looks, the worse it works. There's a reason haute couture is French.

3. Rules for buying food and produce:
    a. At the moms and pops, they touch the food and weigh it, and I better not;
    b. At the weekly public market, I touch the food and they weigh it, unless the food is behind a counter, on a spit, in a cage, a tank, a freezer, or on ice. Then they touch it and weigh it, and I watch;
    c. At the *supermarché*, I touch the food and I weigh the produce, except at the *Intermarché*, where they weigh it. I don't know why. There are some things I have to accept;
    d. The concept of a quick, one-stop, 7-Eleven, AM/PM run into the shop, find what I want, buy it, and run out kind of store doesn't exist. French people have some of the longest life expectancies in the world, so time doesn't matter so much. Shopping, apparently, is how they choose to spend it.

4. Under no circumstances forget the word for "cone" when buying ice cream and ask for "un con." Don't ask why, just don't do it.

5. Customer advocacy does not exist. I have no rights, but I do have a philosophy: expect to be disappointed, and I won't

be too much; and its corollary: if—or when—I get what I want, be thrilled; and its corollary: even if it's not exactly what I want, be happy with what I have; and its corollary: I could have done worse.

6. Persistence and perseverance: I've learned to be determined like an idiot, not willful like a boss. If I'm willful, I'm dead. If I'm an idiot, I have a chance. *As* an idiot, I've had several chances and have made the most of many of them.

7. It's best to begin a transaction with a question. A statement can and likely will be challenged. A question confirms my ignorance and need for help—two traits guaranteed to bring out the kindness and charity of French people.

8. *Supermarchés* no longer provide free plastic bags for carrying purchases. Customers have to bring their own bags or baskets, which is fine if I remember, and not so fine if I don't. I now keep several bags and a wicker basket in the car so I'm prepared for any sudden bursts of shopping. The problem is when I pick up friends and their luggage at the train station or airport, go to the beach, or buy something large, I remove the bags and basket, and forget to put them back, which returns me to the terrible days of people behind me grumbling, days I prefer not to relive.

9. The hours posted on the front door or window of a business are accurate and precise. If the sign says the store closes from 1200hr to 1400hr, entering at 11:55—especially to shop for something big, like a TV, refrigerator, or stereo system—is a no-no, something only a foreigner like me would do, thinking, it's a sale, a big one, maybe the biggest of the day or the week, why wouldn't the salesman want to see me? He does, but during regular, posted business hours. Between 1200hr and 1400hr, he wants lunch. The

same is true in reverse for restaurants. If the sign says lunch is served between 1200hr and 1400hr, don't get hungry at 1100hr or 1500hr and expect to eat. French people take their rules very seriously—except, of course, when they don't, like when they're driving. The trick is to know when and how the rules can be broken—and by whom. As a foreigner, I know I'll never know, which is why I do my best to follow them—no matter how nutty they seem.

10. Shopping on Amazon.fr is easy, but not politically correct, as the few French people I know who do it tell me. Shopping at other e-locations and paying bills online *is* politically correct, but it isn't easy, so few people do it. I tried to pay my electric bill online and found I could not access the information I needed from EDF, the gas and electric company. Sharon tried, and she couldn't either. Gilles, who works professionally in IT, also tried and could not do it, and when the Wi-Fi connection at his house was disrupted, it took multiple repair visits and over a month to get it restored, which is odd, because France is totally wired. My house, in a village of six hundred people, was wired with underground fiber optics more than a decade ago. Wi-Fi is everywhere, online shopping *should* be simple and more common, but it's not, which is why I continue to shop in actual stores, communicate with real people, and look forward to more and greater humiliations, surprises, and lessons—especially at my bank.

Money, Money,
Money, Money

Every year I wire money to my account from the U.S., and every year I worry about it getting there, because once—the first time—it didn't. It went to Corsica. There's never been a problem since, but you never can tell, and that's double the case in France, because I really can't tell—or ask. Worse, I never know my account balance. I don't know it in the U.S. either, but there I have a clue, and I can ask.

In the U.S., if I bounce a check, I pay the bank an enormous fee for the $2.50 I'm short, and everyone—the depositor, the bank, and I—is happy. I assume it's the same in France, especially since people I've never met before and will never see again willingly and gladly accept and cash my checks—for all sums—without requesting a photo ID, thumbprint, or cheek swab. Clearly, I'm not French, not from around these parts, don't speak the language—and on occasion have not even known how to write the amount of the check in words, and the person it's going to has to write it for me. Even then, no questions asked, they accept my check.

For years, I thought it was because of overdraft protection, and because I look honest, friendly, simple—a Forrest-Gump–type nice guy who would never steal, so people trusted me—but now, thanks to Sally, Martin, and Louise, I know the truth, and it doesn't set me free. It scares the hell out of me.

Martin, Louise, and Sally

The first clue that I didn't know anything about French banks should have been the year I arrived and discovered the equivalent of one thousand dollars missing from my checking account. My first thought was the money I wired hadn't arrived; then I thought I added or subtracted wrong and didn't carry the one; all of which were possible, and none of which happened.

It took me a week to figure out my friend Martin had it. He needed the money to buy supplies and material for work he was doing on my house. He walked into the bank, explained who he was and what he was doing, and walked out with a thousand dollars worth of euros *and* a copy of my latest bank statement, complete with the balance, account number, and all my identification information. Even Martin, who lives in Plobien, was shocked, though not as much as he would be when it happens to him.

He and Louise decide to open a *brocante* and sell English antiques out of their garage. To do it, they need to buy a van, refinish their garage, and purchase goods, so they go to their bank. They're English. They've lived in Plobien for three years after moving from Australia, where they'd lived for several years after leaving England. Neither has a regular job. Based on that, the bank loans them a goodly sum to begin their business. That's the good news.

For two years, Martin makes multiple trips to England, taking the van on the ferry from Roscoff to Plymouth, driving around Cornwall and Devon, buying furniture and knickknacks at jumble sales, and bringing the truckloads back to Louise, who cleans and polishes everything, repairs what needs mending, and arranges, displays, and sells—but not very much.

The problem is French people are not terribly interested in buying old English stuff when they have plenty of their own old French stuff lying around. These are rural people, people who do not discard things lightly, and their houses are already jam-packed with generations of goods. After three years and a gallant effort, Martin and Louise close shop, which brings them back to the bank. That's the bad news.

They pay back the loan, but there is a dispute over their credit card payments. The next time Martin goes to the bank, he discovers his account balance is substantially reduced. He asks about his missing money and is told he owes it, and the bank took it—no hearing, notice, letter, appeal—it's gone. The next day Martin returns to close his account before they can take any more and finds he's already a day late and more than a few euros short.

With powers like these, no wonder banks are so willing to make loans—and no wonder people all over France accept my check without ID. After I sign it, any mistake is mine, *and* any mistake, and I'm dead. Like Sally.

She's English and has lived in Plobien for years. She got married in the village and patronizes all the local stores. She's fluent in French and has a doctorate from a French university. Everyone knows and likes her—she's the Perle Mesta of Plobien—and she bounces a few checks and goes over her overdraft limit, and her bank cuts her off in a snap. That's it. Over. No more. Au revoir. This is the bank she's banked with from the start. All those smiling, young, happy-to-see-you *bonjour*ing-and-*bonne journée*ing tellers don't mean a thing. Neither does knowing the bank officers or Monsieur le Président. She writes a few checks for a few more euros than her overdraft allowance, and her account is shut. It takes her a long, long time with lots of forms signed and promises made before another bank will open an account for her.

From this, I understand French people are serious about their money in ways not comprehensible in the U.S. And I also understand this: if it takes Sally, who is French-fluent and a long-term resident, a long time to find another bank, it would take me forever. Even Madame P, I'm sure, could not break that barrier. Sally's story is a lesson learned, and I hope not repeated—at least by me. From that moment on, the bottom line moves to the top, which is why the first thing I do the first day I'm in Plobien is go to my bank in Loscoat.

Getting Money from My Local Bank

In the U.S., I've been going to the same bank for fifteen years. It's been bought and changed names three times, but the same tellers and manager are still there. This is Oakland, a city of four hundred thousand people. In Loscoat, a village of six thousand people, the tellers change every year, in the middle of the year, even during the summer.

Still, I expect *someone* from the previous year to be there. After all, we shook hands, exchanged news and stories, laughed, became friendly—and I'm looking forward to seeing them and catching up on the events of the year.

I walk in, look around, and don't see *any* familiar faces. There's a new, younger, smiling face at the counter waiting to greet me.

"Bonjour," I say, putting out my hand to shake. The good news is there's always a young, seemingly younger every year, teller or trainee or intern in the bank who speaks English very well. The bad news is he or she is never there when I am. I can't tell if this new, younger teller—the one I just said "bonjour" to—is the one who speaks English, and from my "bonjour," he probably can't tell I don't speak French. I begin, as I do every summer, full of hope.

"Parlez vous anglais?" I ask, hoping he is the designated English speaker of the year.

"Non."

"C'est le personne ici parlez anglais?"

"Non. Elle est malade aujourd'hui."

"Bon." I mean "good, I understand," not "good, she's sick," but there's no way I can explain that, so I hand him my checkbook, saying, "S'il vous plaît, Monsieur, le total."

He doesn't move.

I reverse it. "Le total, s'il vous plaît, Monsieur," and make a writing motion with my hand . . . I later learn the word I want is *le solde*, not "total."

The lad taps my account number into the computer, writes a number on a piece of paper, and shows it to me. It's lower than I thought (it's *always* lower than I think), but it's in the ballpark (it's *always* in the ballpark), and not far enough away to quibble about even if I could.

"Merci," I say, "merci beaucoup."

"De rien," he replies, pleased to have helped and ready to move on.

I tear a check from my checkbook that I've already made out to myself and hand it to him—just as I did all last summer—and say, "S'il vous plaît." I do it this way, fill it out in the safety and privacy of my house, because when I'm in a hurry, I usually do it wrong. I write the name of the party to be paid on the top line—in this case me, Mark Greenside—which works fine in the U.S., but not in France, where the party to be paid is the second line. In France, the top line is the amount, which is another reason to write the check at home—I have to look the number up, like "deux cent quatre-vingt dix-huit" for 298 euros. And that's not the trickiest part. The trickiest part is on the bottom of the check, the place and the date, which I usually reverse in two ways: on the line where it says *Fait à* (made at) I write the date where I should write the place, and on the line for date, where it says *Le*, I write the place. Worst are the days and months. In the U.S., dates are written m/d/y. In France, it's d/m/y. So when I write 7/27/12, it's a date that doesn't exist. This is why I fill out the check before I get to the bank. It's embarrassing being a grown man with a house and bank account who is unable to write a check or know the date. It's also suspicious.

In the U.S., a drowsy, unshaven stranger walking into a bank with a checkbook and fully made out check would be detained. The teller would think the check has been lost or stolen, and the stranger would have to answer a gazillion questions and show a dozen pieces of identity. In France, the tellers are thankful. It's one less task for them to do. In Oakland, every time I enter the bank is like the first time, and by the time I leave—after I've refused to take out a loan or get a money market account—they act as if they hope it's the last. Not in France, or at least in Brittany. Here, they act as if they've known me for life. The lad looks at the check I just gave him, says, "Bon," and hands it back to me saying something I don't understand.

Now it's my turn not to move.

"Monsieur," he says, and points to the sign on his desk, *Information*, and indicates I need to get in line to see a teller, which was what I did *two* years ago. I'd walk in, say "bonjour" to the person behind the *Information* desk, and wait in a wedge for a teller who was sitting behind a desk. Then last year, while I was waiting in wedge for the teller, I was told to go to the *Information* desk, where I handed the person my already made-out check and got cash. For the remainder of the summer, I did that. Now, it seems, I have to go back to the teller . . .

I get in line, which really is a line, not a wedge, because only one person is ahead of me. Unfortunately, she wants to go through all of her records going back to the war—Two, I hope not One. In the U.S., they'd open another desk or send this person somewhere else, or just sit there laughing. In France, they do what's necessary. It's 11:45. The bank closes at 12:15 for the obligatory lunch, and the line behind me is becoming a wedge. It doesn't matter. No one cares but me, and I'm doing my best to hide it.

Finally, she leaves. I leap forward, hand the young lass my check and say, "Bonjour."

She says, "Bonjour," and quickly begins doing paperwork. I've never seen anyone enter numbers so quickly. She prints a piece of paper, gives it to me to sign—which I do—and gives me a receipt. Perfect: fast, efficient, pleasant, and pretty, but no money. I look at the receipt. It's a deposit slip. She's deposited my check from this bank into my account at this bank. If only it were so easy . . .

"Madame," I say. I know I should say "mademoiselle," but I can't. It makes me feel like Humbert Humbert. "C'est moi." I point at the name on the check and then at me. "Je voudrais d'argent." I want money. In the U.S., that would probably bring out the security guard. Here, there is no security guard, and everyone is patient beyond reason. She looks at me like, well, duh, who doesn't? I try again. "Je voudrais *cashe* le cheque . . . Changer le monnaie . . . " Miraculously, it works. She redoes the paperwork, gives me something to sign—there's always something to sign, something to prove whatever errors there are, are mine, not hers, the bank's, God's, or the world's. I sign, and she hands me two hundred euros and wishes me "bonne journée." I thank her and leave as fast as I can, managing to avoid eye contact with the wedge of people now out the door.

The rest of the summer I do the same. I walk into the bank, wait in line or wedge until it's my turn, then go to the teller and say, "Bonjour," shake hands, and hand over my check, which is already made out to me. The teller then begins the paperwork, gives me the waiver of all my rights to sign, shakes my hand, hands me my money, and I leave, both of us singing hallelujah, hallelujah, "Bonne journée." *Très simple*, and that's how it is until the day I need twenty-five hundred euros, about three thousand dollars, to pay Martin for work he's done on the house.

I enter the bank as usual with my check filled out, announce "Bonjour," and hand it to the smiling teller behind the desk.

He says, "Bonjour," looks at the check, and his face crinkles. It's like watching a Renoir turn into a Picasso. "Un moment," he says, and walks to an older teller, a girl of twenty-five, sitting at another desk. She takes the check, leaving the woman she was working with, who is now glaring at me like she hates me, and goes to an office in the back of the bank—always a sign of trouble. If they go to the back, it's doom. Sometimes they never return. After a few minutes, I see the girl go from the back office to another office further back. Finally, all of them, the now not-so-smiling fellow, the older twenty-five-year-old girl, two men I've never seen before, one dressed like casual Friday, the other like opening night at the opera, no one over thirty, come toward me. The fellow in front, casual Friday, is holding my check. He hands it to me and says, "Demain."

"Demain? Tomorrow?"

"Oui."

"Pourquoi?"

"C'est beaucoup. Je n'ai pas d'argent."

Unbelievable! This is a bank, one of the largest in Europe, and they don't have twenty-five hundred euros on hand. No wonder they don't have security guards. Why bother? What are thieves going to steal, the desks? I want to ask Casual Friday, Monsieur Sportif, if they don't have it today, why will they have it tomorrow? Where will it come from? And most important, what's the cutoff, at what amount do I need to make my request in advance? Instead I say, "Demain matin," planning to be there at nine sharp.

"Non. Après-midi."

So much for the saying money never sleeps. "Bon," I say.

"Bon," Monsieur Sportif says.

"Bon," says the girl.

"Bon," says the boy.

The guy dressed like he's going to the opera says, "Demain. Tomorrow. *After* midi."

The next day at two o'clock, *après-midi*, I walk in. The fellow at the *Information* desk is not the fellow who was there yesterday, plus he has no *Information*. He directs me to the desk where the twenty-five-year-old girl was yesterday. She's not there either. No one is. The bank seems empty. Yesterday it had no money, today it has only Mr. *Information*, who, at least as far as I'm concerned, has none. I sit on a comfortable leather chair and wait. I look at brochures for life insurance, house insurance, travel insurance, the bike race the bank is sponsoring, brochures on everything under the sun except banking, which is all I give a damn about. A young, well-tanned, shiny-faced, right out of a Norman Rockwell kid—how do they find them?—appears. In the U.S., everyone I know looks like a character out of a Hopper, and on a bad day, a Lucian Freud. The kid sits behind the desk and smiles. I'm bracing myself for the worst. He puts out his hand, and beams, "Hello."

"Parlez-vous anglais?"

"Oui. Yes," and he really does. We talk about his studies in England and travels to New York, New Orleans, and Florida. For some reason, every French person I've spoken to who has been to the U.S. has been to Florida. Not Chicago, Boston, Philadelphia, L.A., or D.C.; not the Grand Canyon, Zion, Yosemite, or the Tetons; but Florida—and not the Everglades, Little Havana, or Key West, but Orlando and Disney World. He asks how I like Brittany, Finistère, and Plobien, and I answer as effusively as he did about Orlando. Eventually, he gets to the point.

"In France it is normal," (Ah! *Normalement*) when withdrawing large sums of money to make an appointment in advance."

"How large?"

He shrugs. "It depends."

"OK," I say. "I understand," though I don't. "Next time. La prochaine fois."

"Bon," he says and he hands me an envelope thick with euros. I think he's going to open the envelope and count the money. He doesn't. He gives me the waiver to sign, which means if it's not correct, I'm screwed. I know I should count the money, but I also know it would be rude. I'm in France, so I opt for manners—the right gesture—over prudence, and sign, but all I want to do is rush to the car and count my money.

"Merci," I say, and stand, put my hand out to shake, and sit back down when he doesn't get up.

"I see," he says, "you have quite a bit of money in your checking account."

"Oui." I have about fifteen thousand dollars worth of euros to pay Martin for work he's going to do on the house.

"It's not safe."

"*What?*"

"It's not safe. It's possible for a hacker to get into your account and take the money."

This is my bank telling me this! Is it a secret? Does anyone else know? Does *everyone* else know? Is this a joke? "It's insured, isn't it? It's protected?"

"Yes, yes, of course, but you should have it in a savings account."

I don't bother asking why a savings account at the same bank is safer—hacker-free—than a checking account, because I know there will be an answer and a reason that will make its own logical illogical sense to everyone except me.

"Also in savings, you'll earn interest."

"OK." What the hell. I agree to put ten thousand dollars worth of euros into a savings account. Actually two savings accounts, because for another reason I'll never know, the maximum amount I can put in one savings account is the equivalent of six thousand dollars.

So I now have a checking account I need to make an appointment to use, two savings accounts I have no idea how to access, and a PIN number I can't remember. I leave the bank with what I hope is twenty-five hundred euros, totally bewildered, and the guy behind the desk is delighted. I've made his day.

Three weeks later, I go to the bank to get money for a stay at my friends Bob and Loni's house on the Île aux Moines, where I'm dog-sitting for a week. I enter the bank, nonchalant, wait my turn in the wedge in front of the teller's desk, and notice nobody looks familiar. I'm not surprised. It's August, and all the regulars are on vacation. I step forward when it's my turn, say, "Bonjour," and hand the new younger person my check already made out to me for three hundred euros, about four hundred dollars.

The lad says, "Bonjour," hands it back to me, and directs me to the front counter, which no longer has the *Information* sign, but is once again, as it was *three* years ago, a teller. This teller, I see, is for withdrawing money. The other teller, the wedge I was in, is for depositing money and problem solving. Upstairs or in the back is for loans. The order, simplicity, and clarity of the design are assuring. It doesn't even bother me that I've already waited in one wedge, and now I'm waiting in another. This is France, and my turn will come. When it does, I step forward with aplomb, sing, "Bon-jour," and give the pretty young girl behind the desk my already made-out check.

She hands it back to me without even looking at it.

"Non, non," I say, thinking I've been through this before. "C'est moi," and point to my name on the check and then myself, and hand it back to her, adding, "Je voudrais d'argent."

"Oui, oui," she says, and quickly hands it back to me, pointing to the checkbook sticking out of my shirt pocket.

"Oui. C'est moi." No one has ever asked for identification before. "Parlez vous anglais?"

"Non." Then, not knowing what else to do, she plucks the checkbook from my pocket and rapidly begins tapping numbers into the computer.

I get it. She doesn't need my check, just the checkbook. No more wasting paper or writing out checks for withdrawals.

It's amazingly un-French: simple, clear, efficient, streamlined. For a moment I think Deutsche Bank must have bought Crédit Agricole. "Bonne journée," she says, handing me my checkbook and a green plastic card.

All I can think is, please God, not something new. The girl smiles, relieved, thinking she's made it through, and I'm gone. I stand there, dumbfounded. If I wasn't a man and she wasn't so young and pretty, I'd cry.

She takes the card from my hand, walks around her desk, and leads me to the foyer where there are three machines. They all have words and signs above them. Two are the same, the third is different. The girl goes to one of the two, slides the plastic card into a slot, showing me it goes red arrow facing in and up, saying, "Très simple, très simple." I don't know if she's referring to the machine or me. She waits a few seconds and pushes one of the three buttons, but she's blocking my view so I can't see which one. All of a sudden money comes out. She hands it to me without counting it. I put it in my pocket without counting it—happy to be out of there with what I hope is enough money to get me through the week, and hoping I won't have to get any more while I'm gone. If it's difficult getting money from my own branch, I can't even imagine how it will be somewhere else . . .

Getting Money from a Branch of My Bank Outside of Loscoat

I'm visiting the Parc du Morvan in Burgundy. To my amazement—I don't know why, because they're everywhere—I see a branch of my bank as I drive to my hotel in the village of

Anost. In the U.S., I would not care less. My bank spends millions of dollars a year to convince me it's my friend, but I know better. If they really were my friend, they'd lower their fees and hire more tellers so I could get out of there faster and on with my life—which is odd, actually, because I spend more time in wedges at Crédit Agricole than I do in lines in the U.S., and I consider the French bank more of a friend. It's like I have a friend *and* they left the light on for me. I, who thoroughly distrust banks, bankers, globalism, multinational corporations, profits, the free market, Milton Friedman, the entire Chicago school of economics, stocks, Wall Street, the prime, and the invisible hand, feel comforted that there's a branch of my bank in this village. Talk about being desperate for friends.

I decide to be prudent—thanks to Sally—and check the balance in my account in the morning. I wake early and eat breakfast—coffee, baguette, croissant, butter, and jam—and wait for the bank to open. At nine o'clock, when it's supposed to open, no one is there. By nine fifteen I worry. Has this branch closed? Did Crédit Agricole fold? Has there been another international monetary crisis in the last twenty-four hours? A kid on a bike whizzes past me and yells, "Lundi."

Right. In the blur of travel, I lost a day and forgot it's Monday, and banks are closed.

I drive through the *parc*, hike, eat a yummy Burgundian meal of Charolais steak with pinot noir, pass out again, wake, and have breakfast—same as the day before, always the same as the day before. Don't French people ever want anything different? Pancakes, two eggs over easy, *French* toast, for God's sake, where is it? I have never even seen it in France. At nine o'clock, I go to the bank. There's a wedge of people waiting to get inside.

When it's my turn I step forward and say, "Bonjour."

"Bonjour," the smiling teenager sings.

"S'il vous plaît, le solde," and I hand him my checkbook.

He looks at the checkbook, then at me, and stops smiling. He's staring at me, bewildered.

"Voudrais vous écrie, s'il vous plaît . . . " and I make a writing motion with my hand, "le solde pour moi?"

"Anglais?"

"Américain."

"Bon." He calls a young lady over who explains in perfect English that my account isn't at this branch.

Now it's my turn to look at them, bewildered. Do they really think I don't know where my bank is? Do I look and sound that out of it? "Oui," I acknowledge. "My *branch* is in Brittany, Finistére, Loscoat," and I show her the address on the checkbook.

"Oui, oui," they both nod, happy to have that agreement, in a way that tells me this conversation is over. Things are so bad, it drives me back to French.

"Monsieur."

"Oui."

"C'est Crédit Agricole."

They look at each other, then at me. I now know how the kids in special ed feel, and it isn't very nice. "Bien sûr," they say to each other, both of them pointing to the sign that says Crédit Agricole.

"Et c'est ne pas possible j'ai le solde pour cette compte?" It's not possible I have a total for this account?

"Non."

"Pourquoi."

"L'information n'existe pas."

This is a national bank—*international*—one of the largest in the world, and they can't access their own account from another branch of their own bank. Holy, holy cow. It's unbelievable.

I then do something even more unbelievable. "Bon," I say, and hold out my hand for my checkbook. The young lady cheerily hands it back. I open it and write my name, then the date and the village—both in the wrong places, and m/d/y instead of d/m/y—and "deux cents euros," about two hundred fifty dollars worth, and hand it to her, saying, "S'il vous plaît."

She immediately begins filling out papers. When she's finished, she gives me the ubiquitous waiver to sign and hands me ten twenty-euro notes. As usual, she doesn't look at my passport or ask for any ID. Everywhere I go in France, it's the same. Getting money is as easy as that . . . Until the day it's not.

Donna and I are in Paris, dining at an old, expensive restaurant, celebrating her birthday. When the bill arrives, I hand the waiter my Visa card and watch amused, surprised, and embarrassed as the card is rejected once, twice, three times. I hand him my American Express card, which is also rejected. So are Donna's MasterCard and Capital One.

I pay by check, which they gladly accept without ID, no problem, but just in case—because we're low in cash, the cards could be rejected again, and I don't want to run out of money—I decide to go to the bank first thing in the morning to get more euros.

I wake early, wondering if I'll have to make an appointment, if they'll even have money, if they'll cash my check. Thinking about these and worse things, I'm the first person at the bank.

A neatly manicured, unruly-haired fellow in a black suit

rolls up the metal barrier. As soon as it's up, I blurt, "Monsieur, j'ai une compte avec Crédit Agricole . . . " I show him my checkbook. "Voudrais-vous donnez moi le caisse pour le chèque?" Will you give me the cash for a check?

"Quoi?" What?

"C'est nécessaire j'ai fait un appointement pour d'argent?" I find out later *appointement* doesn't mean appointment, it means salary, which *is* about money, but not what I want to ask. The word I want is *rendezvous,* but I can't say it without thinking of illicit sex . . .

He's looking at me as if I'm crazy. I persist, because the way he's looking at me is nothing compared to how Donna looked at me in the restaurant, and I never want to see it again.

"C'est possible vous donnez-moi d'argent aujourd'hui?" It's possible you give me money today? Anywhere else and I'd be in cuffs.

"Aujourd'hui?" he says, which I take as a yes.

I follow him to his desk and hand him my checkbook. "S'il vous plait, je voudrais mille euros." I'd like one thousand euros, please.

He looks at the checkbook, and says, "Le maximum est huit cent euros." Eight hundred maximum.

He has no idea if I'm Bill Gates's uncle, Madonna's lover, or vice versa, or how much money I have in my account. "Pourquoi?" I demand, outraged.

He gives me a long explanation, which I take to mean, "That's how it is," take it or leave it, and concludes with "par semaine."

Eight hundred euros *a week*! That's all I can take out of my own account! It *is* outrageous. Meanwhile, he's tapping numbers. Then all of a sudden he leaves and goes to the back.

Oh, merde . . .

He returns in five minutes with his colleague, an older, fashionably unshaven fellow wearing the same black suit. "Mr. Greenside, désolé, désolé."

An apology, about time...

"Le maximum est quatre cent euros par semaine."

"*Four* hundred euros a week! Pourquoi?"

He hands me back my checkbook and points to my name.

"Pourquoi je suis américain?" Because I'm American?

"Non." He points at the address beneath my name and the postal code. "Vingt-neuf."

"Oui. Finistère."

"Exactement. Le maximum pour une personne qui habite en Bretagne est quatre-cents euros par semaine." The maximum for people who live in Brittany is four hundred euros a week.

"C'est different si j'habite à Nice?" It's different if I live in Nice?

"Oui."

"Et Paris est different aussi?"

"Bien sûr."

If this was the U.S., I'd scream, "Discrimination!" but in France discrimination is a good thing, a sign of culture, intelligence, and class—so I shut my mouth and take my four hundred euros, thankful we're in Paris just five more days. I spend those euros vigilantly and reluctantly—and only *after* asking, "Acceptez-vous les cartes de crédit américaines?" If the answer is no, I walk away, pay by check—or if Donna really wants the purchase, with my rapidly diminishing cash.

The following summer the same thing happens in La Rochelle: our credit cards work, work, work, and then don't work. I go to the bank to get a thousand euros and leave with my four hundred euros for the week.

That's when I decide to get a French debit card.

I go to my bank in Loscoat and rendezvous with the new designated English speaker, who replaced the old designated English speaker, who had been at the bank for a month as of three weeks ago.

"Bonjour," I say, and hand her my checkbook. "I'd like to get a debit card for when I travel. Do I qualify?"

She taps my account number into her computer, and says, "Yes, of course," and hands me a remarkably short, simple form to fill out.

While I'm filling out the form, she's telling me the terms, none of which I pay attention to—figuring it's bank-talk, informing me about my rights and privileges and all the ways the bank can violate them—when I hear her say, "The maximum cash withdrawal is four hundred euros a week."

"Four hundred a week from the card *and* whatever else I withdraw from my checking account, right?

"No. Four hundred total each week."

"I can withdraw that much cash right now with my check-book. I need the card so I can withdraw *more* when I travel—like I do in the U.S."

She makes a pouty motion with her lips and shrugs, telling me this isn't the U.S., it's France. "You can withdraw more at *this* branch. When you're traveling, the maximum is four hundred euros a week."

"Merci," I say, shake her hand, and leave.

Donna and I now travel armed with my Visa card, her credit cards, my French debit card and checkbook—and more euros than either of us want to carry. As long as people cash my checks with no questions, ID, or the correct written sum, date, and location, we're OK—and so far, it's worked. But how long can that go on? That's what I wake up at night wondering and worrying about. How much longer before I make a mistake and am caught short, like Sally, Martin, and Louise? It's a question I hope never gets answered.

Buying Euros

At least once a week, I search the internet for the best possible exchange rate, certain if I wait just a little bit longer a better rate will come along—until I wait too long and it passes me by. The truth is no matter when I buy I wish I'd bought sooner or later or more or less than I did. That's capitalism for you: a perpetual nagging that someone somewhere got a better deal, and that I paid too much. That's the bad news.

The good news is *when* I buy, I pay the lowest possible fees and get the best possible exchange rate for that particular nanosecond, because actual money never touches actual hands. It's a virtual experience, which apparently is what the banks like best. I fax a check to American Foreign Exchange in Los Angeles, and they wire a cable to my account in Plobien—and voila!—euros are waiting for me when I arrive, except for the time they went to Corsica.

It's different, though, for friends and family who visit. Mostly, they use the ATM to get euros and are shocked when they return home and discover the fees for the transactions and the percentages taken for the conversion, not to mention the exchange rates, are usurious. It's even worse if they use a debit card—which is odd, because the money is immediately deducted from their accounts, and for giving that privilege and convenience to their banks, they're charged an additional two to three percent. The only thing more expensive is cash. It should be the reverse, simpler is cheaper: you hand the teller a hundred-dollar bill, and she hands you eighty euros. Ha! You're more likely to get seventy, and if you're at Thomas Cook, American Express, an airport or change kiosk, sixty. You're better off donating the money to Doctors Without Borders and taking a tax deduction.

Every exchange costs money. The banks have made sure of that. They've also made sure it's impossible to know how much: some charge a flat fee per transaction, some charge a percentage, and some charge a combination of both. Nothing is posted. There's no way to know the full cost of the exchange without asking, and there's no one to ask, unless you call an international 800 number and wait thirty to eighty minutes to be connected with someone in India who will put you on hold while he or she searches for a supervisor who's probably in London or New York. Worst, the rates and percentages change at will—the bank's will—so the card you used last year because it was the cheapest is now the most expensive, unless you used Bank of America, which every year is exorbitant. Given this, what's a tourist to do? It's a question I'm regularly asked by friends—like LeRoy. He's coming to visit and wants to know what he should do about money.

"Bring some," I tell him. "A lot." Then I tell him what I tell everyone. "Pay for everything you can with your credit—not debit—card, because even with the fees, it's the best exchange you're going to get—and bring traveler's checks. The exchange rate is terrible, but they're one hundred percent safe and secure if stolen or lost, *and* they're not eatable by hungry, angry, hypersensitive, malfunctioning, or hacked ATM machines, as credit and debit cards are."

This is what I tell LeRoy, and it's what he does, and why two weeks later we're standing in a wedge at the *Poste*.

I used to take people to the bank to cash their traveler's checks, but a month ago, when I was waiting in a wedge to buy stamps—waiting an inordinately long time even in France—the woman in front turned around and said to the person behind her, in English-English, "It's worth the wait, it's the best exchange rate around." Now, four weeks later, LeRoy and I get to find out.

We arrive at ten thirty, and the wedge is huge so I feel completely at home. LeRoy's French is worse than mine, so I spend the minutes waiting, practicing what I'm going to say. "Je voudrais changer d'argent. Je voudrais changer monnai . . . Je voudrais caisse le cheque de voyager . . . " What gives me courage is knowing, unlike in the U.S., once it's my turn I can have as much time as I need, and no one in the wedge, except maybe another American, is going to hate me or wish me dead.

Ten minutes later we step up to the counter, and I say, "Bonjour, Madame. Je voudrais changer *d'argent.*"

She looks at me like I'm from England or Mars.

I try it slower. "S'il vous plaît. Je . . . voudrais . . . changer . . . d'argent . . . "

She shakes her head no and begins speaking for two minutes very quickly.

I stand my ground and point to a tiny sign I've never seen before that says, *monnaie,* and put three of LeRoy's one-hundred-dollar traveler's checks on the counter.

She looks at the checks as if she's never seen anything like them before, and as if neither the checks nor I exist. It's enough to make me falter, thinking maybe there's another French rule I don't know about: no money before noon at the *Poste;* nothing over one hundred dollars. Who can tell? But in my bafflement, I hold my ground.

She does, too, but eventually realizes I'm too stubborn or stupid to leave. She picks up the checks and sneers at them. For a moment, I taste victory—until she groans, reaches down, and drops a New-York-City-size phone book on the counter. She opens the book—it's filled with photocopies of zillions of brands of traveler's checks from hundreds of banks in dozens of countries—and slowly starts turning the pages, looking for a match. The good news is LeRoy has American Express, so they're sure to be there. The bad news is American Express starts with an A, and she's begun from the back. Then I think *U.S.*, *U*nited States, and feel bad about my bad thoughts until I remember it's "États-Unis" in French, and I know I'll be here until noon.

After five minutes of searching, she finds American Express. If LeRoy had some obscure, local, Oakland bank checks, we'd still be in line or jail. It takes her another several minutes to verify the checks in her hand match the photocopy in the book. We're lucky. The checks in her hand are hundred-dollar checks. The check in the book is a hundred-dollar check. I can't even imagine what would happen if the denominations didn't match. She turns to her computer to find the exchange rate for that particular nano-moment, and I figure we're on the way, but the paperwork has only begun.

She writes and writes and writes, filling out forms, rechecks her computer, and writes some more. When she's finished, she calls to a younger, bald, chubby fellow, who appears to be her supervisor. As soon as he sees what she's doing, his face becomes sepulchral, as if this is his personal money or his Christmas fund, and she's about to give it away. He looks at the book of sample checks, sadly verifying the authenticity of the check. He confirms the exchange rate, which thankfully has not changed, reviews LeRoy's passport, the information on it as well as the photo, which unfortunately was taken nine years earlier, causing Monsieur to squint and look and study until finally, reluctantly, probably seeing prison in his future or having to personally pay for this mistake, this signature, for the rest of his and his children's lives, he sadly but floridly—he is after all a supervisor and in his penmanship his authority lies—initials the paper. Seventeen minutes from start to finish and we have three hundred dollars' worth of euros in our hands.

Three weeks later, LeRoy and I return, and I say, "Je voudrais changer d'argent." The same woman looks at me with an expression of annoyance, contempt, disregard, disbelief, and awe—and acts as if the *Poste* does not change money, she doesn't know how to do it, and she's never seen me before in her life. Then she proceeds to change the checks. The last time I was there, with my mom, the telephone book of check samples was gone, and everything was computerized, which I thought would make things easier—but there are new obstacles now, and easier, I can tell you, doesn't exist, and the process takes just as long.

ATMs *are* quicker and cheaper, but if you lose your card (as X did), or it's stolen in Paris (as Y's was), or the machine devours it (as with Z), you're in serious trouble. For me, there's my checkbook. For family and friends, there's begging, explaining (which most of them can't do in French), and prayer, which to me are more embrassing, tedious, and time-consuming than losing a few euros in the exchange. Safe is better than sorry. I know, because over the years I've been sorry a lot.

Paying People for Work

When I bought my house, I knew it would require maintenance. How much maintenance, I—a renter for life until then—had no idea. Who knew faucets regularly and repeatedly leaked, sockets had to be rewired, plugs added, wood re-painted and re-painted and re-painted, gutters cleaned, walls re-plastered, windows re-glazed, grass cut weekly, trees trimmed yearly— and most amazingly that I'd want—desperately—my floors refinished, rooms refurbished, cabinets built, a terrace, stone wall, a flower garden? I didn't think about any of these things when I bought the house, so I didn't worry about them.

What I did worry about was Peter Mayle and the other English and American writers I'd read and their horror stories about the difficulty—seeming impossibility—of finding reliable people to work on their houses: people who showed up, worked a full day, and finished on time. Luckily, (thanks to Madame P, who knows everyone, Jean who can fix anything, and Martin and Rick who can build anything), that's not been a problem for me. My problem has been how to pay them.

English people are easy. Soon after I arrive in Plobien, I call Martin, Louise, Jon, Chris, Ella, and Rick, to pay them for work they've done on the house during the year: repairing shutters, painting the terrace, tiling the bathroom, plastering . . . I call them, they tell me what I owe, and I pay. It's as easy as that.

Not so with the Bretons. If I call and ask for the bill too soon (as I've done), the transaction becomes commercial. If I wait too long (as I've also done), there's the unspoken fear I might forget. The timing has to be just right. That's probably why there's all that small talk about the weather and

haricots verts, pommes de terre, and *tomates* every morning in the
boulangerie—to take the sting from the commercial, to soften
or hide it, and transform it into something else. So after I call
and pay my English friends, I wait.

When Monsieur Charles visits I comment on his work in
the garden, the yard, cutting the grass, cleaning the gutters,
fixing the fence. "C'est beau . . . Belle . . . Parfait . . . " and I
thank him profusely, "Merci, merci, merci beaucoup," thereby
acknowledging (1) I know the work is done, (2) done well, and
(3) I appreciate it. Then we talk about family, the past year,
the world, the weather, his garden—everything and anything,
except money.

Finally, after several weeks of repeating this, usually about
halfway through the summer, sometimes starting with the
weather, sometimes ending with it, but always in the middle of
some other topic, where it is heard but not emphasized, I once
again compliment Monsieur Charles on his work, and add, "Je
vais à la banque demain. S'il vous plaît, donne moi le facture
pour votre travaille." I'm going to the bank tomorrow. Tell me
what I owe you for your work. At least, that's what I think I'm
saying.

"Oui, oui," he says, and waves me away, as in not yet, not
yet, but visibly pleased and relieved that I remembered, and
that I brought it up so he won't have to. I do this two or three
more times over the next several weeks, and each time it's the
same—until the time I say it again, as casually as I can, exactly
as I've said it before, and he removes a slip of paper from his
pocket or wallet and hands me a detailed, itemized-down-to-
the-centime list of hours and minutes worked, materials bought,
and additional costs, such as renting a backhoe or hiring a tree
surgeon.

The same thing happens repeatedly. Hugo, the floor guy, works three long weeks repairing and replacing my floors and waits eight months to give me a bill. Jean and Sharon's son, Noé, rewires my house, and I have to call him numerous times and finally drive to his house—forty minutes away—to pay him. Monsieur C, the plumber, regularly does emergency work on my tired old furnace when renters are at the house and have no hot water, and he never sends me a bill. I have to track him down, and when I do, he says, "La prochaine fois," but next time has yet to come. Eric, the son of the oil guy, refills my oil tank whenever it needs it, whether I'm in France or California. Each time he fills it he advances me eight hundred to a thousand dollars. There's no prepayment, autopayment, or pre-authorization. He does it, because it needs to be done.

If I am foolish enough to offer a down payment (as I've done), people wave me away as if I'm nuts: madame in the pâtisserie when I preorder a cake or tart; Stéphanie in the restaurant when I reserved a room a year in advance for my party; Hugo when he worked on my floors; Monsieur B, who trims my trees. No one wants or expects a deposit. The only time I've ever put money down in advance was to pay for expensive supplies, equipment, and tools that were needed for the job. In France, or at least Plobien, where people don't want to pay for anything they haven't yet received, a deal is sealed with a handshake. In the U.S., it requires a down payment and a multipage contract. Having done both—shaken and signed—I know the handshake is worth more than the paper the contract is written on.

France gave us the word "bourgeoisie" and made it a pejorative, something to aspire to and despise. What else is there to say about money?

10 Things I've Learned about Money in France

1. I like to think of myself as a humanist—"From each according to his abilities, to each according to his needs"— and in most things I am, except when following the value of the euro. I read the newspapers secretly hoping for problems in Greece, Spain, Italy, Ireland, and Portugal, because if the value of the euro drops, I'll have a few centimes more . . . This is how capitalism works: I hope for someone else's loss so I can gain. The good news is I have not had to feel bad about my bad thoughts because since Bush II and 9/11, *I've* been the loser most of the time. That's also the bad news. On the other hand, the euros I have in the bank and the value of my house have increased. If capitalism doesn't get you coming, it gets you going, or the other way around, or both.

2. Before buying anything expensive, I make sure the establishment accepts U.S. credit cards. This is especially true at fine restaurants, because unlike jewelry and clothing, the food I just ate is not returnable in any form they want. In the U.S., I carry my Visa card and driver's license everywhere. In France, it's my checkbook. I've seen French people write checks for the equivalent of a dollar-fifty *and less*, and the clerk or owner happily accepts them.

3. The sales tax is 20 percent. The good news is the posted price includes the 20 percent, so I don't see or feel it when I pay it. The bad news is I'm paying a 20 percent sales tax. The best news is I can get much of it returned at airport customs when I leave France. The worst news is there is only one person handling a line of hundreds of people waiting for their reimbursements. Mostly, they're people from Asia,

people who know how to wait forever and entertain themselves with electronic devices. I figure this is part of France's
grand economic recovery plan: pay one person the minimum wage to handle the never-ending line, and pay out as
little as possible. To facilitate that goal, the customs official
has multiple breaks to ensure the line never shortens. It also
helps that signs to the "Douanes" are harder to find than
the elevators at Charles de Gaulle, Terminal One. Unless I
have hours to kill and I'm saving thousands of dollars (neither of which I do) it's not worth waiting—so I and thousands of others don't, and that's worth millions to France.
Not so happily, I'm paying my part.

4. I am no longer fooled by Duty Free signs in shop windows
in Paris and other cities. Those places will promise me a full
refund of the 20 percent sales tax and will fill out all the
paperwork to qualify me—but I still have to wait in that
line to get it, which means I never do. I'm not fooled by
Duty Free signs at the airport anymore either. I bought a
bottle of Wild Turkey and a bottle of Jameson at the Duty
Free shop at San Francisco International Airport on my
way to Paris, Charles de Gaulle, where I had to change
terminals from 2E to 2F for my flight to Brest. At 2F—
ninety dollars and sixteen hours after the purchase, not to
mention the twenty-five-minute trek lugging my comput-
er-laden briefcase and the two liter–size bottles of booze—
the *douane* tells me I can't carry the Duty Free bag onto
the plane. He tells me this by confiscating it. "Pourquoi?"
I demand, outraged. The answer, I think, is Duty Free is
for international flights, but now that I'm in France (Paris)
and I'm flying to Brest (France) Duty Free does not apply.
I could pack the bottles in my baggage, and that would

be OK, except I don't have my baggage—it's on the plane going directly to Brest. I board the plane alcohol free and vow never to shop Duty Free again.

5. France has two great machines that barely exist in the U.S. The first is a handheld computer that accepts, or in my case, rejects my credit card at my table so everyone around me thinks I'm broke. The other device is a cash register that fills out my check. It prints the name of the store, the amount of the bill, the date, and location. All I have to do is sign it—a great boon for people who don't know how to write the date or their numbers. Why it's in France, one of the most literate countries in the world, I don't know—but the local shopkeepers and I are happy for it. I try to shop wherever they have that machine.

6. In the U.S., you are what you do, though nothing that you do really matters. In France, it doesn't matter what you do— even if it's nothing, especially if it's nothing—and everything matters, is judged, rated, and critiqued. In the U.S. people say, 'What do you do for a living,' meaning 'What's your job?' In France, people talk about life and living the good life and never once does it refer to work. In the U.S., living and job are used interchangeably. In France, the two rarely meet.

7. In France, it is illegal to turn off a household's utilities in winter but perfectly fine to close a bank account if it goes over the overdraft limit. In the U.S., my bank carries me if I bounce a check or two or three, but Pacific Gas and Electric will cut me in ninety days—no matter that it is January, freezing, ice on the ground, a baby in the house, and I'm ill. In France, it is better to not pay the bill than to bounce the check. In the U.S., it's the opposite. A bounced

check, at least the first or second time, shows good will and intentions. Knowing the difference is like having money in the bank when you don't.

8. Money has changed three times in France since 1960: from the old franc to the new franc (100 old francs = 1 new franc) to the euro (1 euro = 6.55957 new francs). The result is no one who has been through those changes is comfortable speaking about large numbers. Euros have simplified things a little, as there are no old euros or new euros, just *the* euro. Unfortunately, however, in an attempt to make things easier for people, something France doesn't excel at, all prices are *required* to be written in euros *and* francs—*new* francs, which are now old, and have not been legal tender since 2002. The result is many older people translate the euro price into francs—*ancien* and *nouveau*. So when someone over sixty tells me a new front gate will cost *soixante mille*—60,000—I drop two zeros and hope it's right, though I live in fear that one of these days I'm going to agree to something I can't afford. Then I'll have the Sally experience, or worse, I'll learn about French bankruptcy laws and debtor prison—and whether or not they have laws protecting the mathematically challenged and other mental deficients—all things I hope not to learn.

9. French people are schizo about money: they love what it can do, what it buys—they are shoppers and consumers par excellence—and they disdain it, especially ostentatious displays of what other people have and they don't. France is a generous, social welfare, neosocialist state—and I've never been so vigilant with money in all my life.

10. In France, as elsewhere, nothing causes more trouble between people than bad money and good sex. Luckily, I've managed to avoid both with my friends and neighbors.

I'm Eating What?

Most people know France is foodie heaven. It's haute cuisine land, home of Escoffier, Carême, Ducasse, Bocuse, and the eleven-hundred-page Larousse Gastronomique, all of which are salivating-exciting if you're an explorer of taste like Donna, but daunting if you're a culinary coward, like me.

I won't eat eel (the thought of it), sweetbreads (the source of it), and organs (except liver in foie gras) are off the chart. I'd rather spend hundreds of dollars on Springsteen tickets, good theater, or a baseball game than a meal at French Laundry or Boulud. For me, eating is more comfort and sustenance than adventure. I prefer the familiar, which is why ten months of the year I go to the same Vietnamese, Thai, Japanese, Chinese, Indian, Mexican, and Italian restaurants and order the same dishes, and to the extent nothing has changed, I'm happy. Then I go to France, where every summer is a gastronomique adventure.

Pig

I'm on the train from Paris to Brest, avoiding the Périphérique. It's lunchtime, and everyone is eating but me. I'm reading Genet, waiting to go to the club car to buy a chicken sandwich, *un sandwich poulet*—one of the few things I can identify *and* pronounce—when the lady in the seat across the aisle from me hands me a chunk of something that looks like sausage and smells like death. All I can think of is *The Jungle*, sawdust, roaches, rat droppings, and body parts. In the U.S., under no imaginable circumstances short of torture or starvation would I put anything that smells like this in my mouth, let alone my stomach, not to mention my hand, where it is, because the lady put it there before I could pull away.

Genet in one hand, I-don't-know-what in the other, I look at this friendly, middle-aged lady who could be Babette, Charlotte Corday, or a French version of Jeffrey Dahmer. She points to my hand, and says something that sounds like, "And we."

I know she's telling me something important, but I have no idea what. I bite it, because all the other options I can think of are worse, and swallow. The good news is it's not as bad as it smells. The bad news is it smells like a toilet in a gas station that hasn't been cleaned in a month. The amazing news is I finish it without gagging and thank the lady profusely, while declining more.

I gag later, when I find out "andouille" is French for pig intestines.

I've been back in France less than five hours, and once again I've eaten something I would have leaped to avoid stepping in if I'd seen it on the street. If I am what I eat, I'm in trouble.

Crustacean

Madame P has invited me to dinner with her, Monsieur, and her grandson, Daniel. We've had apéritifs and nibbles and are sitting at the table, in the center of which is a huge covered bowl. The settings are simple: a plate, a glass for water, a glass for wine, a tablespoon, dinner knife and fork, and tiny picking implements that look to me like dental equipment. I know Brittany is oyster land, but July is not a month that ends in an R, even in French. Besides, the only oysters I eat are baked, like oysters Rockefeller, or fried—never raw. Raw, they remind me of phlegm. Madame uncovers the bowl, and Daniel goes over the top when he sees what's inside. I do, too, as I look at dozens of the ugliest shrimp I've ever seen piled on top of each other like a massacre. Then, what I see next is worse.

Madame digs into the bowl with her bare hand, grabs a handful of these orangey-pink things, and drops them in a mound onto my plate, saying, "Langoustine."

It's what the Lionel girl was playing with at Leclerc, and what I vowed to avoid. I look at the pile in front of me: bulging bodies, appendages akimbo, whiskers, feelers, tiny irridescent orange eggs, and big, shiny, beady black eyes staring up at me. I sit there with my hands in my lap, staring back.

The good news is they're not moving. The better news is neither am I. No way am I touching them, let alone eating them. The andouille lady got past me, but not this. Then, I watch horrified as Daniel breaks the head off one of them and sucks on the thorax with delight. He lifts one of the picks and scrapes the insides out like a dentist cleaning plaque. Madame and Monsieur begin to do the same. Everyone is happy—except me.

I know it's rude not to eat these things, or at least taste them, especially since Madame cooked this treat, this specialty straight from the Atlantic still breathing and crawling when she got out of bed early this morning to buy them, for me. I also know it's not polite to throw up on the table, and that's what will happen if I put one near my mouth.

Monsieur passes me the bread. I cut a piece and butter it, pretty sure there's no going wrong with that. Crispy baguette and rich, creamy butter—forget Campbell's soup: *this* is "Mmmm, mmmm, good."

I chew my bread and watch Madame, Monsieur, and Daniel demolish the mounds in front of them and reach into the bowl for more. Piles of black beady-eyed heads, pieces of pink exoskeleton and carapace, shell splinters, whiskers, feelers, and glowing teensy orange eggs litter their plates and the table all around them, making a mess. The space in front of me is spotless. Until this moment, I thought cleanliness was godliness to Madame. Now I see there's a higher order, and gustatory pleasure and need trumps all: clean plate tops clean house. Meanwhile, Monsieur keeps filling the wine glasses, and I keep emptying mine.

Finally, Madame reaches across the table and removes my plate. Thank God, I think, as I watch her snap the heads off a dozen more of these guys and gals, crack their torsos between her thumb and forefinger, and peel away the shell and carapace to expose the corpse. I'm elated—until she puts the plate back in front of me with a look that says, "I made this for *you!*"

Daniel and Monsieur stop eating and watch.

On my plate are small chunks of white meat that look like brain or tumors or worse. I fork the smallest piece possible and drown it in Madame's homemade mayonnaise, bite, chew, and swallow. The mayonnaise is great. I oyster-fork another piece and dip it in the mayonnaise. It tastes like lobster, crab, and shrimp combined. I fork another and another and another and clean my plate.

The langoustine are followed by lotte, a dense, chunky white fish, like halibut. I clean my plate again. It's lucky for us I've never seen a lotte or heard of it, because when I do, I see it's one of the ugliest fish in the world—all head, no body, which means what I ate were cheeks. Fish cheeks! Holy Christ! What's next?

More Pig

In the U.S., I eat pork rinds, which are more Monsanto than meat, the occasional ham sandwich and pork chop, sausage, and ribs. The only pork I eat regularly is bacon in a BLT. This makes me a bad Jew. For a Jewish guy—even a nonobservant, secular Jew by DNA—pig and shiksas are the no-no's supreme. For a Jewish girl, it's pig and non-Jewish guys. Muslims and Jews, at war for generations, agree on one thing: pig is dirty, devil food, poison, and not to be partaken. Grandma Esther wouldn't eat in our house because once every decade, my mom, her daughter, would lapse and let bacon into her kitchen. Somehow, Grandma Esther knew, and it kept her eating her own-made egg salad out of an empty mayonnaise jar she brought from her house while the rest of us ate chicken or turkey or brisket. All of this is written. It's the Eleventh Commandment: Thou Shall Not Eat Pig.

Unfortunately, pig is the national animal of Brittany. There are more pigs in Brittany than people; more pigs than chickens and cows. Pork isn't the *other* white meat, it is *the* white meat, and a good cut of pig, like a free-range chicken, is very high-end. As I'm already halfway to hell with a non-Jewish wife—Donna is Buddhist—the rest of my fall is easy.

I'm driving through a neighboring village at eleven o'clock on a Sunday morning and see a high-rise erector-set construction of metal racks stacked in front of the church. It looks to me like the start of a new Inquisition, so I speed up and leave.

On my way back, I see the racks are five rotisseries, and each one has a huge—more evenly bronzed than an Antibes or Ibiza beauty—two- to three-hundred-pound pig turning desultorily over the flames. That's one thousand to fifteen hundred pounds of pig! A sign in front of the racks says the fête begins at seven o'clock. The fragrance is mouthwatering, so I park and get out of the car. The pigs are grinning, like they're happy to see me and happy to be here; they've given themselves up to the grandest of French causes—gastronomic pleasure—and they're just plain tickled to serve. I buy a ticket for seven euros, about ten dollars, and go home.

When I return at seven thirty, the village is barricaded and thousands of people are in the streets. I park a half mile away, walk into town, and stand in a food line that looks like 1950s photos of life in the Soviet Union or a painting by Hieronymus Bosch. Hundreds of people of all ages are standing in multiple squiggly wedges, each person holding a paper plate, looking as if he or she hasn't eaten in weeks.

By the time I get to the table, all that's left of Piggie Number One is a smile.

Piggie Number Two is on the cutting board, half gone. All I can think is, Which end did the rotisserie rod enter first?—as if the answer will affect the taste, hygiene, or whether I get trichinosis or some other piggy disease. That's what I'm thinking and worrying about, *feeling* that rod sliding through me (through *what? Andouille!*)—when the guy with the knife says something I don't understand.

"Oui," I answer, knowing my odds of answering correctly are fifty-fifty. Years before, when I took the SAT exams, I decided any answer I didn't know was *b*. That gave me a 25 percent chance of getting it right. Here it's 50 percent. Already I've doubled my odds. The guy says something else, and when I don't answer, he cuts a square of pig and hands it to me on the point of his knife. I look at it thinking, pigskin—gloves, suitcases, shoes. I pull the meat from the point of the knife and bite it. It's crisp, not greasy. I swallow. It's delicious. I bought a slice of grilled pig once before at the village market and didn't like the stuffing, but this—I've never tasted anything like it. The skin is brittle—crackling! The inside is juicy, meaty, and sweet, no gristle or fat. I thank the man profusely, "Merci, merci, merci beaucoup."

He cuts me a huge chunk of pig, making sure I get plenty of skin and juices, and points me on to the next person, who gives me a gigantic scoop of creamy scalloped potatoes and an even bigger scoop of ratatouille. I buy a demi-carafe of local cider and sit on a bench at a long table under a tent, eating a wonderful meal with hundreds of other full and contented neighbors. When I leave at ten o'clock, they're cutting up Pig Number Four. If there's such a thing as piggie addiction, I have it. If there are piggie idolaters, I'd be one. If Moses had been in Brittany, it would have been a golden pig. *That's* how good it is!

So later that summer when LeRoy is visiting and we drive past a restaurant named Cochon Grillé—"Grilled Pig"—I stop. I want him to know what I know.

It's noon, *midi*, and Cochon Grillé is empty, which is not a good sign in any country, but is especially bad news in France. I'm thinking health inspectors, or worse, pig plague. I'm ready to leave when a gruff, bearded fellow comes from somewhere and says, "Messieurs."

"Vous êtes ouvert?" I ask. Are you open?

"Non."

LeRoy looks at me like, *Let's go*—but I really want him to taste and experience grilled pig.

"C'est un restaurant, oui?" It's a restaurant, yes?

"Bien sûr."

"C'est possible faire une reservation?" Can I make a reservation?

"Combien de personnes?"

"Deux," I say, pointing to LeRoy and me, and holding up two fingers to be sure.

"Deux?" he repeats, making it a question. At least I think that's what he says, not "duh!"

"Deux. À quel jour?" *I'm* asking *him* when we can eat there, he's not asking me when I want the reservation. In fact, he's acting as if he couldn't care less. I figure he's a stereotypical, disgruntled French waiter.

"Mercredi," he says, "À midi, la semaine prochaine."

It's Tuesday, and he's telling me to come the following Wednesday, nine days later, at noon. "Bon," I say. "Je m'appelle Greenside."

He walks away not writing anything down.

The following week, LeRoy and I arrive a little before noon. The parking lot—which is huge—is empty. As far as I can see, we're the only people there. LeRoy looks at me like, this does not bode well. I'm thinking *E. coli* and Black Death.

"Let's go," LeRoy says, and buckles up.

I start the engine. The waiter sees us and walks to the car to greet us. He's happy and full of cheer. LeRoy shakes his head like doom. I'm thinking at least I know how to get us to the hospital in Quimper. The waiter knocks on the window, saying, "Entrez, entrez," and tries to open the door, which, thankfully, is locked. It's our last chance. LeRoy looks at me, knowing in the U.S. I'd be out of here. I turn the engine off, and LeRoy groans like Chewbacca. He's got a sensitive stomach, an irritable bowel, and is lactose intolerant. If this turns out as bad as it seems, I'm going to have to replace the plumbing in my house. Still, it's France, and we're here, and I've yet to have a bad meal—and the guy is holding onto the door handle.

Reluctantly, we get out of the car and death-row-walk our way toward the front door, which is closed. Monsieur le waiter walks behind us to keep us from bolting. He opens the door and leads us to a full bar. It's 11:50 a.m. All I had for breakfast was coffee. LeRoy had some fruit. The guy uncorks a bottle of something and fills three glasses.

"No, no, no, no," LeRoy and I decline, in harmony.

"Si, si, si, si, si," he persists.

"No, no, no, no," LeRoy solos.

Then Monsieur le waiter, now Monsieur le bartender, says the words that make it impossible to decline. "C'est gratuit." It's free—which either means it *is* free, it's a gift that we can't refuse, *or* it's part of the price and experience, and since we're paying for it anyhow—about fifty dollars each—we should drink it.

I take a sip and gasp. It's firewater. No wonder the Indians lost Manhattan, the lands east of the Mississippi, the plains, and the entire Southwest. LeRoy takes a sip and looks like he's going to cry. He puts his hand on his belly, instinctively, as if that will stop his intestines from disintegrating. Meanwhile, Monsieur le bartender downs his in one gulp. "Nurse it," LeRoy whispers, "nurse it, it's our only chance."

It's noon. We're nursing. There's not a single nibble to absorb or dilute whatever it is we're drinking—and no one else has arrived. We've managed to discover the only restaurant in France that's empty at *midi* and doesn't serve food with drink.

To kill time—rather than us, because clearly he doesn't know what to do with us, Monsieur le bartender asks, "Vous êtes de quel pays?"

"Nous sommes Américains," I say, and instantaneously he becomes ecstatic, joyous, thankful—for help in the World Wars, NATO, cream cheese, Sylvester Stallone, who can tell?—and pours us another drink.

LeRoy slumps on his stool.

I'm about to tell him we're really Brits, or Belgians, Arabs, or Germans, thinking, best-case scenario, he'll throw us out; worst, he'll hold back on the booze.

That's when the bus arrives. Not a mini bus or transit bus, but a huge touring bus. A bus for the Stones, The Beatles, Gladys Knight and every Pip she ever had, John Madden's bus. There are more mirrors on this thing than in a cheap hotel in Las Vegas. The door glides open like it's greased with butter, and eighty people pour out as if they were hostages who hadn't eaten in days, instead of the two hours it's been since breakfast. Everyone is neatly and casually dressed and perfectly coifed. The men are wearing pressed pants, polished shoes, and are freshly shaved. The women are in flowery dresses and high heels. They're all in their seventies and eighties. It's a retirement tour group, I figure, and we're in for pork purée.

The men head straight for the bar, where LeRoy and I greet them with, "Bonjour, bonjour," as if we're regulars, part of the official welcoming party, and we've been waiting for these guys forever. Monsieur le bartender fills their glasses from the same bottle he filled ours and charges them, which for some reason pleases me a lot. The women are met and greeted by a smiling lady who suddenly appears—Madame la bartendress?—and escorts them through two doors into a huge room filled with tables.

That's when the second bus arrives—bigger, and with more mirrors than the first—and another group of eighty people pour out, looking just as determined to eat as their compatriots. They too are well dressed and coifed and in their seventies and eighties. Talk about being early! It seems LeRoy and I came to a senior citizens outing a dozen years too soon.

The men from Bus Number Two go straight to the bar, where LeRoy and I and the men from Bus Number One greet them with, "Bonjour, bonjour," as if we're regulars and part of the official welcoming party, and they're our long-awaited friends. I almost feel like I fit in. The women go through the double doors to the room in the back and mingle with the women already there.

LeRoy and I huddle up. We hug the bar and nurse our drinks, resuming an animated debate about the Giants and A's, hoping in the pits of our empty, alcohol-laden stomachs that no one will be foolish or brave enough to talk to us, and the bartender will leave us alone. Monsieur le bartender pours us another drink, our third. Neither LeRoy nor I drink this much on a Saturday night or New Year's Eve, but today, on a Wednesday, at noon, we're looped.

Monsieur tops everyone's glass and leads us into the back room, where the women are chatting, mingling, *and* nibbling, thank God. There are a dozen long rectangular tables, each one holding serving dishes, chafing dishes, platters, trays, pots, tureens, bowls, and large and small plates of pig: pig parts, pieces, and particles; chopped pig, mixed, minced, diced, shredded, and smashed; gelled, smoked, salted, sweetened, fenneled, and thymed—a cornucopia of spices, herbs, nuts, fruit, and vegetables in every kind of pâté, cold cut, and wet and dry sausage imaginable, and some that aren't. No two tables are alike.

LeRoy and I and the 160 dig in. He and I have no idea what we are swallowing, and we're probably happier and better for it, as it's our only hope of getting sober.

We're eating whatever we're eating—ears, snout, knuckles, feet—trying to avoid conversations we won't understand, talking to each other as if it's really important, like about nuclear arms and where the bathroom is, when the music, which has been playing softly in the background, suddenly blares, and men and women, who are on opposite sides of the room and who have had nothing to do with each other since they arrived or the last thirty years, couple up and begin to dance.

It's nice, these seventy- and eighty-year-olds gracefully fox-trotting around the pork-laden tables. They dance, nibble on pig intestine, and dance some more.

A lady in a blinding yellow floral dress walks over and takes my hand. Her buddy in blue takes LeRoy's. We're sloshed, can barely move, and here we are dancing with two French ladies whose husbands are probably watching. LeRoy is a better dancer, so he's twirling his partner. Mine is lucky I'm wearing sandals so I don't break her toes when I step on them.

By one o'clock, I've had four drinks, danced, and eaten parts of pigs I didn't even know were edible, let alone existed. LeRoy is burning the dust on the dance floor. I'm ready to go home and nap. Madame la waitress opens another set of doors and leads all 162 of us in a single line—like at a state funeral—past a giant fireplace in which a whole three-hundred-pounder with that same happy-to-serve-you smile is turning and roasting, skin popping, on a spit. It's like we're paying final homage and saying thanks for a job well done.

I'm about to ask LeRoy which end he thinks the rod entered first, when we enter a long, narrow room with tables arranged in parallel lines, set for 160 French people, LeRoy, and me. Spaced evenly down the center of the tables are baskets of bread, plates with hunks of butter, and carafes filled with red and white wine and water. "Looks medieval," I say to LeRoy, "maybe there will be jousting."

"Or the plague . . ."

People sit in no apparent order, except LeRoy and me. We wait for Monsieur le waiter-bartender to place us, and he does, in the middle. Except for the three glasses, the place settings look normal. I know the glasses are for red and white wine and water. What I don't know is which goes with which. The fellow next to LeRoy reaches over and fills the biggest glass with water and the smallest with white and solves that problem.

Everyone is talking to someone. The lady next to me asks where we're from. I tell her California, and the word goes up and down the table, and across to the other side. "Americans are here!"

Finally, the pig is rolled in. It looks to me like a patient on a gurney going to surgery. I wonder what the old folks think of this, but from the looks on their faces, all they're thinking about is eating.

A guy in a stark-white three-story chef's hat, snug-fitting stark-white chef's apron, and more gold chains and medallions around his neck than Mr. T, steps forward, and I see it is Monsieur le waiter-bartender, now Monsieur le chef, and probably the owner, Monsieur *le propriétaire*, and Madame, his wife.

Monsieur begins speaking—a welcome? A blessing? A prayer that none of us gets ill? Maybe he's telling us the history of this pig, from artificial insemination to birth to gurney? He pauses, lifts the largest of the medallions from his chest and holds it out for us to see the picture of him in the middle. I get it! He's talking about himself, establishing his bona fides as chef, sommelier, *propriétaire*, as Monsieur Cochon Grillé. He makes the first cut, and a murmur goes out from the crowd.

Monsieur cuts and carves like a French Benihana and places a juicy chunk of pig on a plate. Madame adds ice-cream scoops full of ratatouille and scalloped potatoes, which seem to be *de rigueur* with pig. The plates are passed hand-to-hand down the row like a human conveyer belt. People help themselves to bread and butter, which are limitless, as is the wine. There's enough food for seconds and thirds, and enough red and white wine to loop 162 full, sated, satisfied diners. I happily note the table is a mess and people are eating with their fingers, elbows on the table, occasionally talking with their mouths full of food.

I turn to the lady next to me and say, "J'aime beaucoup le cochon." I love the pig. I say it as if the pig is my secret lover, or I'm into some strange kind of porcine worship.

"Oui," she says, and turns toward the sane person on her right.

The food keeps coming, until even the French can no longer eat. "I'm beat," LeRoy says. "I just want to crawl under the table and sleep."

"Me too." But just when I'm hoping for nap time, Monsieur Cochon Grillé returns with a floor mic and places it at the head of the tables, next to what's left of the pig.

"What's this?" LeRoy asks me.

"I don't know."

I ask the lady next to me. "Qu'est-ce que c'est?"

"Le chant," she says.

"Chanting," I say to LeRoy. He's Catholic, I figure he'll understand.

"Who's chanting? What?"

Two good questions, neither of which I answer.

We all sit there staring at the mic, waiting for something or someone to appear. Heads turn, people look down their row, left and right, across to the other side, at the doors, the windows, floor, ceiling. It's like being in school when the teacher asks a question and no one knows the answer, and everyone's thinking, 'Please, God, not me,' and hopes, if they don't make eye contact they won't be called. That's what we're all doing, when an old fellow—late seventies, early eighties—wearing pressed yellow slacks, a bright-blue shirt, and sandals pushes his chair back and walks from the back of the room to the mic. I'm wondering if this is a setup, if he's a ringer like the "volunteers" at Cirque de Soleil, or if this is for real.

LeRoy looks at me and I shrug.

I ask the lady next to me, "Qui est ce là?"

She shrugs. I don't know if this means she doesn't know who he is, or what I asked. I could ask her again, but I've already stepped on her toes and told her I'm in love with a pig. It's probably best to leave her alone. I look past her, to the man at the front of the room, and watch as he lowers the mic like a professional.

"Bonjour," he says.

We all say, "Bonjour," back, like some sort of call and response.

He begins to speak in a voice like Johnny Cash—basso profundo, French—the kind of voice that no matter what is said sounds godlike, end-of-the-world, the-Four-Horsemen-are-coming, serious. He says a few pleasantries about the food and his tablemates, gets a few laughs, and gets serious again. It takes me a while to realize he is reciting a poem. A long poem—ten minutes' worth—from memory. When he finishes, he waves, says, "Merci," and goes back to his seat. Everyone, especially LeRoy and I, applaud.

He's followed by a woman who looks like Joan Rivers, frosted face, hair, and skin, and is just as funny—at least to the French. She's cracking jokes and telling stories, making fun of "le Président" and "le pape." She returns to her chair to much applause.

As soon as she sits down, a couple in matching plaid shirts bounce up and practically skip to the front of the room. They look at each other, at us, each other again, nod their heads in unison, say, "un, deux, trois," and sing in beautiful two-part harmony. There's harmony all around us, as the lady next to me fills my glass with red, and I fill LeRoy's, and he fills the fellow's next to him, up and down the table, and we all applaud when they're done.

It's like "France Has Talent" or "French Idol," except everyone here is a winner.

People get up and sing, dance, play instruments—harmonica, accordion, spoons—tell jokes and stories and recite poems and speeches. I know from Tatjana and Marie and other French friends who are teachers that French students are required to memorize speeches, poems, and sections of literature and to recite them in class. They still take Latin, elocution, and rhetoric. To become a teacher, it is necessary to pass written subject matter exams as well as orals: tough, long, grueling orals, not something perfunctory like in the U.S. The result is people enjoy performing—and they're good at it.

After twenty or so people have performed, Madame Cochon Grillé returns with huge bowls of red leaf lettuce bathed in vinaigrette. Somehow, the laughter and entertainment have made us hungry and thirsty. The salad is ravaged, more wine is consumed, and the people are getting happier and happier, though LeRoy and I are beginning to slump.

Periodically, as if possessed or cattle-prodded, another person stands, goes to the mic and sings or speaks or recites. Each person is greeted warmly, and everyone, no matter his or her talent, gets an applause. It's like an AA meeting. Thank you, Jacques, for performing. Hello, my name is Pierre, and I'm going to sing for you.

"Qui est cette groupe?" What is this group, I ask the lady next to me, pointing at both rows of tables, thinking they must be from the same church or village. "La même ville ou église?"

"Non."

"Qua," a word I made up on my own.

"Nous sommes touristes."

"Touristes?"

"Oui."

"Ne connie pas cette personnes?"

"Non."

I'm amazed. These folks are acting like family—like the Le Blanc family picnic—and they've never met before this trip. The only tours I've been on in the U.S., people huddle next to the people they know and ridicule the others.

To be sure, I ask, "C'est le première fois vous êtes ensemble?" This is the first time you've been together?

"Oui."

That's bonding for you. They must have met several days ago in Belgium or Strasbourg, Metz or Nice, and quickly became a group. I know families in the U.S. who aren't this close.

"Vous êtes habiton où?" Where are you from?

"Quiberon."

"*Quiberon?* En Bretagne?" I ask this because Donna and I were once invited to a wedding in Montauban. I brought a suit, tie, dress shoes, and a gift from California. Donna brought a dress, jewelry, four pairs of shoes, and a gift. All summer she asked, "Are you sure you know where it is?" Twice, I showed her on the map. "It's a tiny village near Rennes. Two hours away. No problem." It wasn't until Donna gave the invitation to Gilles, who studied it exceedingly closely and discerned a thin, very lightly drawn squiggly line that I thought was a smudge or a decoration with the tiny word "Tarn" written next to it. Tarn, it seems, is a river in the south of France, and *that* Montauban was a long, nine-hour drive away. Since we were returning to California the day after the wedding, we missed it. So I repeat, "Quiberon ici, en Bretagne?"

"Oui. Bien sûr. Nous nous sommes tous rencontrés ce matin."

All of these people just met *this* morning. They are on a one-day activity—eating—and they're returning home tonight.

"Et les autres?" I point to the people from the second bus, sitting across from us.

"Morlaix." She says it as if they're a different species, the same way Manhattanites refer to Brooklyners. "C'est pareil."

They also just met this morning. Not only have they bonded as Quiberonnais and Morlaisiens, but in the time they've been together, about an hour and a half, they've all bonded as Bretons. Except for a two-week tour to Japan, every tour I've been on, I've come away despising and loathing the other tourists. At Williamsburg, I got into a nasty argument with the tour guide and other tourists over slavery and just how lucky the house slaves actually were. *These* people, though, are really enjoying themselves and one another. And I am, too. It's been a thoroughly enjoyable day, but I'm ready to say, "Bonne journée," and "Bonnes vacances." It's three thirty, and I'm beat. "How about it?" I say to LeRoy.

That's when Madame Cochon Grillé begins serving cheese. LeRoy and I look at each other like, *is she kidding?* Even some of the more sportif-looking French people wince. The ensemble is becoming quieter and slower.

A woman stands, walks to the microphone, and sings a beautiful song in a language not English or French. The lady next to me whispers, "Breton."

I turn to tell LeRoy, who's busy trying to tell the fellow next to him five glasses of wine is enough. "Oui, oui," the fellow says, and fills LeRoy's glass to the brim.

The lady next to me stands and begins talking. I don't understand anything until I hear "Américains," and see people nod to LeRoy and me and make gestures of welcome—at least, I think they are gestures of welcome. When she finishes, everyone appears to be waiting. For what? For us! They expect us to do, say, or sing something. LeRoy does a great Curly and I do Moe, but without Larry, it just isn't worth it. We confer, and the only song we can remember is "Take Me Out to the Ball Game." It's either that or the Gettysburg Address. Luckily, Madame arrives with dessert and coffee, and we demur—why ruin a good meal with us!

Dessert is consumed quickly, as if the buses are going to leave, or enough is finally enough, and it's time to go while it's still possible for most of us to walk.

By five o'clock we're finished—in every sense of the word. LeRoy and I walk along with everyone else back to the buses and wave goodbye, calling out, "Bon voyage," "Bonne chance," "Bonne vacances," "Bon mercredi," "Bonne journée," "Bonne santé," and "Bonne nuit." Then we wobble back to the car. The good news is we're less than thirty minutes from the house. I open the car door. Monsieur Cochon Grillé, who's been largely invisible since carving the pig and showing his medallions, comes out to shake our hands.

"Avez-vous bien manger?" he bellows. Are you full?

"Oui, oui," LeRoy and I nod.

"Bon temps?" he inquires. Have a good time?

"Oui, oui."

"Bon." Then he wraps an arm like a moose leg around each of our shoulders and steers us back toward the restaurant.

LeRoy looks at me. I look at him. "I don't know," I say, "maybe we're supposed to tip." LeRoy shrugs, which actually isn't easy with two hundred pounds of meat on his shoulder. We do what we can, which is nothing, so we follow. Monsieur leads us back to the bar, and announces, "Un digestif," as he plops three glasses on the counter.

Holy Christ! Any more alcohol and I'll be antifreeze. LeRoy will be embalmed. That said, we each down two shots of something, and my stomach feels better. I can't see straight, but my digestif system is *très bon*—and, as with the apéritifs, Monsieur *le propriétaire* refuses to allow us to pay.

Finally, through some miracle or divine intervention, we get home at six thirty. By 6:35, LeRoy is asleep in the attic and I'm dozing off in my bedroom. Six hours of eating is what French people consider a day in the country. No wonder they spend a greater percentage of their income on food and drink than any other people on Earth. In France, food is the national pastime: it's religion, art, sport, science, entertainment, security blanket, comfort, and pleasure combined.

In the U.S, I know what I eat, and I eat what I want, and I'm satisfied. In France, Brittany, Finistère, where I don't want to displease, disappoint, annoy, or offend any more than I do, I eat what's given to me, and the results are often startling. After eating langoustines, lotte, and grilled pig, *some* other foods go down surprisingly easy.

A Mollusk

I'm visiting my friends Bob and Loni at their home on the Île-aux-Moines, the French version of the Hamptons or Cape Cod. We're taking a short hike around the island, on our way to a picnic, though we have no food with us, only two bottles of wine and a baguette.

We're on the coastal path, and I'm marveling at the three-story stone houses, roses, hydrangeas, and geraniums blooming everywhere, ferns growing next to palms next to evergreens next to fruit trees, and the spectacular, changing-with-the-light, lapis lazuli, star sapphire bay. It's gorgeous, idyllic, perfect for a picnic—if we had any food.

That's what I'm thinking when we stop at a shack, and a weather-beaten, batten-down-the-hatches fisherman-type guy, complete with rubber hip boots and veiny red nose, steps out of a tank of water and greets us with a hearty, "Bonjour, bonjour," as if he's expecting us.

I look at Bob, who sings, "Bon-jour," right back, shakes the guy's hand, and gives him the two bottles of wine. I don't get it. This isn't a restaurant or café, and the guy doesn't look like a sommelier, but for some reason, or no reason, or all reasons, he has a corkscrew in his pocket—maybe all French men do, and I'm just discovering it—and he opens both bottles of wine. For another reason I don't understand, he takes four glasses from a shelf that's holding at least a dozen more, places them on a rough plank of wood perched across two sawhorses, and fills each glass to the brim.

This must be some strange Île-aux-Moines ritual, I figure, and I'm being welcomed and initiated. I'm sipping the wine, waiting for who knows what, watching an old, wooden, two-masted shallop with rust-orange sails tack across the bay. I turn to show Bob the boat, and I see behind him, walking slowly toward us, Monsieur le Fisherman, arms outstretched, holding a large, round, dripping wicker basket filled with . . . *OYSTERS!*

Oh, no! *He's* the oyster man! *This* is the guy Bob and Loni have been talking about—and we're going to eat oysters for lunch. *I'm* going to eat oysters for lunch. Raw oysters, not Rockefeller. That's what that tank is: an oyster bed. *This* is our picnic! He puts the basket down and pulls a huge rubber glove over his left hand, quickly cuts open a dozen oysters, and serves them to us on a wooden platter.

Bob and Loni smile and glow as they down one, then another, and smile and glow even more. The happier they are, the happier the oyster guy is. I'm the only one who's glum. I know oysters are a treat, a delicacy, supposedly an aphrodisiac—which I don't need, since Donna is in California, and I'm alone. But I also know they are raw and alive. I've eaten sushi and sashimi—thanks to Donna—but those are fish, not mollusks, and they're dead.

I'm debating: on the one hand, I didn't want to eat langoustine, and now I love them. The same is true of sushi, sashimi, roast pig, and lotte. On the other hand, I still won't touch gizzard, brains, tongue, frog, horse, blood sausage, andouille, or his cousin, tripe . . .

Bob and Loni and the oyster guy are waiting. I'd wait, too—forever if I could, but it's clear I can't. I squeeze half a lemon on the smallest oyster to cover the taste and see if it moves. It doesn't. Bob and Loni slurp down their third and fourth. The oyster guy downs two of his own. I pick up the half shell—it still looks like phlegm to me—put it to my lips, tip my head back, and pour it down my throat, hoping it goes all the way to the end without stopping.

Bob and Loni and the oyster guy are laughing and waiting. I'm perplexed. I don't know if I like it or not. The only thing I taste is the ocean. It's like drinking the sea. I have another and another and another, and I order a dozen more, "Un douzaine, s'il vous plaît," and the four of us down a half dozen each, along with the baguette and the two bottles of Muscadet-Sèvre-et-Maine-sur-Lie . . . Oh, happy day!

I'm even happier, when a month later, for my birthday, Donna takes me to Cancale, the oyster capital of France, where we eat sea-dripping oysters for breakfast, lunch, and dinner, and scientifically test their aphrodisiacal qualities under numerous imaginative conditions at night.

I'm still not like Donna, though. She asks questions about what she's eating, where it came from, and how it was prepared, and I prefer "don't ask/don't tell." As far as I'm concerned, there's nothing to be gained by knowing I'm eating fish eyes or cheeks or pig's toes—and plenty to lose, possibly all over the table. I'll taste anything now—that's the good news—as long as I don't know what it is. For culinary cowards like me, the unexamined meal is best.

10 Things I've Learned about Eating in France

1. *Dégustation* means "tasting," not "disgusting"; *poisson* means "fish," not "poison"; *terroir* means a product of the land—like "turf" in surf and turf—not "terror"; a person with a napkin tucked under his chin is a gourmand, not the pretentious, gluttonous slob I think he is in the U.S.

2. Cutting cheese: I used to cut cheese any which way until one night at Jean and Sharon's house I cut the tip of a Bleu d'Auvergne, and Jean went nuts. "Marc, Marc you cannot cut the cheese like that." Jean explained there are rules for cheese cutting—as there are for everything else: if the cheese is round, cut a triangular wedge, if it's square or rectangular, slice from the sides, and if it's a triangular cheese— like the Bleu d'Auvergne—cut from either of the two sides, and never, *ever* from the tip, where, according to Jean, the best of the Bleu resides, though it looks blue throughout to me. It doesn't matter how big a piece you cut—as long as there is plenty left for others—or how tiny, as long as you taste it. Cheese is a basic food group in France. It's important to get this right.

3. Coffee is another major food group in France, meaning there are more rules to follow, which in this case, I don't. It's like the furniture in my house: I'm willing to change lots of things about myself when I'm in France, but not my aesthetics, and not the way I drink coffee. For reasons I'll never understand, French people drink *café au lait* or *café crème* only with breakfast. After some unspecified hour in the morning, it becomes a moral and culinary lapse to have milk or cream with coffee. It's like eating cottage cheese with ketchup, it's wrong—which is how I feel three or four

times a day when I add milk: like a recidivist Philistine reprobate.

4. Eating the mussel: Monsieur P teaches me to eat mussels like a local. Nonlocals eat with a fork. Locals use the two halves of the mussel shell like chopsticks. Monsieur holds the half shells with the fingers of one hand, like pincers, and the mussel he's going to eat in the other. He pries the mussel open with a shell, plucks the meat out, places it in his mouth, and chews. Simple, easy, convenient, and clean—if you're Monsieur. Laundry and bath time, if you're me. I now eat mussels using the shell if the meat is large and easy to extract, and using a fork if it's not, marking me as the semilocal I am.

5. Food from every major culture and country in the world is available in France—but Paris, Lyon, Marseille, and Lille are the only urban areas with more than one million people. I have to remember that when I arrive in a village and want *enchiladas verdes* or pad thai, and if I want eggs for breakfast, or cereal, or yogurt, fresh fruit, smoked salmon, toast, or oatmeal—or things most French people consider disgusting, like peanut butter, hot sauce, or sweet butter (which Jean and Bruno refuse to eat, calling it "hospital butter")—I have to eat at home or go to a high-end Anglicized hotel. Otherwise, breakfast is what it always is: half a baguette, a croissant or two, maybe a brioche or *pain au chocolat* (French people are nuts for chocolate in the morning), a couple of choices of jam, probably strawberry and apricot, lots of salted butter, maybe a small glass of OJ, and either a single cup or a two-cup pot of coffee with steamed milk that will cost between ten and fifteen dollars *per person*—for bread and coffee!

6. Never eat anything called *Américain*. I once ordered an "Américain" sandwich. It was a foot-long hunk of baguette, sliced and smattered with a slab of butter on each side, filled with a single slice of ham, another of gruyere cheese, and half a hard-boiled egg, all buried under lettuce, tomato, mustard, and mayonnaise, topped off with a heaping scoopful of fries. One bite and I was transported back to two-year-old land or forward to Alzheimer's—with food all over my face, hair, and clothing.

7. The only quick meal in France is at home or takeaway. If I sit at a table, I kiss one to three hours goodbye, which is fine and delicious if I want to, but not so fine if I don't. The fastest sit-down eating is at a café, *salon de thé*, a bistro, brasserie, McDonald's, KFC, or Domino's pizza. The only way to eat when I want and what I want is to eat at home.

8. Everyone eats two-handed: fork in the left hand, knife in the right, knife used to cut and shovel, fork to spear and eat. Only I shift my knife and fork back and forth, left hand to right to left. No one makes mention of it, but it feels like a disability or worse, a character flaw.

9. None of the food or dining experiences, in homes or restaurants—even in Michelin one- and two-stars—are anything like those I've experienced in fancy French restaurants in New York, San Francisco, or New Orleans. I go to those restaurants and I'm embarrassed by not knowing which knife, fork, glass, or spoon to use; where to put my elbows; when to eat with my fingers; what to order; how to pronounce it; what *it* is—from the sea, land, air, or Genentech—and where *exactly* in the body *it* originated. Even worse, are the waiters: the waiter who never appears, who I have to implore to come to the table, thereby proving

he's superior to me; or the know-it-all waiter, who lectures me in French, Franglish, and heavily accented English, informing me about the restaurant, menu, and chef, telling me all of this as if there's going to be a quiz at the end of the meal—like what secret ingredient did Maître Charles cook with the quail—in a tone that tells me he doesn't expect me to pass, thereby proving he's superior to me. When the food arrives, the meat is too raw, the vegetables too cooked, the desserts too rich, and the coffee too strong. I spend more time trying to avoid what I don't want to taste, see, or smell than enjoying what I do—none of which happens in France. Eating French food in the U.S., especially in New York City, is intimidating. Eating French food in France is eating. In France, except possibly at state dinners, no one seems to care which glasses or dishes are used, or which cutlery. Waiters don't lecture me and only ignore me when I ask for the bill. People eat with gusto, shovel food with their knives, eat with their fingers when necessary, talk with their mouths full, make a mess, and never seem to go to the bathroom. Given the prodigious amount of liquid consumed with French meals, this last is what distinguishes me most—not my etiquette or miserable French.

10. Bruno, my next-door neighbor, is devoting his life to teaching me about wine. I'm learning how to drink enormous amounts and not get drunk. I've watched amazed, as he sends back wine served by a friend as not the right complement for the food we are eating—*at* the friend's house. I've seen Monsieur P refuse his own wine as "too young." Bruno has given me a map of the wine regions of France that identifies the varietals. He's embedded 2008, 2009, 2010, and 2014 in my brain as the years for great

Bordeaux. Since he and Françoise visit Donna and me often, he's determined I get this right. I am, too—but the bottom line for him is the continuous bang! of the ongoing explosions of taste as he swallows; for me, it's ten euros a bottle. Between these perimeters, we live.

I Cooked This for You

Eating French food is one thing. Cooking French food is another—and cooking French food for French people is something else. Lesson Number One: you cannot feed a French person the way you'd feed an American.

In the U.S., it's no big deal to experiment with food on friends. In fact, it's an honor: LeRoy's such a good friend, I can cook something new for him. If it doesn't work, and worse comes to worst, we'll go out. Not in France. In France, cooking and eating are not about taste and nutrition. They're a combo of religion and sex. It's tantric, merging pleasure and spirit, but only if done right—right ingredients, preparation, presentation, and flavors. The result is I approach every meal I cook for my French friends with nervousness and trepidation. More than anything, I want to do this right. I can't speak properly, wait patiently, dress, act, or look French, but please, God, let me feed them well: bien manger. *And, please, please God, let no one leave the table ill or get sick within twenty-four hours of eating at my house. That's my prayer before I start. Then I plan and prepare like for D-Day.*

It begins in the kitchen, my favorite room in the house and also the most dysfunctional. In California, my kitchen is a commuter kitchen, a single-guy kitchen, even after Donna moves in. It is not a room for eating, sitting, visiting, talking, reading, thinking, or hanging out. When people visit, we sit in the living room. In France, it's the kitchen all the way, with its oak parquet table, soft, leather-covered chairs, whitewashed walls, beamed ceiling, 100-plus-year-old tile floor, and the summertime view through the window of red geraniums, verdant trees, and the river. It's a room that's ready for anything—except cooking.

First, there's the baby fridge: five feet short, as wide as one of the doors of a double-door American fridge, with a freezer the size of a mailbox. There's also a baby dishwasher and a baby sink. The dishwasher is a Bosch and actually holds a lot. The sink does not. One medium-size pot and it's full. That, and its back-breaking lack of height and the ridiculously low angle of the faucet, makes it an uncomfortable place to work. According to Margaret Fox, daughter of my friends Harold and Anne Fox and former cook and owner of Café Beaujolais in Mendocino, "It's the worst-designed kitchen in the world."

The sink is in one corner, the fridge in another, the stove in a third, and an old English oak cupboard with my dishes, pots, and utensils in the fourth. I'm lucky the room's not an octagon. My kitchen! This is where the damage gets done.

A Salad

I take six eggs from the fridge, a pot from the cupboard, fill it with water at the sink, and cook the eggs on the stove. Monsieur and Madame P and their son and daughter-in-law, Henri and Renée, are coming to dinner tonight.

It's unseasonably warm, so I'm going to make a huge garden salad, like I do in the U.S. I wait till after *midi* and drive to Loscoat to buy the veggies and bread last-minute fresh. I also buy a wedge of Tomme de Savoie and a half kilo of *fleur de sel*, *demi-sel* butter—1.1 pounds! It's France: there can never be too much butter—as long as it's not sweet. I buy another bottle of Muscadet-Sèvre-et-Maine-sur-Lie, because there can never be too much wine either.

I spend the afternoon washing and shredding red leaf and butter lettuce from Madame P's garden and cutting, slicing and dicing tomatoes, mushrooms, olives, red and yellow bell peppers, cucumbers, zucchini, radishes, oranges, and cheese;

I mince shallots and slice the hard-boiled eggs I made in the morning—and put everything in the fridge to chill. I set the dining room table for dinner and the table on the terrace for apéritifs—the one part of the meal I never fret about, because I do exactly what everyone does—and wait.

They arrive forty minutes late, which is on time in France. I point to the side of the house, and say, "À la terrasse," and lead them there, because no one will go on his or her own, even though everyone has been there before. As soon as they sit, I start passing bowls of peanuts, Chee-to-like and bacon-bit thingies, sliced dry sausage, olives, and baby, thumbnail-size radishes still warm from the earth of Madame P's garden; I take orders for drinks and mix black currant or peach liqueur for Kirs, cider for Kir Breton, water and Ricard for pastis, and serve them along with beer, white wine, and red. As long as everything flows and nothing runs out, apéritifs are a success.

After an hour of *de rigueur* nibbling and drinking, I excuse myself, "Je vais fait le salade," and go into the house to mix the salad. In the U.S., someone, usually Donna or another woman—out of politeness or self-defense—always offers to help. In France, only Sharon offers—probably because she's Canadian and has eaten a lot of my cooking. In France, the kitchen is a private space. Basically, there's an invisible sign on the door that says, "Keep out!" I know, because every time I offer to help serve or wash dishes—as every woman I've ever known in the U.S. has demanded I do—I'm stopped. It was five years before I was allowed into Madame P's kitchen, ten years before I visited the second floor of her house. I waited three years to use her bathroom, and then only because it would have been worse if I hadn't . . . So I mix and dress the salad myself while everyone gets in the last of their nibbling and drinking.

I fill two large bowls and set them on the table along with three baguettes, the half kilo of butter, two bottles of water, and three bottles of red. Then I call everyone inside, "Asseyez vous, asseyez vous," sit down, sit down.

Everyone enters, sits, and looks at me like, 'What's this?' Nobody says anything, and nobody moves—not even to unfold a napkin.

That's when I remember I've never actually been served a salad as dinner in any French person's home—and I see from the confusion and disappointment on their faces that ninety degree heat and eighty-five percent humidity don't mean a thing: it's dinnertime, and they want and expect the full seven courses—which means I'm five courses short.

"Bon appétit," I say, serve the salad, and hope for the best.

Out of politeness, hunger, or both, everyone digs in, except Madame P. She pokes through the salad, searching for chunks of mushroom, spears them one at a time, and places them on the side of her plate.

"C'est bon," I say. "C'est frais," telling her they're either fresh or strawberries.

"Oui, oui," she says, and then says something else, the only word of which I understand is *champignons*, mushrooms.

I look at Henri.

"She says they're not cooked. Mushrooms have to be cooked. You can't eat them raw."

I start to explain that we eat them like this in the U.S., then remember we're the ones who brought them McDonald's and Cocoa Puffs, and realize it's probably not the best argument.

I fork a large chunk of mushroom and put it in my mouth,

chew it slowly, and rub my belly, moaning, "*Mmmmmmm*. C'est bon."

Madame makes a face like I'm eating poo. Monsieur, making the decision to not get involved, bites through a wedge of tomato. Henri asserts his independence and wantonly eats the mushrooms in public defiance of *maman*. Renée doesn't. The following day, Henri tells me no one actually liked them raw, and next time I should cook them. He also tells me cheese does not belong in a salad, and a salad is not a meal.

Madame is teaching me to be French, or at least not to offend the French, especially their taste buds, and most especially hers. The result is I am very careful about what I serve, though often not careful enough.

After numerous attempts to be creative or fanciful or playful—like making a face out of tomatoes and carrots—I understand salad is lettuce. *C'est tout.* Salad comes after the entrée and before the cheese, is basically a palate cleanser and digestif. That's it. I've got it. What I don't have is the dressing.

Luckily, I served olive oil and red wine vinegar as the dressing for the garden salad, so that turned out OK. Since then, I've made Russian, blue, Thousand Island—even French—and failed with all of them. It seems only oil and vinegar is universally accepted. I get it, but I still can't do it. It's like going to 31 Flavors and always ordering vanilla.

I add shallots to the oil and vinegar, and no one removes them, gags, or complains. That's the test. French people, compliant and accepting of so many things, are very vocal about what they'll put in their stomachs—or mouths, actually, because I've gotten lots of things in their mouths that never made it to their stomachs. Jean won't eat my green beans. They're too al dente—he wants them soft. He also dislikes my mayonnaise. He wants me to make it myself with a raw egg and olive oil the way he does, but all I see when he shows me how to do it is salmonella. So I continue to buy my mayonnaise at the store, and he continues to ridicule me.

I add a quarter teaspoon of Dijon mustard to the shallots, which is also OK. I increase it to half a teaspoon, and one third of the people at the table refuse to eat it. It's too strong, *piquant*, a word that seems to be the equivalent of "crap". I switch to mustard "à l'ancienne" and it's worse. What are those seeds, and why are they in my salad? It's like I'm running a scientific taste lab or Julia Child's kitchen, which unfortunately for all of us, I'm not.

The biggest decision is which vinegar to use, because there are zillions to choose from: red wine, white wine, cider, with orange blossom, lemon zest, strawberry, raspberry, thyme, shallots. They all work, until I get to balsamic. First, there's the color. Why is it black? What's the trick? What are they hiding—the *they* now includes me. Madame P approaches it carefully, remembering the mushrooms, I'm sure. She forks a piece of lettuce that is barely coated with olive oil and has a drop of balsamic glistening on the leaf.

"Mmmmmmmm," I say, "C'est très bonne. Espécial. Italien." I figure I'd have better luck with that than saying it's American. She tastes it and gags like it's poison.

"Qu'est-ce que c'est?" she demands. Her voice full of horror and betrayal—as in, "How could you do this to *me*!"

"C'est balsamic."

She repeats it, "Balsamic," saying it in a way that tells me she never wants to say, see, smell, or taste it again.

I *know* lots of French people like balsamic vinegar because I've eaten it in other people's homes, and I see it in all the stores—but that's not the point. This is: if you want to feed *all* of the people at your table *all* of the time, you have to do what everyone does, and this is what surprises me most. People in Plobien and Loscoat, *French* people, are like me— *not* adventurous eaters. Their range is broader than mine— they'll eat intestines, brain, horse, gizzard, feet, knuckles, tongue, all the organs, and things that once were family pets—but anything out of their range, like peanut butter, hot sauce, sour cream, and Russian dressing is as alien to them as andouille is to me. Pizza is OK, probably because it comes from the neighbor to the southeast, isn't English, and is made with flour, tomatoes and cheese, three of the all-time French favorites. The same with paella, which comes from their neighbor to the southwest, isn't English, and is made with rice, chicken, pig, langoustine, and mussels, all of which are familiar and comfortable to French people. That's the main point, being comfortable and familiar, not new or different. From the northeast, Belgium, there are *gauffres*—waffles— which are basically crêpes, only thicker, and not English. When people want to be exotic or brave, they eat Chinese or Vietnamese, which also serves to remind them of their Asiatic colonial past, isn't English, and has been French- ified to remove most of the interesting spices and all of the *piquant*. Couscous, tagine, and merguez sausages are colonial reminders from their North African past. And to remind them of their colonial past in North America, there's a new McDonald's, which most people don't want to be reminded about, which hasn't made the wedge out of the door any shorter.

I know all this, and still I persist.

Le Barbecue Américain

I invite Madame P and her family to an American-style barbecue even though I know it's impossible. To start, there are no all-beef hot dogs. No Nathan's, Vienna Franks, or Hebrew National, or anything like them. This is pig land. There are sausages, but not American sausages like bratwurst, kielbasa, linguica, knackwurst, sweet Italian, or hot links; no designer chicken-apple, garlic, Thai, or jalapeño either. What Plobien has is andouillette, the foul-smelling little sister of andouille, and *boudin noir*, blood sausage, made from pig's blood, fat, bread crumbs, and seasonings. The only *edible* sausages are the finger-thin merguez, chipolata, and herb, but I need to eat at least four of them to be full, and because they're so thin I usually burn them when I cook them. Hamburger, thankfully, is ground sirloin.

Hamburger, mustard, ketchup, tomatoes, lettuce, and onions, that's it! There are no buns, baked beans, sour relish, dill pickles—only sweet gherkin-like *cornichons*—or sauerkraut that I've found. This is potato land, but there are no thick-skinned Idaho russets, only thin-skinned boilers and broilers.

The *only* reason I'm doing this "Barbecue Américain" is corn. It's one of the foods I miss most in France: sweet, fresh, buttery, summery corn on the cob . . . There are millions of acres of corn in Brittany, and *all* of it for animals. Chickens get their corn on the cob. People get theirs in a can from Del Monte. I don't know why, but that's how it is and has been for years. Then one day, like magic—the same way Volvic water suddenly disappeared—a cellophane-wrapped package of six ears of yellow corn on the cob appears in the dairy section of Leclerc. I buy two packages and call Madame P to invite her and her family "pour le Barbecue Américain." It's a testament to their gastric strength and our friendship that she accepts without even saying, "I'll call you back."

Dinner is at 8:00. They arrive at 8:30. The good news is I expected this and haven't started cooking. The bad news is the charcoal is ash. I replace the briquettes and rekindle the fire.

By 9:30, people are getting restive. So far, all they've had is alcohol and chips. To let them know what's happening, I announce there are no crudités—"Pas de crudités. C'est une Barbecue Américain."

Madame's face falls, probably remembering the mushrooms and balsamic. I can see her thinking, "I knew I should have eaten before coming here . . . " In the U.S., whenever I cook, I feel like Wolfgang Puck. In France, I feel like puck.

Thankfully, Henri and Renée appear to be thrilled by whatever it is they will be eating, and keep repeating, "Le Barbecue Américain." They have no idea what it is, but they're willing to try it—and hopefully soon. It's 10:00, and all they have eaten is chips. Luckily, we're in France, and everyone is too polite to make up an excuse to leave.

When the potatoes are finally ready, I scoop them from the coals, unwrap the tinfoil, and place them in a glass bowl. I remove the hamburgers and sausages from the grill and put them on platters. I bring out six baguettes, mustard, mayonnaise—French people seem to eat mayonnaise with anything—ketchup, which only I use—everyone looks at me suspiciously—along with salt, pepper, and butter, a staple like water and air. Then, *la pièce de résistance*. I go inside and drop the dozen ears of corn in a huge pot of boiling water, wait two minutes, put them on a platter, and carry them to the table, beaming. Everyone stops talking and stares. It's a look I'm becoming familiar with.

"What's that?" Henri asks, knowing full well, since it grows everywhere in Brittany.

"Corn."

"Yes, but it's on the cob."

"Oui . . . Une surprise," and I place the platter on the table. "Bon appétit."

No one moves, something else I'm becoming familiar with. I figure they don't know how to eat it and don't want to appear foolish. I lift an ear from the tray, bite a mouthful—and immediately want to gag. The kernels are dry, hard *and* mushy, no sweetness, no juice—other than remnants of the boiled water— with the texture of wood or the shells of sunflower seeds. No wonder they don't eat it. The corn on the cob is garbage. The big hit of the evening are the baked potatoes, even though they're not russets. Madame P eats four, as happy as if they were a Poire Belle Hélène or banana split.

Monsieur and Madame P and their family; Jean and Sharon and their boys; Jean-Pierre and Joëlle and their girls; Mr. Charles, Bruno and Françoise; Gilles and Tatjana, Louis and Jocelyne, and Hugo and Nadine and their families, these are my friends and my French family, and short of poisoning one of them, things will be OK. The larder is full, and it will take more than raw mushrooms, green beans al dente, balsamic vinegar, sweet hospital butter, or corn on the cob to empty it. I think . . . I hope . . . I worry . . .

Dinner for Six

Hugo and Nadine are coming for dinner. I've eaten at their house three or four times, so it's my turn to cook for them. In the U.S., this wouldn't be a problem. I'd make a salad, grill salmon or steak, boil or broil some veggies, and serve Ben & Jerry's Cherry Garcia for dessert. Every course except the Ben & Jerry's would be on the table at the same time. My friends would arrive at seven and leave by ten, none asking for cheese, most not wanting coffee or tea, half not wanting dessert, and no one expecting a digestif. Not so in France, and definitely not Hugo and Nadine.

The last time I ate at their house, it was the full seven courses. Apéritifs included Nadine-made *warm* nibbles—like hors-d'oeuvres at a wedding or an embassy dinner. Alcohol included all the regulars plus Suze, thirty-year-old port, and American cocktails. I had to pace myself, which is the key to surviving a French meal: eat a little of each serving, because there's always a lot, and the eating goes on forever. Crudités were from Nadine's garden: butter lettuce, tomatoes, radishes, mint, *nasturtium petals* . . . The entrée was a whole sea bass—*bar*—that had been bathed in sea salt, baked whole, and filleted at the table—the moistest, tenderest, most flavorful fish I've ever eaten, and I'm a beef guy. Salad was followed by five cheeses. The only ones I recognized were a chèvre and Morbier. I tasted all five because Jean told me it's mandatory. Desserts were served after midnight: homemade apple tart, Breton butter cookies, fresh fruit, and ice cream, all of which I also tasted, followed by tea and coffee and cognac. We finished at 2:00. I left at 2:30. *These* are the people who are coming for dinner.

My first thought is to order out: paella, Vietnamese, charcuterie deli food, but even I know that's not right.

My second thought is to take them out—crêpes or pizza or *fruits de mer*, but that would be lazy *and* ostentatious, plus they would feel they have to reciprocate and take me out. It would also send the message they're not worth spending four thousand hours to cook for.

That leaves option number three: wait for Donna to arrive, which is what I do. I invite Hugo and Nadine and their son Johann and his girlfriend, both of whom speak English and can translate, for the Saturday following Donna's Thursday arrival. I know she'll be tired, but I also know I need all the help she can give.

Meanwhile, I plan. There is no doubt this will be the full seven-course French meal: hors-d'oeuvres, crudités, entrée, salad, cheese, dessert, coffee, tea—with appropriate booze at every course. The possible choices are immense, and so are the possible faux pas.

Apéritifs and hors-d'oeuvres are easy.

Appetizers and crudités are trickier. Langoustine, which I now love, is a favorite, but I've never actually cooked them. I know you drop them live into boiling water to kill them, then put them in the refrigerator and eat them chilled with homemade mayonnaise. But I'm afraid I'll drop them in the water and they'll scream or scramble out and I'll undercook them and everyone will get sick and die, or I'll overcook them and everyone will get sick and gag. I know I can buy them precooked, but I don't trust the freshness, and everyone says it's a rip-off. So no langoustine for Hugo and Nadine.

Melon. They're juicy and sweet, the color of cantaloupe and the size of a large grapefruit. Each person will get a half. To make it more interesting, I'll fill the hole where the goop and seeds were with port. This is France: you cannot go wrong with alcohol.

The biggest decision is the entrée. It has to be cooked well, presented right, and tasty. It also has to be plentiful, and it cannot be cheap—like mussels or a plate of pasta. Nor can it be too easy or simple to make. What you cook illustrates how you feel about your guests, how much you respect and value them, unless, of course, they are practically family, like Monsieur and Madame P and Jean and Sharon; then you can be a little more informal and experimental, but not a lot: think green beans, raw mushrooms, and balsamic.

Rich and fancy are also out, thank God. Ostentatiousness—say lobster—will make Hugo and Nadine feel bad, like why didn't *they* serve me lobster. The same is true of prepared food from the charcuterie, Picard, or anywhere else—unless you're cooking for family. It says, "I don't have the time to cook for you." It also says, "Money is no object," as prepared food is always expensive, and will once again make Hugo and Nadine feel bad they didn't serve it to me, and next time they will, which guarantees they'll hate me *and* my next visit—*if* there is one.

I settle on chicken, the Greenside family bird. Every Friday night, every woman in my family served her family a chicken. It didn't matter in the least that it was inedible, bland, dry, and spiceless. It's the one meat—besides hamburgers, hot dogs, and steak—I'm comfortable with. In the U.S., chicken is considered a so-so meal, cheap, and low-end. Not in France. In France, chickens—at least the nonindustrial chickens—are prized and expensive but not so expensive as to be ostentatious. It's also relatively easy to cook—just put it in the oven. I'll add green beans because everyone loves them (except Jean) and tiny pota-toes, baked in the dish with the chicken, soaking in the juices.

Salad is salad—lettuce, olive oil, red wine vinegar, salt, and pepper. *C'est tout.*

Cheese is like the color of flowers, Jean told me: any mélange will do. They will not clash or diminish in effect, as long as there is an ample variety in terms of texture (soft, hard, runny), taste (mild, strong, stronger), and smell (honey, lavender, and toilet). Three to five types will do.

Dessert is *obligatoire*. In the U.S., half the people I know won't touch it, but in France no meal is complete without it. Fresh fruit is acceptable: strawberries with crème fraîche, or cut pineapple, but they feel too unspecial for Hugo and Nadine. The local specialties are Gâteau Breton (a shortbread-like chewy cake), Far Breton (a pudding cake combo of clafoutis and flan), and Kouign Amann (crusty, bready like a puff pastry, covered with caramelized sugar), all of them made with eggs, sugar, and gallons and gallons of butter. I decide to get a *tarte aux fruits*, a preordered, bakery fruit tart. This is *not* considered ostentatious. It says, "I planned and called ahead and had this specially made for you." It's also guaranteed to be yummy, beautiful, and tantalizing—three things that always succeed in France.

Add fresh bread, lots of butter, coffee ("caff" and "de-"), tea (herbal, black, and green), and lots of booze—from apéritifs to digestif—and there it is, the meal for Hugo and Nadine.

That's my menu. I check it with Jean and Sharon and Madame P to make sure it's appropriate and no one will be offended or disappointed. It takes me three days to finally decide, half the time it took God to create the world. Given the results, I don't know if that's something to worry about or not.

On Wednesday, three days before the dinner, I go to the pâtisserie to order the tart. "Bonjour," I say, "Je voudrais une tarte pour samedi soir." Everytime I say this it sounds to me like I'm looking for a loose woman.

Thursday, I go to the weekly village market in Loscoat to get fruit, veggies, cheese, and maybe the chicken. "Bonjour," I say to the fruit and veggie lady, "Je voudrais haricots verts et tomates grappe"—green beans and tomatoes on the vine—"pour huit personnes," and hold up eight fingers. Only six people are coming to dinner, but unlike the U.S., where when you ask for portions for four people, they give you enough for six, in France, when you ask for portions for four people, they give you enough for three, maybe two—so I always add a few more. "Pour samedi soir," I tell her. I also buy one large yellow onion for stuffing the chicken and three melons. Then I go looking for the potato guy.

He sells nothing but potatoes. He looks like a potato. He's dressed in brown from shoes to cap and is always a little dusty, like he just emerged from the earth. He has a dozen varieties in different sizes, colors, tastes, shapes, texture, and skin—everything except russets. "Bonjour, Monsieur," I say and point to the tiny, round, almost translucent-skinned light-brown broilers. "Pour huit personnes." He fills a bag, weighs it, and charges me two euros.

The cheese lady is last. "Bonjour," I say. "Je voudrais un mélange du fromage pour le poulet." I know I just asked for a variety of cheeses for a chicken, like I'm feeding cheese to a chicken. Basically, I'm relying on her—on everyone—to realize I'm not as stupid as I sound, I don't always mean what I say, that they need to fill in the blanks and the logic. Anyone else and she'd ask questions: how is the chicken being prepared? What seasonings? What kind of chicken? What veggies, sauces, wine, etc. With me, she just selects. She chooses a local round chèvre dusted with ashes, a Tomme de Savoie, Bleu d'Auvergne, and a Livarot: soft, hard, blue, and stinky. Perfect. It's not until later that I realize she's chosen the same cheese I usually buy to be certain I won't be disappointed.

The big question is the bird. Should I buy it now, on Thursday, at the market, or wait until Saturday and buy it at the local charcuterie? The birds are so fresh they lie on the slab with their innards, heads, and feet intact—for all I know their hearts are still pumping. I decide I don't want a Thursday bird, which may be a Wednesday bird, for Saturday, even though in the U.S., I would have bought it a week ago and frozen it. *These* birds are killed daily. If the insides are still there, it was killed in the last twenty-four hours. I want the freshest bird possible for Hugo and Nadine, so I decide to wait until Saturday.

I return to the house and start cleaning everything for Donna. I finish at five o'clock and drive to the airport in Brest to get her. I know she'll be exhausted from the twenty-one-hour, door-to-door journey, and from the all-nighter she pulled, because her clients always pile on the work before she leaves. She'll be wired when she lands and asleep in three hours. Except for getting up to nibble and go to the bathroom, I won't see her awake until sometime Saturday—and that's only because Hugo and Nadine are coming for dinner. Otherwise, she'd sleep until Sunday or Monday . . . And so it goes.

She gets up just before noon on Saturday, and the first thing she says is, "We have to clean the house for Hugo and Nadine." It doesn't matter that I just cleaned it for her. If *she* doesn't clean it, it's not clean.

We scrub the kitchen I cleaned, the sitting room no one will sit in, and the dining room, even though I plan to eat outside. I draw the line at the first-floor bathroom. "No one *ever* uses the bathroom. No matter how much people eat and drink, no one goes. Trust me."

She doesn't.

It's when she begins bleaching the *second*-floor toilet—a room I haven't visited all summer—that I leave to get the tart, bread, and the bird.

I push open the pâtisserie door and call, "Bonjour."

Madame says, "Bonjour," and disappears. She returns holding a cake box with a picture of a yellowy creamy cake on the lid. I'm the only person in the store, but she lifts the lid so only I can see what's inside—like it's a peep-show dessert and she's embarrassed, even though it's gorgeous. The apricot halves shimmer like perfect egg yolks, the strawberries are the "fraises de Plougastel," sweeter than candy, so red they look fake. "Mmmmm," I moan, knowing she'll understand and appreciate *that*. She closes the lid, ties the box shut with a yellow ribbon, and hands me the bill: ten euros, about thirteen dollars.

I put the tart in the car and drive to Loscoat for the bread and the bird. I could have bought the bread at the pâtisserie— in the U.S. I would have bought everything in the same store— but in France, land of specialization, I go to the pâtisserie for dessert and the boulangerie for bread. I buy three baguettes— half a baguette a person. I place the bread on the back seat of the car and walk to the charcuterie for the bird.

"Bon-jour, Madame," I sing, thrilled to see several birds in the case. "Avez-vous le poulet noir?"

"Non, Monsieur."

"Le poulet rouge?"

"Non, Monsieur."

"Le blanc?"

"Désolé."

I point to the four in the case. They look like *poulet* to me. I peer in and read the label—"poulet fermier, élevé en liberté": free-range chickens from a farm. Exactly what I want.

"Qu'est-ce que-c'est?"

"Des poulets, mais ils sont tous réservés."

"Reserved!" Holy shit. You can't just walk in and buy a chicken. You have to reserve it in advance. A chicken!! It's as bad as the bank, where I have to wait a day to withdraw my own money.

"Combien jour avante c'est necessaire pour réservés?" So I know for next time.

"Un ou deux jours."

I leave shaking my head and go to the other charcuterie in Loscoat, where I rarely go, and it's the same. All the *poulets* are *réservés*, as if this is some fancy resort and it's holiday season and all the rooms are taken. It's three o'clock. Hugo, Nadine, Johann, and his girlfriend are arriving at 7:30, and I don't have the main dish. I'm American and a man—I know they will make many allowances for both of those failings—but not having a main dish is not one of them. They are invited for dinner, and that is what they will expect.

I have three choices, none good. (1) I could go to Leclerc and buy an industrial bird, which I won't do. (2) I could cook beef, pork, lamb, or fish, which I don't want to do. (3) I could drive twenty-five miles to Quimper where the odds are I can find a *poulet fermier* in the large indoor marketplace. In the best-case scenario, I'll be back at 4:00 with a bird. Worst case, all the birds will be *réservés* and I'll have to cook something else. It can't be fish, because that's Nadine's specialty, and I wouldn't do her or the fish justice—which takes me back to beef or pork.

I race to Quimper and go to my favorite secret place to park. It's full. I go to my second favorite secret place. That's full, too. It's a beautiful summer day, and the old town is jammed. Anywhere else, people would be at the beach or a park. Not in France. If there's an opportunity to shop, people shop, and if it's *soldes* time, as it is, there's a mob. I finally find a parking place on the other side of the river and run to the market. There are at least four *boucheries* and *volailleries* at the market, so I'm feeling confident.

I stop at the first *boucherie* I see, almost out of breath from running, and call out. "Monsieur, avez-vous le poulet rouge?" The guy must think I'm addicted.

"Non, Monsieur."

Shit. I'm dead.

"J'ai du poulet noir."

"C'est vrai?" I almost shout. *Noir* is the best.

He looks at me like, Is this a joke. Is he on *Candide Camera?* Why wouldn't I believe him? Why would he lie? He lifts one from behind the counter.

"Pour huit personnes?"

He puts it back, lifts another, and weighs it: 2.7 kilos, 5.9 pounds. It looks to me like a Fiat 500. "Bon," I say. "S'il vous plaît, voudrais vous coupe le tête et les pieds et nottoye?"

"Oui. Bien sûr."

He cuts off the head, leaving lots of neck, then the feet. He opens the bird and removes the insides, placing the liver in a plastic bag, and hands it to me like it's a gift. He wraps the bird in paper, puts it in a plastic sack and tells me to cook it at 180 degrees for an hour to an hour and a half, until brown. That's all, he warns. *"C'est tout!"*

I pay him the equivalent of thirty dollars in euros—and I'm happy to do it. This is why, unlike the U.S., chicken is not considered a low-class, cheapo meal. In France, chicken can be more expensive than beef or pork.

I return home the proud hunter, with a headless, footless, interior-less bird (as if I'd done it all myself), three baguettes, and a tart.

Donna has the glasses, dishes, silverware, and serving platters laid out on the dining-room table. "Let's eat outside," I say.

"I don't know," she says, "It could rain." Being with me has made her less optimistic.

"It hasn't all day, it's been beautiful."

She looks at me and shrugs. "It's *your* party."

"OK. Let's prep and see how the weather looks."

I wash and tear the lettuce and scrub the potatoes. Donna washes and French-slices the green beans. The lettuce and green beans go in the fridge with the chicken, tart, white wine, and water, filling the baby fridge. The freezer is full with six trays of half-the-American-size ice cubes. The cheese is on the fireplace mantle, at room temperature. Two bottles of red are open and breathing on the table.

By six thirty, we're prepped and ready. In that time, the weather has changed from sunny to cloudy to dark to overcast to sunny. To be safe, we set up for dinner inside and apéritifs on the terrace. While we're setting the table, Nadine calls to say Johann and his girlfriend had an emergency and can't make it, which means a five-hour meal without a translator. Now, it's *totally* up to Donna, who's still groggy from her trip. I place two dictionaries on the table. If I were a religious person, I'd pray.

Hugo and Nadine arrive early, which is less than forty minutes late. I lead them outside and leave them on the terrace with Donna. This is our division of labor: she cleans the toilets and takes care of the guests. I shop and cook and serve. Both of us will clean up at the end.

At seven thirty, I put the bird and potatoes in the oven. Fifteen minutes before they're done, I start the green beans. All night, I clear and serve, clear, and serve again, using every glass, dish, knife, fork, and spoon in the house. Everything is going great. Donna is awake and alert enough to speak and translate—including telling jokes and explaining U.S. trade policy, which almost makes sense when you're half-sloshed and groggy.

With each course I serve and every plate I remove, I notice Nadine nudging Hugo and nodding toward me. When I bring out the chicken, she elbows him and points at me. When I bring out the cheese platter, she starts talking about studying English. By dessert, she's toasting American women and making plans to visit us in the U.S. Hugo, who used to be my friend, does not look happy. Every time she nudges him, he squeezes her close, and says, "Cher-ie," basically telling her, *No way!* He'll do *almost* anything for her, but not cook (except barbecue), serve (except alcohol), or clean (except the car). I figure from now on, we'll be eating at their house . . .

Hugo and Nadine leave at one thirty. Donna and I clean up and go to bed at two thirty. As it turns out, only she and I used the bathroom.

The following week, Jean-Pierre and Joëlle are coming for dinner. The last meal we ate at their house was a delicious, ocean-tasting, never-been-frozen, home-cooked *fruits de mer* platter of crab, oysters, clams, langoustine, shrimp, lobster, and ugly, crawly, chewy-like-rubber sea snail thingies called *bulots*. On Monday, Donna and I will start to prepare . . . This is what it means to cook for French people, and why I always worry about failing or committing faux pas.

10 Things I've Learned about Cooking in France— and Another 10 I've Learned about Entertaining

1. Measurements are different: (Fahrenheit-32) x 5/9 = centigrade; .035 ounces = 1 gram; 28 grams = 1 ounce; 34 ounces = 1 liter; 1 liter = 1.056 quarts; 1 quart = 896 grams = .896 kilogram; a centimeter = .393 inches; electricity is 220 volts, not 110, and gas for the stove can and does run out *anytime* if you use the metal, impossible-to-know-how-much-gas-is-still-inside the tank of butane, as I do.

2. Ingredients are different: hardly any hot, sour, or piquant spices; prepared sauces are few and mostly packaged and dehydrated, as French people won't pay for something they can make better and cheaper at home. Veggie and fruit choices are much more limited than in the U.S., as they're seasonal and regional, not frozen: there's no Caesar salad in summer, because there's no Romaine lettuce, and corn on the cob and russet potatoes don't exist.

3. Cuts of meat are different: no T-bone, porterhouse, New York, or chuck, but there is horse, frog, bunny, goat, sheep, and every part, internal and external, of pig—which is probably why filet mignon in France is pork, tender as Kobe beef, and the most popular steak is a *faux filet*.

4. Birds are different: sold complete with heads and feet and internal organs, and sometimes a few feathers as well. Chicken quality is designated by the color of the bird's feet—white, red, or black—which hopefully is their natural color and not the result of something they stepped in.

5. Fish are different: often whole, not filleted, or in parts and pieces that look like brains and intestines and things I've never seen before and don't want to see again, and with a

few exceptions, like—sole, *saumon,* and *maquereau*—are not recognizable by name, so I have to shop with a dictionary to determine if *roussette, morue, aiglefin,* and *grondin rouge* are really the fish I want—or don't.

6. Quick meals: When I'm alone or with American friends, like LeRoy and Peggy, I rely on *French Cooking in Ten Minutes* by Edouard de Pomiane, a former medical doctor and research assistant at the Pasteur Institute in Paris. According to Ed, all I need is a frying pan and thirty minutes and I can cook anything. I have three frying pans—so I'm set. The preface to his book says, "I am writing this book for students, dressmakers, secretaries, artists, lazy people, poets, men of action, dreamers, scientists, and everyone else who has an hour for lunch or dinner but still wants thirty minutes of peace to enjoy a cup of coffee." Bruno and Françoise scorn Ed and his book. Jean and Sharon agree with them, but Ed is my kind of guy.

7. Making crêpes: Madame P has wasted many hours of her time trying to teach me how to make hot-from-the-griddle, crispy-brown-at-the edges, melt-in-your-mouth, chewy, moist crêpes. My batter is either too thick or thin. My crêpes rip or glob—and when I try to flip them over, I scorch my thumb and drop the crêpe, burning it on one side, leaving it gooey and half-cooked on the other, an incredible, inedible blob.

8. A meal without alcohol is breakfast . . . usually . . .

9. My new stove is an engineering marvel—and scares the hell out of me. It's marvelous because it has three gas burners, one electric burner, a rotisserie, and a large, three-shelf, electric convection oven. It scares me because all of the automatic cooking settings are computerized and

the instruction booklet is in French and not even Sharon can figure out how to set the automatic timer. If anyone changes the current settings, it's not my dinner that's going to be cooked, but me.

10. A good meal is a respite from time itself—unless I'm the one cooking it. In which case, I watch my clocks and set my mechanical timer.

On Entertaining . . .

1. What to serve: nothing new or different. French people want to know what they're eating. If they do not like a single ingredient, they may not eat the entire dish. Unfortunately for me, there is no hold-your-nose, gulp, swallow, and smile-to-be-polite routine in France. French people—*friends*—who are normally curious, friendly, and helpful, have publicly told me my green beans stink, and I use the wrong kind of butter.

2. Equality and Fraternity: Whom to invite to dinner? I invite everyone—intellectuals, professionals, artists, artisans, craftsmen, laborers, farmers, the unemployed, unemploy-able, those too young to work and those too old, people working under the table and people working over the table, those who read everything, and those who read nothing, Gaullists and Socialists—I just don't invite them at the same time. In the U.S., I bring friends together. In France, I keep them apart: every relationship is unique, and everyone wants to keep it that way. The more diverse the group, the more uncomfortable everyone is, and the more diminished each person feels. What kind of party is that?

3. Cheek kissing: Whom to kiss, how many times, where, and how? French people don't actually touch when they cheek kiss. It's an air kiss, but I figure unless I make contact, why bother, and depending on whom I'm with, I put lips to cheeks two, three, or four times, the fourth always eliciting a "Quatre?" which tells me the person is either pleasantly surprised, or I've crossed another line. When greeting people, I always kiss women and children at least once on each cheek. If I really like the person I'll kiss three times, and if I *really* like them, four. If I'm a very good friend or feel like a member of the family, I'll kiss the men once on the cheek, head, or neck—otherwise it's a handshake. I do the same when leaving, and if I had a good time, I up the ante a kiss or two, but never, ever to more than four. I don't want people to think I'm excessive, desperate, or worse.

4. Viewing the house: In the U.S., when people visit for the first time, I show them around so they know where everything is and they can help themselves and leave me alone. In France, people don't help themselves to anything. At meals, nobody will move until the host says, "Bon appétit," and even then some people won't move until they are served. Madame P finally let me carry the dishes from the dining room table to her kitchen because it was two in the morning, and she was too tired to say no twenty times as she usually did when I picked up a plate. I saw her faltering at the tenth no, and in her moment of weakness, I carried on. Rule Number One: if you're a guest, sit—there's nothing you can do to help. Rule Number Two: if you're the host, pray someone breaks Rule Number One.

5. Bathroom doors: In the U.S., I always keep the bathroom door open to indicate it's not occupied. In France, the door

is always closed and often lockless, which means there's ample opportunity for being walked in on or walking in on someone else, both of which I've done. I now knock—loudly!

6. Bathroom smells: A box of matches and an open door work fine in the U.S. In France, where the doors are closed, there are more air fresheners with more scents than there are breakfast cereals in the U.S. It's astonishing. I go to the toilet, usually a tiny, windowless room the size of a broom closet, and I come out smelling like I've been to Yosemite.

7. Open windows: When it's warm and sunny, people open their windows letting in fresh air, sunlight, and flies. For some reason I'll never understand, French houses and apartments have no screens. Flies come in and out like guests. French people, renowned for their obsession with cleanliness, eat with flies buzzing around their heads and food. They hang sticky-honey fly strips from their ceiling and light fixtures, and place dishes of powdery yellow fly poison around their rooms, and still, flies zoom and buzz and hop from plate to plate as people eat. There's a tolerance for nature that's beyond me. At my house, windows are shut while eating and open when sleeping, the reverse of most people in the village.

8. At the table: Elbows on the table are OK. Using the wrong glass, dish, and silverware are OK. Even talking with your mouth full—if you have something interesting to say—is OK. The only person I've ever seen chastised at the table is the cook.

9. To stack or not to stack: As a guest, I know I'm not supposed to enter the kitchen or offer to help. What I don't know is if that includes stacking at the table. So far, as far as I can tell, which isn't very far, it seems to be OK. The

problem is I can never discern if the host *intends* the dishes or silverware to stay or go. Sometimes, I stack them and see they're not going anywhere. Then I have to unstack them, remembering the order in which I collected them, hoping Monsieur A's plate did not contaminate Madame B's, or their spoons did not touch or get mixed up, in which case I'll offer to wash everything, which the woman of the house will refuse, thereby either (1) giving her more work to do, or (2) not giving her more work to do and infecting Monsieur A and Madame B. Other times I don't stack them and end up eating dessert with a fish fork. Now, after eating several fishy-tasting fruit tarts, I do what everyone else does. That way I'm not alone, which in France is worse than being wrong.

10. Bring the host a gift: *Any* gift will be appreciated, as it's the thought and gesture—*le bon geste*—that count. I know, because I've brought liquor to a recovering alcoholic, chocolate to a diabetic, and roses to an allergic-asthmatic—and have been invited back to each home again and again and again.

A Hypochondriac's Delight

(And it's even better if you're really sick)

I grew up with a Jewish mother, two Jewish grandmothers, and an aunt who married a Hassid. Every cough I had was possible bronchitis, influenza, or diphtheria; every ache the first signs of polio; drooling, probable cerebral palsy—and, I can tell you, my people have nothing on Bretons, a people as fatalistic as the Jews.

Anything I say about my body, medicine, aches, pains, sprains, bites, and bruises is taken seriously. No pooh-poohing here. Rudyard Kipling and the stiff upper lip are damned. These are a people who respect pain—wherever it is, whatever the source, no matter how minuscule—and they're proud to say it, show it, feel it, even honor it. The only thing shameful is to deny it. My kind of people, for sure.

In France, the body and bodily functions are normal, hence bare breasts on beaches, nudity on TV, open and visible pissoirs, men peeing in public, male and female toilets next to each other and interchangeable, toilets without doors, without seats, without toilets . . . Everyone pees and craps, so what's the big deal? I've been in line at the boulangerie and listened to the most disgusting private ailments being publicly discussed. Once, the man in front of me lifted his shirt to show everyone the scar from his hernia operation. All I could think was, what if he had hemorrhoids? Another time, I listened to a discussion about constipation, including a lively debate about the best remedy. The winner was a concoction of warm water, lemon, honey, and stewed prunes—with or without lambig (Breton whiskey), I'm not sure.

Given this interest in all matters concerning health, I should not have been surprised when one morning, in passing, like the way we talk about the weather in the U.S., I responded to four separate, "Ça vas?" in four different telephone conversations by telling each person I hadn't slept well the previous night and I had a headache. Three of them came to the house within an hour. The fourth was Sharon, who's Canadian-Irish, who said, "Go back to bed." Not the

French. They arrived with something in hand: food (if I'm going to live), flowers (if I'm not), offering sustenance, support, camaraderie, care—and drugs. Even Monsieur P, who rarely leaves his house, hooked up his oxygen tank and drove over with his personal cache of medications, which is ample.

I have a neighbor who will not leave her house without a plastic sack the size of a medicine cabinet filled with prescriptions, as well as over-the-counter medications for fever and shortness of breath; stomach, back, head, muscle, heart, liver, and kidney ailments; pains, cramps, bruises, cuts, and bites. Her sack, plus two cell phones, and she'll go anywhere. Without them, she won't go to Leclerc. For all I know, she's got oxygen tanks and a defibrillator in her car. She's her own personal pharmacy and EMT, and the happier and more secure for it. Best of all, everything except the nonprescription medications are reimbursed by Sécurité Sociale, the amount varying depending on whom I ask—and I ask and observe a lot, because someday, Donna, family, friends, or I may need them.

There's a Doctor in the House

I'm driving home after watching *Midnight in Paris* in Quimper, and I see the kitchen lights on and the front door open at Monsieur and Madame P's house. Usually, their shutters and door are closed after dark, so I park in front of their house and look through the kitchen window. It's summer, hot, maybe eighty degrees Fahrenheit, and Madame is sitting at the table with a scarf around her neck. I knock on the doorframe, call, "Bonsoir," and enter. Monsieur and Henri are sitting in a corner chatting, and a guy with a stethoscope around his neck is writing on a pad. I don't know who he is, but the one thing I'm sure of, he's not a doctor.

"Marc, c'est Docteur M," Madame says, introducing me.

He stops writing—the stethoscope swinging from his neck like a snake—shakes my hand, and says, "Bonsoir." Then he places the stethoscope on Madame's chest and listens to the left side, the right, upper, lower, her back . . . It's almost midnight on a Friday night, and a *doctor* is making a house call: not a registered nurse, a licensed vocational nurse, a home health aide, or a student intern, but a *doctor*! As far as I can see, there is no emergency. There is no imminent birth or death or child or older person in trouble, no blood or protruding bones. Henri is here without his ambulance, and *he* certainly doesn't seem concerned. What's up?

The doctor finishes listening to Madame breathe, says, "Bon," gives her a shot in the arm, some pills, three prescriptions, and after much conversation, many "Bonnes nuits," and shaking everyone's hand, leaves at 12:15 without money being exchanged or leaving a bill. In the U.S., this happens only if you're dead.

"Is this usual?" I ask Henri.

"What?"

I guess it is, but I ask anyway. "A doctor coming to the house at night?"

"Yes, of course. C'est normal."

"Was there an emergency?"

"My mother couldn't sleep."

"Couldn't *sleep*!"

"Yes. She has a cough. It keeps her awake so she called the doctor and he came. C'est normal." He looks at me like, 'How could you not know this, and why would it be otherwise, and isn't it like this in all civilized countries in the world?'

I don't have the heart to tell him. All I know is if I woke my doctor at eleven thirty at night because I couldn't sleep, he'd send over an anesthesiologist to finish the job. "How much was it, the doctor's visit?" I ask.

"Don't know. Maybe thirty U.S. dollars."

"Ah, bon." For some perverse reason, this pleases me.

"The doctor will send my mother the bill, she'll pay it and be reimbursed by Sécurité Sociale."

I don't even bother to ask how much.

Later, I figure this must be the reason French people have a reputation for being hypochondriacs. The rich worry about losing their money. Healthy people worry about losing their health. People worry about losing what they have, not what they don't have, and the French are among the healthiest people on Earth. In the U.S., the people most obsessed about their health are the health-food nuts. The sickies know what they have and are dealing with it, the health-food nuts suspect what they could have, and imagine it's worse.

Two weeks later, I knock on the open front door, call out, "Bonjour," and walk into Madame P's kitchen, which is also the all-purpose family room, complete with TV, radio, and stereo, and see Madame sitting at the table with a blanket over her head and a chunky middle-aged woman grinding tiny brown seeds into powder with a mortar and pestle. Madame lifts the blanket and introduces me: "Marc, c'est Docteur D."

The table is covered with branches, leaves, twigs, herbs, seeds, berries—God knows what else, maybe frogs. If Madame

D is a doctor, she's a witch doctor. She goes to the stove and removes the lid from a huge pot, and I realize the burning rubber smell I thought was brakes or tires is coming from Madame's kitchen and being brewed on the stove. Dr. D ladles a huge spoonful of goop into a cup and places it in front of Madame. Madame inhales the steam, covers her head and the goop-filled cup with the blanket, and moans a long, satisfying, "Ahhhhhhhh."

This too, I learn, is reimbursed by the national health system: homeopathy, thalassotherapy, acupressure, acupuncture—everything, it seems, except counseling and voluntary, non-mandated, therapy, which are apparently too bizarre to be covered. All of it, except thalassotherapy, which requires the ocean, is available in the privacy and comfort of your home when you need it—or when you think you do.

It's almost (but not quite) enough to make me want to try the system myself—and then I do.

At the Pharmacy

I wake scratching between my toes and discover I have athlete's foot. God knows why. I certainly haven't earned it. I show Madame P, and ask her what to do. She tells me to go to the pharmacy, which for some reason has a flashing *green* cross above the door, not red.

I walk into the shop, get in the wedge, and say, "Bonjour" when it's my turn.

"Bonjour," the pretty lady in a white lab coat responds.

"S'il vous plaît," I say and point to my left foot. It's bare because I'm wearing flip flops—because I still haven't found a Mephisto store with the shoes or sandals I want in the right size, color, or model.

"Ah oui," she says, "champignons."

Mushrooms? I look at my foot. What does she see that I don't? What does she *know* that I don't? She's now changed how I look at mushrooms—and eat them—forever. Why couldn't she have diagnosed my ailment as Brussels sprouts? Given what French people think about Belgians, I'm surprised it's not . . . She hands me a tube and charges me five euros—about eight dollars. I don't know if I should put it on my foot or a salad. I stand there clutching the tube like an idiot. Madame, professional that she is, recognizes this symptom. She swings around the counter, pries the box from my hand and destroys it after it fails to easily open at the place marked clearly in red, "ouvrir ici." She punctures the mouth of the tube with the point of her pen, squeezes a generous amount on my foot and rubs it in with her naked fingers. It feels so good I want to return three times a day.

"Merci, merci," I say. Except for the non-kiss cheek kisses, it's the first time a woman has touched me since I left Donna in California. "À bientôt," I say, and to put her at ease add, "Au revoir."

A month later, I return with the *aoûtats*. At first, I thought it was a horrible bug bite. Then I found out it's worse: it's horrible *and* disgusting, and painful as hell. I show Madame P a welt the size of a jumbo shrimp under my armpit. "Qu'est-ce que c'est?"

"Les aoûtats."

This is the first I've heard of it. *Mouches* (flies), *moustiques* (mosquitos), *abeilles* (bees), *chauves-souris* (bats), *puces* (fleas) sure, but the *aoûtats*? "Quece que c'est?" What is it? And more important, "Où est ce la?" *Where* is it? And most important, what does it look like: "C'est possible, je regarde?" This is one creature I need to avoid.

Madame says, "C'est invisible. C'est un microbe."

Holy shit! "Une microbe!"

"Oui."

"Il habite à où?" Where does it live?

She points at me.

"No, no, *où* habiton les aoûtats?"

She takes me outside and points, "Le jardin (garden), la pelouse (grass), la terre (land), les fleurs (flowers), et toi (me)!" Then she explains in great detail what the *aoûtat* is and what it does. I don't understand much until she says that magic one-in-every-three words that's the same in English: "larve," larva, the singular of larvae. Holy, holy shit! Living baby *aoûtats* are growing inside me and eating me up—and *that's* not even the worst of it. The welt I showed her is the visible one, the polite one. The others are in the corners and creases of my warmest, moistest, most private parts, which they apparently like as much as I do. No wonder I've been scratching my crotch for a week. And a week, believe me, is enough, so I'm back in a wedge at the pharmacy.

"Bonjour," the same lady sings when it's my turn. "Comment sont les champignons?"

"Bien. Bon, au revoir."

"Bon," she says, wondering, I'm sure, what today will bring.

"S'il vous plaît," I say, and scratch my hip. *"Les aoûtats."*

It's August—*août*—when the *aoûtats* appear. It's also hot, which the *aoûtats* like, but she's not a clerk, she's a professional, and she's not going to give me any medicine or treatment without seeing what's wrong and making a diagnosis. She walks around the counter, and before I can say "Jean Paul

Belmondo," she's pulling the elastic on my shorts and looking down my pants. Lucky for me—and her—I'm wearing underwear, because until today it itched so much around the elastic I took them off. Three female customers are in the shop. None of them look at me, and none seems to think this is strange. The pretty lady pharmacist touches one of the welts on my hip, and says, "Ah oui, les aoûtats." Diagnosis over, she hands me a box with a tube of cream in it and charges me five euros. It looks like the same box she gave me for the *champignons*. I stand there holding the box, waiting and hopeful, expectant. She smiles and walks away.

Pharmacies are the first line of medical defense in France. They're where you go to get prescriptions filled and to fix anything wrong with your body, head, skin, hair, nails, and mouth, and most important, your digestion—things going down, things coming up, things coming out, and not. So when I'm dog-sitting for Bob and Loni at their house on the Île aux Moines and get the stomach flu, I know exactly what to do. I wait as long as I can—about two days—and go to the pharmacy.

I open the door and see two wedges of people. I join the shortest wedge and wait . . . and wait . . . and wait. There's always a wait for the pharmacist, who by another immutable French law—is there a national test, a pageant, a Catherine Deneuve look-alike contest requirement?—always seems to be a pretty woman of indeterminate age with shiny teeth and glowing hair, perfectly coiffed, made-up, and manicured, as if she personally is responsible for modeling every health and beauty product in the store. This time is no exception, as one of the two women is much younger and prettier than average, and average is about 9.5 out of 10. Normally, I'm hoping for the prettiest one, but not today. Whoever it is, though, please God, make it fast.

An old woman steps forward from the wedge. She's so small I didn't see her. She opens her bag and fumbles through it—it's half her size—separates a piece of paper that looks like a letter from other pieces of paper that look like letters, and hands it to the pretty pharmacist. Oh shit! I know what this means: an hour's wait—and I don't have it in me. Or, I do, but I won't, if I wait.

I know this because I've been to the pharmacy for Monsieur and Madame P and given a letter like that to the pharmacist. The last time I did it, it took an hour to fill the order, because the letter contained enough prescriptions to fill two large shopping bags with medications and supplies, and because shopping at the pharmacy is like every other shopping experience in France: slow.

It doesn't matter that everyone in the wedge is in a hurry, needs something, and usually badly—every transaction takes forever. Each person is asked question after question about his or her needs, history, symptoms, and diet, whether they're buying mouthwash or diuretics. It's like a job interview for your body or a lifetime longevity study—all asked and answered in public, so within fifteen minutes of leaving the pharmacy everyone knows your breath smells, your hair's dry, and you're incontinent. Finally, when you've answered everything to her satisfaction—and only then—the pharmacist will leave the counter, go behind a curtain, and *unlike* any other shopping experience I've had, *always* returns with what I need. These women are one hundred percent thorough and professional, courteous and bright—and if they get to me before I shit on myself or faint, both of which I now feel coming, they'll fix me.

I distract myself by praying—please God, give me the one who looks old enough to have had her own intestinal experiences—and by practicing what I'm going to say if I get to speak to someone in time. Wisely, I looked up the word *and* its pronunciation before leaving the house. *Diarrhée*, pronounced "djare . . . Djareeee, D-jareee . . ." Shit, I'm in trouble.

"Monsieur."

It's the younger, prettier one. "Avez vous le produit pour djaree," I whisper.

"Quoi."

My bowel slips. I can feel it. "Djaree, djareeeee . . . "

Her concern is palpable—she's as serious as Mother Teresa. She wants desperately to help, "Quoi, quoi, Monsieur . . . "

I'm a grown man, an adult, well educated, relatively successful and accomplished, and all I can think is please don't make me have to act this out. I rub my stomach and think of the movie, *La Grande Bouffe*.

"Pour digestion," she says.

"No."

"Non?"

I'm about to say, "l'autre fin," the other end, knowing in my gut it's not right, when she yells, "DIARRHÉE!" like she just won Jeopardy or bingo.

I'm so thankful and relieved I don't even care that the entire village now knows I have the runs.

"Beaucoup?"

Is she kidding me?

"Combien de fois?" How many times?

I blink. I shrug. *What* is she asking?

"Par jour."

"Oh, oh, huit, neuf, dix . . . "

"OOOOO la la."

This is the first time I've actually heard this expression in France. I've been wondering when it's used. Now, I know. The girl hurries behind the curtain. People behind me murmur. I want to tell everyone this never happens when I eat *American* food. The woman behind me taps me on the back and offers me a look of empathy, sympathy, pain, and condolence, as if I'm stage-four terminal, and says, "Désolée."

"Moi aussi," I say. Me too.

The girl returns holding a box half the size of a pack of Gauloises. She carefully explains that I should take two pills now, and she gives me a glass of water to make sure I at least get the first part right and don't ruin her floor or her business. After that, it's up to me. She tells me to drink plenty of liquids and eat "des carrottes," and she explains half a dozen times and writes on the box: "2 tout de suite. MAXIMUM: 6 *par jour.*"

"Or what?" I want to ask, but don't have the time or sphincter power to wait for the answer.

I hurry home, barely get to the toilet, and let loose. For a second, while sitting there, because that's all it takes, I think: she thinks I'm constipated and *want* diarrhea and, she's given me a pill to give it to me. I look at the box. It says "Diarrhetique." It doesn't say stop or start. I remove the pills—they're smaller than Tylenol. I think I should take two more. Then I remind myself, she may look eighteen and like a supermodel actress, but she's a professional pharmacist who knows what she's doing . . . I hope.

She does. It's the last crap I take for five days. I can't even imagine what would have happened—and what the conversation at the pharmacy would have been—had I taken two more. Luckily, none of us will ever know.

At the Doctor's Office

My first trip to a doctor's office occurs with my friend Bonnie, who's visiting me from California. She arrived with a cold and a cough, and is getting worse, hacking and sneezing. After a few days, I do what I always do. I telephone Madame P, thinking pharmacy, drugs, some kind of prescription Theraflu. I call in the morning. In the afternoon, Bonnie is on her way to the doctor's office. Madame's not taking any chances. No American is getting sick on her watch—and since I called her, it is her watch.

The doctor, a Madame K, is waiting for us when we arrive. Clearly, Madame P is taking no chances with my French either, and has already explained the situation. The doctor leads Bonnie into a room the size of a small bathroom, sits her in an armchair facing a poster of cows grazing in a pastoral field, and proceeds to give her a full examination: lungs, ears, nose, and throat, and concludes, "C'est un virus."

It's the same diagnosis I would have made—it's the best disease and diagnosis there is—since it's invisible. It's like stress or anxiety or USD, "unspecific sexual disease." All medical beauts, as far as I'm concerned. Say the word, and *ca-ching! ca-ching!* is the sound of the music you'll hear.

I'm expecting Docteur K to take out her pad and write several prescriptions, as one never seems to be enough in France, and she does. Then she takes out a syringe.

Bonnie looks at me, I look at Docteur K, she looks at both of us like, 'Hey, I'm a doctor. If you want to get better, this is what you do.' She loads up the syringe, bends Bonnie over the chair and drops her shorts—I look away, not out of propriety, but because I hate shots—and that's it. The whole thing is a minor miracle, almost unheard of for anything less than a life-threatening illness in the U.S.: call, appointment, exam, and treatment all in less than four hours, two of which are lunch, with a doctor who isn't your own or a member of your family.

Even more amazing, when Bonnie asks for the bill, the woman refuses to give it. Ah, I think, the notorious French black books, "au noir": she wants to be paid under the table. I start to fish through my wallet, but she waves me away. There is no black book or "noir" or table. It's simply: I'm a doctor. This is what I do.

I don't know if it's charity, good will, or more of Madame P's magic—or if Docteur K is rich, doesn't want to bother with U.S. and French insurance, not to mention Bonnie's English and my French—but whatever it is, not paying for services can't be usual. And it's not: when my brother gets sick and goes to a doctor, he pays.

Jeff and Corinne are celebrating his sixtieth birthday with Donna and me—and celebrate we do, with lots of new, tasty and strange foods for him to eat: langoustine in homemade mayonnaise, cheeses he's never heard of, everything cooked in butter and crème fraîche, whipped cream on ice cream with caramel, and more alcohol than he's drunk in his entire life.

On the third day, he wakes up dizzy, heart pounding, white-faced, feeling numb on his left side. Our father died of a massive heart attack in his sixties, so this is serious.

I call Henri, Madame P's youngest son, who arrives in ten minutes with his ambulance and his assistant, Louis. Henri asks Jeff where it hurts, how he feels, what he ate and drank. "Did you drink rosé and mix it with white and red?"

Jeff groans, "Yes."

Henri and Louis look at each other and nod. "Can you stand?"

Jeff groans, "No."

Henri and Louis help him down two flights of stairs and into the ambulance. They lay him gently on a gurney and drive to Loscoat, where Henri has already called Docteur B, an English speaker who's agreed to leave his office and examine Jeff in the ambulance. Donna, Corinne, and I follow in the car.

Henri parks on the main street in Loscoat. While we're waiting, people stop to shake Henri's hand as if he's running for office. No one asks about the ambulance, who's inside, or what's happening. A tall, thin young man dressed like a car salesman crosses the street and shakes Henri's hand, Louis's, mine, Donna's, and Corinne's. He opens the ambulance door and climbs in. That's how I know he's the doctor. It's perplexing: we're standing next to an ambulance with my brother inside with what could be a heart attack, and only Corinne, Donna, and I seem concerned. No one else, including the doctor, seems worried.

Thirty minutes later, he steps out of the ambulance and writes a prescription. He hands it to Corinne and tells her Jeff has a hangover, and the prescription is for cramps, but the best thing he can do is go home and drink a shot of Ricard, a 45-percent-proof anise-flavored liqueur—the old hair of the dog—go to bed, and wake up refreshed. Jeff does, and he does.

The doctor charges twenty-three dollars for his services. The prescription costs twenty-seven. Henri doesn't charge for the ambulance because we are friends, but if he had, the entire bill would have been $150—for an American! A French person would have been reimbursed for about 75 percent, leaving a bill of about thirty-eight dollars. If the person had complimentary insurance, as French people are now required to do—at a cost of between $600 and $1,000 a year, $50 to $83 dollars a month (depending on the size of the family), the reimbursement would have been 95 to 100 percent, and their *maximum* out-of-pocket cost would have been $7.50—less than the price of a discounted movie ticket in the U.S . . . It makes me want to cry.

So does having to replace my glasses.

The Ophthalmologist

One morning, I bend over to tie a loose, non-Mephisto shoelace, and my glasses fall out of my shirt pocket onto the hundred-plus-year-old tile floor in the hallway, and crack. These are my TV, movie, driving, and seeing-anything-beyond-my-nose glasses. I've worn glasses for more than thirty years, and I've never lost a pair or broken a lens, so it never occurs to me I could or would, which is why I don't have my prescription with me, or a second pair, and why I need to see a doctor to get them replaced. I do what I do best: I call Madame P.

I call her on a Thursday afternoon. Friday morning she drives me to a village twenty miles away, where she's made an appointment with an ophthalmologist, a Doctor C, a tall, thin, pleasant bald man, who speaks no English. He shakes my hand and leads me to his office, where he gives me a complete eye exam—in French. The first part is easy: look at the chart and go thumbs up, thumbs down to indicate seeing better or worse as he changes a dozen or more lenses to determine my sight. Everything moves smoothly until he indicates he wants me to verify what I'm seeing and read the eye chart out loud. I look through the lenses and see the letters clearly. E, U, R, I, A. *That's* easy. The hard part is how to say them. E is pronounced *eh*, I know, so I say, "eh." He looks at me like I'm in pain. "E-*uh*," I repeat, "*e*-uh." *Euw* for U fares no better, and my *wah* (W) for *rrr* (R) is utterly hopeless. He gives up with my *eee* for I and goes back to thumbs up, thumbs down, each of us hoping for the best: me, that I get a pair of glasses that allow me to see well enough to not hit anything when I drive; he, that I don't come back. I spend forty-five minutes with him, for which he bills me the equivalent of twenty-five dollars. I happily pay him on the spot.

It's a little after eleven o'clock when we leave his office with Madame P holding the prescription, probably afraid I'll lose it, and we'll have to start over.

Her goal is to get to the eyeglass store before noon so I can get my glasses, and she can return to the life she had before I called. We race to the optical shop the doctor recommended. It's in Douarnenez, about twenty miles away on small country roads. Madame gets us there in less than half an hour, a time I've never come close to duplicating. We enter the shop, and I start looking through hundreds of designer frames. French people wear glasses like jewelry, as an accoutrement, embellishment, and couture—my choices are wide and varied, from staid, prosaic banker's wire rims to outrageously spectacular look-like-a-raccoon-Elton-John-horn-rims: Dior, Klein, Boss,

Porsche, Vuarnet, Lacoste. I find an emerald green Vuarnet frame that I want badly, but Madame says I look like a frog, "une grenouille," a word I avoid on menus, and convinces me I should get the Calvin Klein tortoiseshell. Since she sees me more than I do, I follow her advice. Besides, she's French and much better at this than I am—*and* my ride home.

Madame hands the tortoiseshell frames and the doctor's prescription to a saleslady, a woman in her midfifties wearing stiletto heels and a push-up bra that puts the laws of Newtonian physics in doubt. She points to a chair behind a table and indicates I should sit there and wait. The good news is it's almost noon, so I know I won't have to wait too long. I think she's going to put the frames on me, quickly adjust them, and get us out of the store as they do in the U.S, but in the U.S., glasses are glasses; in France, they're *la pièce de résistance*.

The saleslady returns with a binocular headset that looks like it's right out of *Star Trek*, the kind of apparatus a not-so-friendly alien would wear or you'd use for protection in a nuclear reactor meltdown. She places it on my head and starts measuring my eyes: length and width, the distance between them, pupil size, forehead, nose, ear to ear, and, for all I know, my brains—like this is some sort of eye-size–intelligence measurement left over from the good old days of endomorphology and phrenology. She writes each measurement on a piece of paper and makes all kinds of calculations and quantifications, like a female Dr. Frankenstein.

While she's working away, I'm watching the clock. If it hits noon before she finishes, we're here for two more hours. She finishes at three minutes to twelve and hands me the paperwork: the equivalent of three hundred dollars for new Calvin Klein tortoiseshell frames and photo-gray glass that I seriously suspect will turn blue, green, or yellow when the sun hits them, not the gray I want.

I pay with my Visa card, knowing if the prescription is wrong or the glass is not photo-gray or the frames don't fit, I can challenge the expense and not have to pay. As she rings me up, I ask, "À quel jour c'est fini?" What day will they be ready?

"Demain. Après-midi."

One day! *Saturday* afternoon. Right! In the U.S., I have to wait seven to fourteen days.

The next day, Madame P picks me up at two o'clock, not trusting me to walk to her house without my glasses—maybe even with them—probably worried I'll fall into the river and she'll have to dive in to save me, and then do my laundry as well. It's easier to pick me up.

She takes the scenic route via Locronan, and we still arrive in record time. She parks in the blue disabled zone, probably feeling justified because of me, and indicates I should get the glasses while she waits in the car. Her confidence amazes me. First, that I'll be able to say what I want, and second that the glasses will be ready.

I walk into the shop. The woman who measured me yesterday, wearing her stilettos and gravity-defying bra, goes behind the counter and hands me a beautiful leather Calvin Klein case. She hands it to me in a way that tells me not to open the case and try the glasses on, that she's a professional, and whatever she did yesterday—the measurements, calculations, formulations—were sufficient, and the glasses will perfectly fit. I'm not so sure. My entire shopping history tells me to put them on, to be sure they fit and I can see across the street, because it's easier to do now, while I'm here, than to ask Madame P to drive me back. What to do?

Trying them on would be to doubt the woman's work, deny her expertise, maybe constitute a public denigration. She's waiting, smiling—and definitely wants me out of there—happy, satisfied, and gone. I put the case in my shirt pocket and leave.

Back in the car, Madame indicates I should put them on, probably because *she* doesn't want to have to drive back if they don't fit. I open the case expecting the worst. They're the right frames. I put them on—they sit well—and I can see, better than with my old glasses, which were five years old. I look in the visor mirror. I look better—the frames are classy—and I see better, *and* Madame can get back to her life. Winners all around. The photo-gray is even gray.

When I tell my French friends about the whole experience, half of them are amazed I saw a doctor so quickly and got specially tinted glasses in one day. The other half shrug and say, "C'est normal." But everyone asks who the ophthalmologist is, and when I give them his name, they all say, "Ah oui. C'est le meilleur." He's the best.

No one and nothing escapes evaluation in France. *Everyone* is a critic, about *everything*—and once again I'm thankful I have no idea what people are saying about me.

At the Hospital

When I return from dog-sitting on the Île aux Moines, Madame tells me Monsieur is in the hospital in Brest, and we're going to visit him.

I'm carrying a shopping bag full of Madame-cooked goodies. She's carrying fruit, nuts, and nibbles in a purse that must weigh at least ten kilos. Side by side, we march into the lobby. The only person there is an old guy in pj's, sitting hunched over on a couch. He has metal crutches on one side of him, an oxygen tank on the other, and a long plastic tube running from the tank to his nose. Monsieur is in the hospital for respiration—breathing problems—so Madame asks the fellow if he knows her husband, Monsieur P.

"Non," the man answers.

"Quelle est la direction du service respiratoire?"

The man points and directs us down the hall, telling us to go to the third floor. Madame leads the way.

We take the elevator to the third floor and start walking down a long, empty hallway. My usual hospital-visiting routine is to peer into every room I pass to see what horrible things can happen to people and hope none of them happens to me. Here, all the doors are closed. It's not like any hospital I've ever been in. There are no wheelchairs, gurneys, or stacks of food trays lining the hall. Even the smells are regular, like those in a Holiday Inn or clothing store—not decaying flesh, bodily waste, or antiseptics. If I hadn't seen the sign—"Hôpital"—I'd swear I was in a government office building after closing, when everything, including the air conditioning, has been shut off because it's sweltering.

I'm sweating through my shirt. Madame is wiping her face. I figure Sunday is not a good day to be ill at "the end of the world," Finistère. I later learn Mondays, Tuesdays, Wednesdays, Thursdays, Fridays, and Saturdays aren't any better—as the air conditioning isn't "off," it's nonexistent in Brittany and most of France. I don't know if this is the result of cost-benefit analysis or another example of planned inconvenience. All I know is it's like a sauna: think 72nd Street subway station in ninety-degree heat and eighty percent humidity, and you're close.

Madame finally stops and knocks on a door. A voice from inside calls, "Entrez," and we do.

Monsieur's wearing his plaid slippers and a bathrobe and has a tube from an oxygen tank clamped under his nose—and he looks great, like he's on holiday, and the oxygen tank is for scuba diving. He's tan, smiling, and happy to see us. Madame kisses him on the cheek and drops her purse on his bed. I kiss him on both cheeks, and say, "Bonjour."

She starts unpacking: peanuts and cashews, chips, apricots, peaches, plums, fresh bread, *galettes*, homemade jam, cake, and still-warm crêpes, as if the hospital is starving him. It doesn't matter that he's just eaten lunch, a bar of chocolate is on his bed table, cherries on the windowsill, and probably more of everything tucked away in his dresser—she adds to the stash. If she didn't, she'd feel remiss. In the U.S., bringing patients food is verboten, the assumption being "outside" food will make the person worse, even though the "inside" food is terrible. In France, it's the reverse. If you *don't* bring food, *you're* verboten, and however good the hospital food is—and it is—food from home is better, even if it comes from Leclerc. In France, it's the gesture that counts. In the U.S., it's the product—think orchids, a hardcover book, or a double CD.

As we're chatting away, the door opens. A crutch enters, a slippered foot, another crutch . . . It's the guy we spoke with in the lobby, the guy who didn't know Monsieur and directed us to the third floor. He's Monsieur P's—Joe's—roommate, making his way to the other bed. He didn't know Joe's last name because family names are private, and nobody needs to know—whereas peeing in public, showing your body parts, and sharing bodily functions with strangers are not.

Madame offers him a plum. He says he'd rather have a glass of wine, and we're off. While we're talking, there's a knock on the door. Everyone, including me, calls, "Entrez."

A svelte, mid-to-late-forties nurse, wearing a crisp, blindingly white uniform—how does she do it in this heat?—walks into the room, says "Bonjour," and asks Monsieur P and Monsieur K if she can take their temperature and blood pressure. *Mine* would go up if she touched me. She finishes her work and thanks them, then adds her numbers to the charts and leaves them hanging from the beds for anyone to see. Madame picks up Joe's, reads it, asks him a series of questions, and admonishes him about his diet, exercise, and smoking, which he continues to do even with the oxygen tank, though not in the hospital. Somehow she restrains herself from reading Monsieur K's chart, though I know she wants to.

After a while, Madame suggests she, Joe, and I go to the coffee shop for *goûter*, afternoon tea time. We have forty pounds of food in the room, not including whatever Monsieur K has hidden, yet we're going down two floors to eat—and so is everyone else. Anyone who can walk, wheel, crawl, or breathe—at least forty people in various stages of repair and disrepair—is in the coffee shop. It looks like a combination of Lourdes and the Oakland emergency room. People are in casts, bandages, neck braces, attached to IVs. Wheelchairs and crutches are everywhere, and one person is strapped to a gurney, chewing and trying to swallow a brioche while lying on his or her back.

We sit at the last unoccupied table. Monsieur parallel parks his oxygen tank beside him. Behind me, someone coughs. I look around. An entire family wearing surgical masks and protective paper gloves and booties—husband, wife, daughter, and two kids—sits with an older woman in a wheelchair who is *not* wearing a mask, gloves, or booties, and who never stops coughing and spitting phlegm, bile, or her insides.

I hold my breath and breathe through my nose. The last thing I want is to eat in this place. It looks like an incubator for hell. Coffee, if the water's been boiled. But no food.

Madame says, "Que voulez-vous manger?" What do you want to eat?

It's taken me years and zillions of calories to learn the one sure answer to getting out of eating is, "Je suis malade," and rub my stomach. Unfortunately, I didn't know it then, so I say, "Rien." Nothing. "*Rien.*"

Madame returns with three coffees and three brioches. She and Joe talk and eat their brioches. I save mine for the proverbial "later." When they are finished talking and eating, we walk Joe and his oxygen tank back to his room and say goodbye to him and Monsieur K.

Monsieur K has been in the hospital four days, Joe six, and there's no rush to get either out. There's no "slam-bam, thank you, ma'am," that will be $750,000. Of course, there is no air conditioning either.

The following year, when I arrive, Monsieur tells me Madame is in the hospital in Quimper. She had surgery six days ago— six days!—and is being discharged in two days. My God, what can it be?

She's in the same hospital where I met Jacques, the fellow whose car I hit when I was driving Peggy to the airport, so finding it is easy. Finding the room is not. None of the signage is clear, at least to me.

After several false starts, I locate the correct wing and head down the corridor looking for the room number Monsieur gave me. It's like when I visited him in Brest—more like a hotel at three in the morning than a hospital. No one is in the halls, not even a custodian.

I see the room number and stop in front of Madame's door, take a deep breath to prepare myself for the worst, and knock.

"Oui. Entrez," comes a cheery voice from within.

Oh my God, it's worse than I thought. In my U.S. hospital-going experiences, the more cheery a patient's voice, the sicker he or she is—unless, of course, they're cured and healed and about to go home. She's been here six days and is staying another two, how good can it be? I open the door expecting doom.

The room is blindingly bright, light, and airy, a double room with Madame the only resident. On her lap is a tray with real dishes (ceramic), silverware (stainless), and a glass-glass, nothing plastic—not even the food: a chicken breast, green beans, carrots, soup, salad, cheese, bread, and crème brûlée. It all looks good, but this is France—everything looks good. It's what's underneath you have to worry about, like my design-perfect thermos that won't keep liquids hot *or* cold.

"C'est bon?" I ask, pointing at the food.

"Oui, bien sûr."

"Bon," I say, surprised, hurt, and disappointed. She has more enthusiasm for this hospital food than she has for mine. Ever since tasting my mustard-balsamic salad dressing, she eats my food with the doubt and foreboding of Stalin's food taster.

"Quand vous êtes retour aux chez vous?" When are you coming home, I ask?

"Deux semaines."

"Deux semaines!" Holy shit. Two *more* weeks! This is

serious, critical, maybe terminal. My God. "Monsieur dit moi vous êtes parti en deux *jours*." Monsieur said two *days*.

"Oui, oui, pour la récupération."

"Recuperation?"

"Oui."

My vocabulary is expanding all the time. It seems the French have this silly notion that after surgery, a patient needs to recuperate. Never mind that they hold you in the hospital five times longer than in the U.S. When they discharge you, you don't go home, you go to another place to be cared for. In the U.S., you're out of there—fast. It doesn't matter that you live alone in a four-story walk-up, there's no food in your house, your neighbors and friends are on vacation, your nearest relative lives five hundred miles away, and you've just had a hip replacement or hernia repaired. The doctor says he's done, and you're gone. You're fixed—the rest is up to you. The only thing worse is if they *do* send you someplace to recuperate—a skilled-nursing facility or rehab center—places run like a factory, a *poorly* run factory, with understaffed, low-paid workers who are angry and tired and not happy to see you, care for you, or hear from you—treating you like the enemy you've become; places where the food is crap and it smells like a toilet or septic tank's overflowed, where you're every bit as likely to get worse as better. Unless you're Bill Gates or Warren Buffett, these are your choices: take care of yourself or go to hell.

Not in France. Madame P is discharged from the hospital in two days and sent to an *auberge*-y building facing the sea in Bénodet—a beautiful resort town, where English and French people pay beaucoup euros to bathe and relax. After another hospital stay, they send her to Roscoff, a beautiful resort town on the "English" Channel.

The French have this idea that a person needs calm, beauty, and relaxation—mental and physical—after surgery, and nothing provides it better than the sea. Madame has her own room and a choice of meals, even a menu. She has physical therapy every day. She's in Bénodet and later Roscoff for ten days, and comes home looking healthy, relaxed, and tan—and it's all part of French universal health care, those socialist fools!

But what about foreigners? Americans? Me! What happens to us? That's what I want to know.

I soon find out.

Jerry and Sheryl are visiting from California. Jerry is a high school principal, retired and on disability after five heart attacks. Sheryl is a gerontologist, also retired and on disability, *and* the recipient of a recent Stanford University Hospital double-lung and kidney transplant. Both use and carry more medication than the average pharmacy stocks. Any change in their health is serious and life-threatening—and doesn't slow them down or deter them a bit. When Sheryl needed dialysis and wanted to visit New Orleans for Mardi Gras, she booked a hotel next to a dialysis center. After Jerry had a stroke, was wobbly and using a cane, he went to the Galapagos Islands, fell, broke his arm, came home, and booked himself an African safari. Now they're visiting Donna and me for a week.

Sheryl comes downstairs from the attic bedroom and says, "Jerry is sick, his stomach hurts, he hasn't slept all night. I think he needs to see a doctor."

It's 10:00 a.m. on a Sunday. There's a doctor on duty every weekend, as there is an open pharmacy and at least one boulangerie—so the French are never without a doctor, medicine, or fresh bread. The doctor's name and phone number are printed in the weekend edition of the local newspaper, as is the pharmacy. The problem is, I don't have the local newspaper, and even if I did, I wouldn't know where to look for the name and number. Anyone else, I'd give him a Tums and encourage him to wait until they returned to the U.S.—or at least till Monday. But I can't do that with Jerry, so I do the only thing I can: I call Madame P. Monsieur answers the phone and I explain, "Mon ami est malade. C'est necessaire le docteur."

"OK. D'accord." That's all he says, but it's enough to assure me the world is right.

Thirty minutes later, there's a knock on the door. A short, slightly balding man who looks like a doctor and says he's a doctor—"Docteur L"— shakes my hand and says, "Bonjour." I can tell he's miffed. I'm wearing my I-have-nothing-to-do-but-lounge-around-the-house-on-a-Sunday-morning-pants, holding a steaming cup of coffee and smiling, which is clearly what *he* thinks he ought to be doing, at *his* home, not catering to me.

"Pas moi," I say. Not me. "Mon ami," and I lead him up the stairs. "Parlez vous anglais?" I ask, hopefully.

"Non."

Jerry and Sheryl speak no French. It becomes Donna's and my job to translate. I figure Jerry's lucky if he gets out of this without a hysterectomy. Donna tells the doctor about Jerry's heart. "Le coeur est très malade. Il a beaucoup de médicaments—il a eu cinq crises cardiaque." The doctor makes that deep sucking sound that tells me he understands, and that it's serious. He asks lots of questions, which to the best of our collective abilities Sheryl, Donna, and I try to answer. It's harder than the GRE. I have no idea how well we've done, what he understands, or for that matter, what we even said. He gives up on us and starts on Jerry. He probes, pushes, and squeezes. Jerry squawks. He repeats everything and Jerry squawks again, louder, clearly in pain. The doctor listens to Jerry's heart and lungs, writes things down, turns Jerry over, and does it again from the back, all the while making those sucking sounds and saying "bon" and "oui" to someone other than us.

He spends twenty-five minutes tapping, pushing, probing, squeezing, pinching, listening to Jerry front and back, periodically saying "bon" or "oui" to himself. Jerry accompanies him with "oh" and "ow" and an occasional howl. Finally, the doctor looks at me and begins a long, detailed diagnosis. Then he gives up and talks to Donna. "Appendicite, peut-être," and "hôpital," are the two things I understand. He takes out his cell phone and makes the call.

Madame P's youngest son, Henri, is the *patron* of the largest ambulance and taxi service in Loscoat. The call will go to him.

Sure enough, ten minutes later, Henri and Louis arrive in a shiny new ambulance. Henri hops out of the driver's side and Louis out the other, and we all shake hands: Henri and me, Henri and the doctor, Louis and me, Louis and the doctor. Sheryl comes down the stairs, and Henri shakes her hand, then Louis shakes her hand, then both of them shake Donna's. When there's no one left who hasn't been shaken, we go upstairs to see Jerry, who looks like he's feeling neglected. Henri shakes his hand. Louis shakes his hand, and the doctor begins his long diagnosis again. Henri translates the French to English for Jerry and Sheryl and Donna and me and translates the English to French for the doctor. The conclusion is the same in both languages: "Appendicite, peut-être," and "hôpital." The doctor writes something on a pad and hands the paper to Henri. He shakes Henri's hand, Louis's hand, Jerry's, Sheryl's, Donna's, and mine.

I walk him down the stairs to his car, a not very fancy Renault. I shake *his* hand and thank him profusely, "Merci, merci, merci," and wish him a "bon dimanche." It's the last any of us see or hear from him. In France, apparently, this is just part of a doctor's job. *C'est normal.*

I go back in the house and watch as Henri and Louis help Jerry down the stairs. Jerry's six foot two and weighs over two hundred pounds—moving him isn't easy. If he falls, stopping him will be even harder. They get him to the ground floor and sit him on a gurney, lay him down, strap him in, wheel him out, and lift him into the ambulance. Sheryl jumps in and rides with him. Donna and I follow in the car.

Henri gets on the N165 heading south, to Quimper, the same hospital where I met Jacques and visited Madame P. I'm starting to feel like a regular. I've now been to this hospital more than I've been to Kaiser in Oakland, where I'm actually a member.

We arrive at the emergency room at eleven fifteen. The intake person, a young blonde nurse, greets us with clipboard in hand, and I wonder how we're ever going to get through, given the required documentation we'll need and in all likelihood, don't have.

The nurse asks Jerry, "Votre nom?" and "Votre age?" That's it. Two questions, and he's in. There's no signing away of his house, retirement, wife, or kids; no questions about insurance, money, bonds, deeds, stock, mortgages, or credit cards. It's like: 'you're sick, you need help, you're in the right place. Don't worry.'

A thin, buzz-cut, sportif-looking doctor arrives and asks about Jerry's medical history. Henri, who has stayed with us, translates for Sheryl. Sheryl tells Henri, and Henri tells the doctor, "He's had five heart attacks and a stroke." The doctor asks what medications Jerry is taking. Sheryl understands the question and tells him. When she stops, the doctor says something to Henri, who explains, "Jerry is taking a blood thinner. Coumadin. It is not possible to operate or do anything invasive until his blood stabilizes and he has regained the ability to clot."

We nod in comprehension. The doctor shakes everyone's hand and leaves to talk to the intake nurse. The intake nurse says, "Oui . . . Oui . . . Bon . . . " picks up the phone and makes a call. Two orderlies arrive in two minutes and wheel Jerry away. Sheryl kisses Henri four times, shakes both his hands, says "Merci, merci," and follows Jerry to wherever they're taking him.

Henri looks at me and shrugs. "C'est normal."

I believe him. He shakes my hand, hands me his card with his cell phone number, and says, "If there's a problem, call me," and he leaves to help the next person.

I walk to the nurse and ask for Jerry's room number. "Quel numero est le chambre?"

She gives it to me and says, "Mais ce n'est pas possible de lui rendre visite maintenant." You can't visit him now.

I want to argue with her, but I don't know how.

On the way out, I see it is 12:15. In two hours and fifteen minutes, a doctor has been called, a house visit made, a diagnosis given; an ambulance called, a thirty-kilometer ride, admittance to the hospital, and a room. All with no money being exchanged—or even discussed—and on a Sunday morning. It costs more and takes longer to eat lunch at the 2nd Avenue Deli.

Donna and I drive back to the house and wait for Sheryl's call. She calls at two o'clock and tells us Jerry has his own room, and she's staying with him. She calls at five to say they've begun testing and examining to determine what's wrong. At seven, she says they think it is appendicitis, but they can't be sure without opening him, and they can't do that until his blood thickens. All everyone can do is wait.

From my visits to Monsieur and Madame P, I know French hospitals do not normally allow wives or husbands or family members to spend the night with a patient in a hospital room. For them, it's another person to answer to and take care of, which means more work. Sheryl, however, is not normal or French. At five foot one inch, one hundred and five pounds, she's cute as a canary and steely as bridge cable. She is not going to sway, let alone budge, and speaking no French, she conveys it. *Do not mess with me.* In the U.S., they would welcome her, tolerate her, or arrest her. In France, they ignore her, which means no one brings her a comfortable chair, blanket, or food. The plan is to starve her out.

Sheryl calls the next day at nine in the morning to say they operated on Jerry the previous night. His blood stabilized around midnight, and they opened him, found the problem—a blockage in his intestine—removed about a foot of it, and sewed him up. He's resting, and she's eating a croissant that one of the nurses snuck her.

In the U.S., that would be the end of it. He'd be walking that day and home the next or the day after. In France, it's just the beginning. In the U.S., surgery heals—so get up and out of bed. You're better, quit lollygagging about. In France, surgery hurts. It's an invasion—something the French know more about than Americans. Remember, the Third Republic: 1871, 1914, and 1940! After you're invaded, you need time to heal, recoup, and rebuild your strength, because one thing is certain: the next invasion isn't far away.

Meanwhile, by the third day, Sheryl has moved into the hospital. She has her suitcase, books, and is sleeping there. Instead of despising her, the doctors and nurses admire her spunk, her willful flouting of authority, even though the authority she is willfully flouting is theirs. It doesn't seem to matter. On the second day, an orderly brings her a blanket and pillow. On the third day, a nurse wheels in a cot. The fourth day, they are bringing two food trays to the room. The fifth day, two menus, and when Jerry tells the nurses about the special diet Sheryl's transplant medications require, they start bringing her specially prepared foods.

By the end of the *first* week, Sheryl is living with Françoise, the chief nurse taking care of Jerry. Françoise drives Sheryl to the hospital early in the morning and drives her home late at night, including the days she isn't working. She shops and prepares special meals for Sheryl according to her medical and dietary needs. Sheryl lives with Françoise for six nights. Françoise speaks no English, Sheryl no French. They become the best of friends.

After ten days, the hospital is ready to discharge Jerry —to Bénodet or Roscoff, or some other beachy paradise "pour récupération."

Jerry says, "No."

I tell him about visiting Madame P and how lovely it is.

Jerry says, "I want to go home."

I appeal to the shopper in him. "Tourists are spending thousands of euros a week to stay there. It's a deal, Jerry . . . a fully paid vacation—room *and* board." This is a guy who listens to four-hour spiels about time-shares in Reno to get a free night in Sacramento.

He says, "No," again.

I try the humanitarian approach. "*Sheryl* needs the rest. Do it for *her*. Hell, do it for me. Sign up and I'll go if you don't want to—as long as nothing invasive is required."

"I want to go home."

I understand, and I don't. Everyone wants to be home, in their own bed, when they're ill. But he's better now—and still in Brittany. He'll be home soon and long enough. Stay, enjoy the gift, the views, weather, sites, and food; take the rest your body needs to heal—but Jerry is adamant, and as much as Sheryl wants to stay, she knows they're leaving. It's part of their agreement: the one who is ill, if and when possible, makes the decisions.

Sheryl begins calling the airlines. Watching her is like watching a trader trying to close a deal: talking, threatening, cajoling, crying, yelling, until she convinces United Airlines to change their flight without paying their usual penalty.

On the twelfth day, Jerry is discharged without paying a sou, leaving a credit card, fingerprint, or body part—other than a foot of his intestine. He goes home healthy, almost healed, and not broke, in debt, or destitute. And he and Sheryl have a new friend, Françoise, who visits them two years later and lives with them for five weeks.

When the bill finally arrives in the U.S., Jerry's insurance pays it. The total is in the low thousands, about what he'd pay for an emergency room visit in the U.S. or a week for two in Cancun.

10 Things I've Learned about Health Care in France

1. Don't get sick or go to the hospital on a weekend or holiday, during the summer or a heat spell, probably not even during *midi*, and definitely not in August, when it's hot, there's no air conditioning, most of the doctors are on vacation, and those who are on duty wish they were not. In 2003, fifteen thousand people baked to death in their apartments and hospitals during a July-August heat wave. If I am unlucky enough to go to the hospital during one of those times, I want to *appear* to be very ill. It's the best chance I'll have of seeing a doctor and getting treated. Think "triage"—a French word, after all.

2. Mental Health Services: They are great if you're standing on the street screaming at passersby or yelling at yourself, or wake up thinking you're Napoleon. You'll be certified nuts, sent to a hospital, see a psychiatrist, and get drugs and therapy, all of it covered and reimbursed by Sécurité Sociale. The same is true with school-age kids with serious mental and behavioral problems: covered and reimbursed by Sécurité Sociale. But if you wake up feeling blue about your life, spouse, job, or kids, or you want to quit smoking or drinking, there are not many neighborhood counselors or rehab centers, especially in non-urban areas, and if you do locate one and utilize the services, in all likelihood you won't be reimbursed. The French attitude toward mental anguish is like the Anglo-Saxon attitude toward physical pain: suck it up—and French people do lots of sucking it up. France has the highest consumption of wine and spirits in Western Europe. Unless you're a kid or certifiably crazy,

it's the mental-health-from-a-bottle treatment plan, supplemented by pills and visits to the local priest.

3. Dentistry: French teeth look more and more like English teeth. Enough said.

4. Disability: If you're ambulatory and not too far below the intelligence norm, you're in luck. French services and supports are great. When Monsieur P was diagnosed with emphysema, the system went into action. He received a stipend to live on, home assistants to do his laundry, shop, and clean house; a visiting nurse on a regular basis; oxygen tanks delivered and replaced as needed; and when it became too difficult for him to climb the stairs with his oxygen tank, the state installed an electronic chair to carry him up the narrow, *curving* staircase to his second-floor bedroom and bath. But . . . If you're not ambulatory or are seriously below the official intelligence norm, there's very little support, encouragement—or *convenience*—to be or become independent. There are a lack of handrails, public benches and toilets, elevators, and powered wheelchairs. This, plus narrow streets, lack of sidewalks, cobblestones, speeding cars, old houses, and lots of stairs, make it not an easy place to be disabled and live an independent life. For that, I'm thankful for the U.S., especially Berkeley, California, and the San Francisco Bay Area, where Independence with a capital "I" is the goal.

5. Senior Services: If you're ambulatory, semi-compos mentis, have money and a large family living nearby who actually like you, you're OK. If not, see Disability, above.

6. General Health: As everywhere, French people are paying more for medical services and insurance and getting less. Still, they have an affordable, universal health care system

that covers 100 percent of the legal residents in France for hospitalization, doctor visits, home-health care, and non-medical support frills like cooking, shopping, cleaning, and driving; prescription drugs and lab tests; nontraditional and non-Western medicine; posthospital recuperation; choice of doctors; ambulance and emergency room coverage; pre- and postnatal care, including fully paid family leave for mothers *and* fathers before *and* after a baby is born; stipends for having kids and subsidized day care for kids under two; vision allowances; hearing aids; and prosthetics. The United Nation's World Health Organization ranks the French medical system number one in the world. The U.S. ranks thirty-seventh. The U.S. ranks thirty-eighth in the world for longevity. France ranks tenth—imagine where they'd be if they had air conditioning!

7. The four cardinal rules of French medical services are also the rules for French life. Rule Number One: *No physical pain.* If you feel it, treat it. If you think you feel it, treat it. If maybe, sometime down the road you could possibly feel it, treat it. Suffering in France is reserved for the mind, the soul, the spirit, the metaphysical and metaphorical heart; it's for poetry and philosophers and chanteuses, not for the body. For the body, there's Merck and Johnson & Johnson . . . When I go to the pharmacy for Monsieur or Madame, I always return with a shopping bag full of painkillers. The first day I visited Jerry after his operation, he was lying in bed, happy and drowsy, pumping away at his morphine dispenser, oblivious to everything around him except his thumb. Physical pain is a no-no. Mental and spiritual pain are inherent to life.

8. Rule Number Two: *No hunger.* Food is ubiquitous, plentiful, and good. It smells good, looks good, and *tastes* good—and

there are seconds, thirds, fourths, and fifths if you want them. Every time I visit someone in the hospital, the food tray is there and something's always on it to eat and drink. When patients are ready, they are given a daily menu offering choices of *poisson, viande, laits,* and *poulet* for *midi.* Some have wine: white, red, or rosé. Others have two desserts. The lactose tolerant have cheese. It's like Air France, except here the seats fully recline and the only turbulent air is your own.

9. Rule Number 'Three: *Privacy and politesse.* Nurses and doctors and orderlies are polite. They address you as an adult, "Madame P" or "Monsieur K," not some infantilized Annie, Bobby, or Jerry. They shake hands with the guests-cum-patients and say, *bonjour,* when they enter the room and *au revoir* or *à bientôt* or *à tout à l'heure* when they leave; *s'il vous plaît,* before they touch you, and *merci* when they're done. They knock before they enter, and wait to hear *entrez* before they do. French people value their privacy and do not like surprises. Hence, all the doors are closed. No one—not even a doctor—can walk down the hall and witness someone's private moments.

10. Rule Number Four: *No rush.* The only way to get out of the hospital in a day or two is not to go in. A splinter in France is not a splinter. It is a breakage of the skin, a rupture, a foreign invasion, and if not an actual problem yet, a potential one: *infection.* And unlike unemployment, strikes, immigrants, or farmers dumping artichokes and milk on the highway, this *is* something they can do something about, so they order more tests and prescribe more drugs. Anything that *could* possibly happen must be explored and stopped and treated so it won't happen—and all of that takes time, a resource French people excel at using.

"Je Voudrais Une Con Avec Deux Boule..."

Before I bought my house in Plobien, I thought French was the most beautiful language in the world. Now, I think it's the most difficult. It's not the language per se—which is no more difficult than Finnish, Hungarian, or Xhosa—but the precision with which it must be used. French people care more about the precise usage of French than they do about the precision of their products, which is why the Académie Française is more important than the French Better Business Bureau, and why I'm a functional illiterate and my thermos and vacuum don't work.

I Am, I Have, I Go

I know words—lots of words—especially cleaning, plumbing, and hardware words. I understand most signs (except road sign directional arrows) and can communicate with anyone willing to listen to me: people with lots of time, goodwill, and fortitude, who are mostly my friends; strangers who don't know better; and shopkeepers who wish to make a sale. I'm like the peasant in those movies set in the dark ages or India who hands a piece of paper to a scribe, asking him—it's always a he—to read it to me and write a reply. If France had a twelve-step program for illiterates, every day would begin like this: "Bonjour. Je m'appelle Marc, et je suis *illettré*." As far as I know, no such program exists, so I don't have to say it, but I think it and feel it most of the time.

I didn't set out to be illiterate anymore than Lou Gehrig set out to have Lou Gehrig's disease. In my dreams, I sound like Charles Aznavour and Yves Montand. I write like a transplanted Beckett. However, between my dreams and my tongue falls reality—and the reality is I can't speak, read, or write anything a French person would consider to be French, though it's not for the lack of trying.

Years before I bought the house and entered my French life, LeRoy and I enrolled in a conversational French class at Merritt College, where we both taught U.S. history. We enrolled to meet women, though we weren't opposed to learning French. We believed learning French was the kind of useless, interesting activity intelligent women were likely to do.

The class was an evening class, and good students that we were, we got to the first class early. The room was full, standing-room only, and lots of good-looking women were there. The teacher, a good-looking woman herself, began speaking French—and never stopped. No English at all. Nada . . . Nadda word. LeRoy and I sat there studiously listening when all of a sudden, a quarter of the students raised their hands. Fifteen minutes, I thought, and I'm already sixteen behind.

"What do you think she said?" LeRoy whispered.

"'Are you registered for this class?' That's what I always ask."

We raised our hands.

The next thing we know, we're sitting in the smart people's group, where we discover the question was, "Who's taken French before?" We then did what every upwardly mobile student driven by success and fear of failure and foolishness does in this situation: we volunteer. We volunteer to find a dozen more chairs. We volunteer to carry the chairs into the class and to set them up. We volunteer to find chalk, colored markers, and erasers; we show the teacher, a Madame Gironde, where the projector is, how to use it, where to locate a screen, get copies made, find the dean, the faculty bathroom, coffee during the break, a water fountain, the mail room, maps. We volunteered so much we were hardly in class. The one thing we did understand was none of the interesting women were interested in us. By the third class, the only question remaining was whether LeRoy or I would be the class dunce. Having no incentive to find out, we quit. I lived the next fifteen years perfectly content with subtitles. Then, I bought a house in France . . .

I returned to California determined to learn French. I began at Alliance Française in Berkeley, where I quit after two months because they were way over my head. Later, I enrolled at the Piedmont Adult School, where I quit because *I* was way over my head. Finally, in the privacy of my home, I watched *French in Action* videotapes, which by lesson number nine became French inaction, because I stopped doing the homework. I never got beyond *être, avoir,* and *aller*—I am, I have, I go. It's my version of veni, vidi, vici, minus the conquering . . .

Bon Usage

I can't pronounce the R, so I turn it into W, making Roissy Woissy, and sound like Elmer Fudd speaking French. My friend Thierry becomes sherry—or worse, *chéri*—which thankfully he never figures out or responds to. To say *pain* and *vin* correctly, I have to hold my nose to nasalize, not the most polite way to shop for bread or wine. Imagine: I walk into a store, hold my nose, and say, "Le pain, s'il vous plaît." How's that going to go over? The only good news is H is silent and I never have to pronounce it, like in New York.

Then there's gender. This is a language where every word has sex. No wonder French people are considered lascivious. Melons and vaginas are masculine and cars and motorbikes are feminine. There's no logic to it. You can't figure it out. You learn it osmotically or genetically by being French. On several occasions, I've introduced myself as an American girl—"Je suis américaine," and I've changed the sex of both of my neighbors, calling Françoise (*Françwaas*) François (*Françwa*), and vice versa, thereby outing them and their heterosexual partners as either very butch couples or transsexuals—and that's not even the worst of it.

The worst is *you*. In English, there's one you—there's only you—which makes speech easier and simpler, though definitely not clearer. In French, there are two, a formal (*vous*) and a familiar (*tu*), thereby acknowledging the complexity of life and making it even more so. You would think having two yous and recognizing different categories of relationships would be helpful, but it's not.

I've asked all my bilingual friends in France—Henri, Jean, Sharon, Gilles, Tatjana, and Bruno—when to use *tu* and *vous*. No one knows. Sure, they all say use *vous* if the person you're speaking with is superior to you in age, education, status, profession, income, and stature, which is easy if she or he is ninety years old with a PhD, a doctor or a lawyer, making 200,000 euros a year, six foot five, with the Croix de Guerre— or a complete stranger. Short of that, there's trouble.

For example, you're introduced to your wife's second cousin for the first time, or a new colleague, classmate, roommate, neighbor, or best friend's girl- or boyfriend, and before you say a word, you have to assess if the person is older, smarter, or richer than you—thereby asking yourself every day, in every new encounter, is this person superior to me? In the U.S., land of equality and individualism, the answer is universally no, and the inferior go around feeling superior. In France, land of *liberté, égalité, et fraternité,* the answer is also no, but the response is yes, because people fear committing faux pas and thereby publicly affirming their inferiority to their inferiors.

The result is I say *vous* to everyone: Jean and Sharon's sons, Noé and Yann; Marie and Gaëlle, whom I've known since they were teenagers; Gilles and Tatjana's two young boys; *everyone,* including my closest friends and Monsieur and Madame P, is *vous.*

Mostly, people ignore me, but Louis and Jocelyne, my former next-door neighbors, tell me it's jarring and grating to hear *vous* when they're tutoyering me. The way they say it, I suspect it might even be offensive. Still, I hold the line and continue to say *vous,* because I know once I cross it, I'll have the same problems French people have, and I need those problems even less than they do.

This works until the day Monsieur and Madame P, who have been tutoyering me for years, demand I tutoyer them *and* call them Joe and Yvonne. I cringe just thinking about it, but not to do so after they ask would be disrespectful—the last thing I wish to be. So I compromise: I continue saying *vous* and call them Yvonne and Joe when I have to, like when introducing them to friends. "C'est Yvonne. C'est Joe." But mostly I try to say as little as possible, and even that often turns out to be too much.

The problem is, if you ignore conjugation, pronunciation, gender, and grammar, as I do, French *appears* to be easy.

For one thing, there are a lot fewer French words than English. The *Petit Larousse* has about 75,000 words; *Webster's Third New International* has 470,000. The average French person uses 3,500 words, with 1,500 being the minimum for everyday life. The average American uses 10,000. For someone trying to speak French, this is a major plus.

Even better, more than one-third of English words originate from French, and many of them are the same: words like bureau, comment, loin, chose, bras, pays, ton, store, and main. Unfortunately, they have different pronunciations and meanings in French. Still, it's comforting to see these words, and it makes French feel familiar and accessible to people who know nothing, like me.

It also helps that French is literal, logical, and rational. You can almost see the language developing: apple is *pomme*; potato is *pomme de terre*, apple of the earth; sky is *ciel*; rainbow is *arc en ciel*, arc in the sky; earth is *terre;* earthquake is *tremblement de terre;* to fall or faint is *tomber par terre;* a butterfly is *papillon;* a moth is *papillon de nuit,* a butterfly of the night; a mouse is *souris,* a bat is *chauve-souris,* a bald mouse. Pretty clear—except for the bald mouse.

The truth is the vocabulary *is* relatively easy. It's the *bon usage*—using the right word, tense, grammar, pronunciation, gender, and form, as well as making incomprehensible chain-reaction-like *liaisons* between the consonant at the end of one word and the vowel at the beginning of the next—that's bewildering. It's like driving: the cars are small, fast, efficient, familiar; the roads are great. I get behind the wheel and everything is where it should be—mirrors, signal, horn, brakes, lights, defroster—and I think, I know what I'm doing, and then I drive in circles and get lost.

In English, I end a business letter with "Sincerely." In French, it's "Nous vous remercions, et vous souhaitons bonne réception de notre courrier": We thank you, and we hope you like what our letter says. This is from a chimney repair person I met once. How do you construct a sentence like that? And why? In French, it is proper, formal, florid, and clear, conveying mood, intent, and content. In English, it's a waste of time, ink, words, paper, and space—and reads as insincere. In American English, people tend to write as they speak, unless they're lawyers. In France, people try to speak the way Proust writes.

In English, *what* a person says matters most: "Je suis ici hier." I am here yesterday. It isn't elegant or proper, but it is understandable to a French person, which is what's most important to an English speaker—and the most important difference between English and French.

In English, if you're understood, make your point, and convey the required information accurately—*Je suis ici hier*— you have successfully communicated. Not so in French. In French, it's *how* you say it, and if you don't say it correctly, properly—and in intellectual conversations cleverly and wittily, not half-wittily, as I do—the message you convey is you arrived yesterday, *and* you're a dolt, which is exactly why so many French people who can speak English won't. They don't wish to be judged and found intellectually and aesthetically lacking.

It used to annoy me that French people who studied English for eight years in school, and who spoke it and understood it better than I ever would French, let me struggle and make a fool of myself. Like most Americans, I attributed it to French arrogance, some inferior French need for superiority, the taking of perverse pleasure, even sadism—the Marquis de Sade was French, after all. But now I know better, or at least more.

French people worry about using the wrong word, pronouncing or spelling it incorrectly, and not knowing proper punctuation and grammar—*in French!* No wonder most people would rather waste hours and painfully struggle to understand my French than make life easier for themselves and speak "bad" English. For me, there is no choice: *Je m'appelle Marc, et je suis illettré.* French people do have a choice and until very recently they've mostly chosen not to speak English. If I were them, I'd be even more afraid of speaking French. Slowly, though, things are changing. Lately, more and more people are speaking English to me—partly because using English words has become trendy, and partly, I think, because I've lowered the foolishness bar so much, they know they can't fall under it. You'd think this new willingness to speak English would make communication easier, but it doesn't. French-English is often more difficult to comprehend than French-French, especially proper names. Add deconstruction, cultural relativism, structuralism, and post-structuralism, and it's a miracle anyone understands anyone—and most especially that anyone understands me.

Savoir Faire and Not

Given *bon usage* and communication differences, it's not surprising I'm an illiterate. What is surprising are the advantages there are to being one—like when Mom and I land at Aéroport Charles de Gaulle and Air France loses her luggage. We immediately go to customer service, where, astonishingly, someone is there who is pleasant, apologetic, and helpful, confirming that indeed we are in another country. The woman assures us she'll have Mom's bag back in an hour and gives us each a coupon for a free lunch.

It's eleven in the morning French time, five in the morning in New York, and Mom and I both want breakfast—cereal, fruit, yogurt—not a ham sandwich, salade Niçoise, or quiche for lunch. I tell Mom to sit at a table and I'll take care of it. Mom speaks French and I don't, but this, I figure, I can handle. I go to the counter and order two bowls of fresh fruit and two containers of yogurt by pointing at them and saying, "Plus pain, beurre, et deux grande café crème," and hand the very professional eighteen-year-old behind the counter the coupons, politely adding, "s'il vous plaît."

He takes them, looks at them, studies them, and becomes serious. His face changes from a nonchalant-on-top-of-the-world-could-not-care-less professional to merde! I feel sorry for him. He probably just began his shift, is happy to have a summer job—maybe gets free or reduced flight privileges—and all he wants is to get through the day without doing anything wrong, and he draws me. He hands me back the coupons and points to the box boldly marked with an X: *déjeuner*/lunch. Then he points to the other boxes: *dîner*/dinner, *boissons*/drinks, and *petit déjeuner*/breakfast. We've been approved for free lunches, not free breakfasts, and he shows me the premade ham and cheese, ham and lettuce and tomato, and ham and butter sandwiches; prepackaged chicken salad, salade Niçoise, and quiche lorraine. There's also croque monsieur and madame and giant hot dogs floating in a huge glass jar, reminding me of a headless Walt Disney and cryogenics.

"Un moment," I say, and walk back to Mom to see if she's changed her mind and wants lunch. She hasn't. She still wants breakfast, as do I.

I walk back to the youth, who looks professionally cool again, though a tad less sure than last time, clearly expecting me to order lunch.

"S'il vous plaît," I explain. "C'est onze heure ici . . . " I hold up two fingers hoping he understands them as eleven, not two, then point to the floor to show him I mean *here*, "en Paris. Mais en New York . . . " I point to somewhere far away, "c'est cinq heur . . . " I hold up five fingers: "en la matin. Nous prefer le petit déjeuner. S'il vous plaît," and I hand him back the coupons.

He refuses to take them and says something I'm probably glad I can't understand, which is another advantage of illiteracy: it keeps *me* in bounds. He stabs at the X in the *déjeunier*-marked box, and says, "C'est tout. C'est tout. Terminé." We're done.

This is ridiculous and absurd. I can have a free ham sandwich or salade Niçoise but not a free fruit bowl or yogurt. "Monsieur," I say. "S'il vous plaît . . . "

"Non." He crosses his arms over his chest. "Ce n'est pas possible."

I've entered the world of no. Neither of us is going to budge. It's the Maginot Line, with me playing the Germans. I'm waving the coupons in the air, repeating, "S'il vous plaît, s'il vous plaît . . . " and he's standing still. Luckily, it is late for breakfast and early for lunch and no one else is waiting.

Another youth, this one a supervisor—I can tell because he's wearing a tie—senses discord, as in 'who knows what foreigners will do?' He walks over to see what's happening, and says something to the lad, who responds immediately, excitedly, in great detail, *now* taking the coupons from my hand and showing the supervisor the marked box, and pointing and gesturing at me. In the U.S., I wouldn't tolerate it, and I'd do my best to one-up him. In France, I can't—so instead of becoming the ugly American I want to be, I become the quiet American I am, and lo and behold, like the Red Sea parting or an episode of *You Are There*, the entirety of French history unfolds before my eyes: from anarchy to authority, protofascism to existentialism, chaos to rationalism, the Reign of Terror to the Rights of Man. *Enlightenment.*

The supervisor, destined for the Pantheon, becomes a combination Talleyrand, Voltaire, Hugo, and Rousseau. He takes the coupons from the outraged youth and slashes a giant X in the box marked *petit déjeunier*/breakfast, and it's done. The supervisor is happy because the incident is over and his authority has prevailed. The lad is happy because *he* didn't make the decision that violated the rule. Mom and I are happy with our yogurt and fruit bowls for breakfast. None of this would have happened had I been French or literate, and it's another lesson learned—illiteracy brings out the kindness of strangers, and, as an added bonus, works well with authority and the stubborn.

Mom and I finish our breakfasts and go back to customer service. The same lady is still there, *and* she has Mom's bag. She found the person who mistakenly took it, called him on his cell phone, and had the bag back at the airport in ninety minutes. Had I been the person she called, I wouldn't have understood a word she said. Illiteracy does have its downsides—like if the French Publisher's Clearing House knocked on my door, I'd probably send them away. Ignorance is bliss, and what you don't know can't hurt you—until, of course, it does.

Le Mal Mot: The Wrong Word

When I first arrived in France, I couldn't say much, so I didn't. I pointed and used lots of nouns, some of which were actually correct, and I spoke in first person present tense, making me the be-here-now-live-in-the-moment kind of guy I always wanted to be in California and an idiot in France.

The good news is every year I learn more words. The bad news is I use them.

One day, in a mood of joyous enthusiasm, I say to Jean, "J'aime beaucoup mon vie en France." I love my life in France. I say it because I can, and it's true.

Jean shakes his head. "Marc, do you know what you're saying? You love your dick. You love your dick in France. *Mon* vie is your dick. *Ma* vie is your life." All the while, he's pointing to his crotch, repeating, "Mon vie, mon vie . . . "

I now say, "J'aime beaucoup ici," I love it here, and leave it at that.

I return from an afternoon at the beach and see Madame lugging a five-gallon bucket of water from the shed to the veggie garden she has at my house—a distance of about seventy feet. I take the bucket from her and make three trips, then drive to Leclerc and buy a hundred-and-twenty-foot hose so neither one of us has to carry the bucket again.

The next day, Monsieur Boom-Boom, the neighbor who cuts my grass every two weeks, stops by to give me three bottles of his homemade cider. LeRoy and I call him Mr. Boom-Boom, because the first time he came to the house and saw the large dining room-living room with its two huge fireplaces, he said, "Deux chambres, deux cheminées, deux femmes, boom-boom," and banged his fist into his palm in one of those universal ways men have of conversing about sex.

I start to tell him about the hose so he won't run over it and shred it when he cuts the grass, but stop because I don't know the word for hose. "Moment," I say and open the English-French dictionary I always keep handy. "Je achete Madame P le *chaussette*."

His eyes become disks.

I knew it was good to get the hose, I didn't know it was *that* good, so I add, "le *longe* chaussette." The long hose.

The disks become wheels.

After he leaves, I open the dictionary again and see *chaussette* is the *second* definition for hose. The first definition, the one I want, is *arroseur*: garden hose. *Chaussette* is hose—short for hosiery. I just told Monsieur Boom-Boom I gave Madame P a pair of stockings . . . Long ones . . . And it gets worse.

It's four in the afternoon, *goûter* time, and I want some tasty-zesty-creamy French artisanal ice cream: two scoops of chocolate in a handmade waffle cone with a dab of whipped cream on top. I step up to the counter and immediately forget the word for cone, which is *cornet*. This happens to me often, and when it does, I do one of two things: I get flustered and frustrated and say anything French that comes out of my mouth—like *bonjour* when I'm leaving. My other, more thoughtful response is to conjure the word. For example, placing the accent on the last syllable of an English word often makes it French: attach-*ment*, continu-*er*, préserva-*tif*—which also unfortunately means condom—conspirat-*eur*, terr-*asse*. It works about half the time, which are pretty good odds until I realize it fails half the time.

This is one of those failed times. The word I conjure for cone is *con*, which *is* a word, but not one you use out loud, in public, with strangers. It refers to female genitalia, which normally don't have much to do with ice cream—unless you're kinky, or me. It also means asshole, as in *You idiot!*

"Monsieur," I say, "Je voudrais une con avec deux boule chocolat et un peu chantilly, s'il vous plaît." I would like female genitalia with two chocolate balls and a little cream, please.

The suntanned fellow behind the counter stands there and stares at me.

"Je . . . voudrais . . . une . . . con . . . avec . . . deux . . . boule . . . chocolat . . . et . . . un . . . peu . . . chantilly, s'il vous plaît," I repeat, a little slower.

In the U.S., I would have been punched in the nose or bedded on the spot. In Brittany, I get two scoops of chocolate ice cream in a cone with a little whipped cream on top—and not even a wink.

Françoise invites Donna and me to her and Bruno's house for apéritifs. Françoise speaks a little English, tries not to, and understands a lot. Bruno is truly bilingual, and Donna, who actually studies and practices her French, is an excellent speaker and listener. In situations like this, as at Monsieur and Madame P's, where their son Henri is fluent in English, we speak French so Monsieur and Madame and Françoise won't be left out. After all, it's their country. Someone periodically stops the conversation and explains to me what's being said, and occasionally I add something that fits, or doesn't.

Bruno is watering the garden when we arrive at seven. Bruno is always working at something: mowing the grass in the dark, cutting trees in the rain, building a barbecue in ninety-degree heat, making a fence, planting, cooking . . . The only times I've seen him sit still are to eat, drink, or read. I've yet to see him wear long pants.

He puts down the hose, and we go into the house to start apéritifing. Bruno has the largest liquor cabinet of anyone I've ever met in France *and* the U.S. He even has twenty-five-year-old single malt Speyside Scotch, which hardly anyone I know drinks in France. Several times he's opened a bottle of fifty-plus-year-old cognac just to offer me a taste. He'll call on the phone and invite me over to try a particular wine, and then tell me all about it, giving me my own private wine tasting, all of which means Donna and I are in for some serious drinking.

Luckily, French people do not drink without eating—except for work, they don't do much of *anything* without eating—so there are sliced dry sausages, cashews, chips, and green and black olives to nibble while we drink white, red, and rosé wines. By nine thirty, I'm sloshed and hungry.

At ten, Bruno begins cooking dinner. He makes individual, fluffy, mushroom-onion omelets, which we eat with bread and butter and whatever wine is best to drink with eggs.

We drink and eat until one thirty, when Donna and I stand while we can. I kiss Bruno once and give Françoise the four-cheek kiss, and say, "Au revoir. Bonne nuit. Merci. La prochaine fois à chez nous. À demain. Merci." Goodbye. Good night. Thanks. Next time at our house. See you tomorrow. Thanks . . . It doesn't get much better than that from me.

The following evening, Donna and I are going to dinner at Sharon and Jean's. I'm waiting for Donna, who's upstairs changing socks or sandals or shorts or shirts, trying to decide what to wear. There's a knock on the door. I open it and see Bruno and Françoise. Bruno is clean-shaven, wearing a pressed

Hawaiian shirt, and pressed shorts—the first time I've seen him do so. Françoise is dressed as usual—clean-pressed slacks, bright, cheery blouse—and smells terrific. I'm perplexed—until I see an Île de Ré brochure in Bruno's hand and remember there was some conversation about their vacation on the Île the previous night.

"Merci," I say, and reach for the brochure. Bruno releases it, looking slightly befuddled.

"Entrez, entrez," I invite them in. "Mai, j'ai dix minutes parce que nous mangon à mes amis ce soir."

Bruno looks at Françoise in a way that makes me wonder what I just said. I repeat it in my head: I only have ten minutes because we are eating with friends tonight . . . It's clear to me, though it doesn't seem too clear to them, so I offer them a beer.

"Une bière?"

"Oui," they say, in unison.

I open two Heinekens, empty them into two glasses, and the three of us sit at the table looking through the Île de Ré brochure, waiting for Donna.

She comes downstairs and looks at them the way Bruno and Françoise looked at me. She kisses them twice on each cheek, says, "Bon soir," and sits at the table. Everyone is obviously confused.

Bruno and Françoise sip.

Donna and I peruse the brochure.

When Bruno finishes his beer, I pick up the glass, put it in the sink, and say, "Bon." I do the same when Françoise finishes hers. I wave the Île de Ré brochure, and say, "Merci."

Bruno stands, and says, "Merci."

Françoise stands, and says, "Bonne soirée."

They leave fifteen minutes after arriving—a record short visit in France.

"You know," Donna says, "I think they think you invited them to dinner tonight."

"No."

"Yes."

"I said 'we have to do this again.' *'Next* time at our place.' Not tonight. *'Next* time,' some time in the future . . . "

She points to the door, at the now departed, clean, and spiffily dressed Bruno and Françoise.

"Shit!"

We hurry next door where Bruno is already watering the lawn. Françoise is standing there, looking lost. "Bruno," I say, "J'ai une question—en anglais . . . Did I invite you to dinner tonight?"

He hesitates and looks at Françoise, who immediately answers in perfect English, "Yes!"

"Why didn't you say something?"

"I was embarrassed. I thought I made a mistake."

He was embarrassed. He's fluent in English, totally bilingual, understands French *and* English grammar better than I ever will, and he thought *he* made a mistake. Oh, my God! The social pressures on these people are unbearable. It's enough to make *me* feel sorry for them.

I invite them for dinner the following evening, and for the rest of the summer we joke about "dix minutes." It's *dix minutes* to do this, *dix minutes* until that, but the truth is I'm mortified I made Bruno feel bad because of my mistake, and I wonder how many others I've made I don't even know about.

You'd think after *mon vie, con, chaussettes,* and *dix minutes,* not to mention buying the wrong mattress cover three times,

I'd have enough incentive to start seriously studying French. Nope. In this regard, I'm like French people: they don't want to speak bad English; I don't want to study French if I can't learn it—and there's no doubt in my mind, I can't.

There's not a single non-French person I know—including those who spent a junior year in Aix, lived on and off in Paris, studied at the Sorbonne, have a doctorate in French from U.C. Berkeley, taught French at San Francisco State—who considers him or herself proficient in French. All of them express concerns that their French isn't good enough, clear enough, current enough, and that some French person will notice and say something, correct their use of an article or an archaic tense, or tell them that what they just said is now said in a new, cooler way and embarrass them.

I listen to all of these people speak French, watch them go back and forth from French to English to French, and I'm amazed at how they not only switch languages but thought processes and paradigms as well. To me, it's a miracle, but they only hear what's missing and wrong.

Peggy is quadrilingual, speaking and reading Italian, Spanish, English, and French. Her husband Larry speaks and reads Latin. Joanna taught herself Tamil and Vietnamese when she travelled to those countries. George taught himself Japanese. Leslie has a degree in French, teaches French at U.C. Berkeley, and has lived in France. Donna studied and speaks Russian and Japanese. *None* of them feels the need for perfection in any language but French. It takes Peggy three days to write a one-page letter for me in French, and that's only because I take it away from her and make her stop. I've seen Donna spend two hours with a French dictionary and grammar book answering a three-sentence email. Even Sharon, who grew up in bilingual

Quebec and has two French sons and is married to Jean and has lived in Brittany for forty years, does not feel fluent. She still makes mistakes in word use, spelling, tense, and gender that Jean and her boys correct. And Rick Steves, who has made a bazillion dollars writing French guidebooks says his French is "terrible," and that he's tone-deaf to French—but *not* to Italian or German.

Knowing this, and knowing I will never, ever (no matter what I do) approach the fluency of these people—and seeing and feeling their angst, doubts, concerns, and fears about what they don't know, I ask myself, who needs it—and I answer, not me.

Especially since the better you speak French, the *more* critical French people are. I've seen it with Donna. Because she speaks French well, people think she'd like to speak better—so they help her, and when they do, she does feel better because she knows more, and then she feels worse, because she'll never know enough. But when French people hear me speak, they say nothing. Often, actually, they're speechless, which personally I prefer, because if they did speak, I'd have to respond.

French people and I seem to have reached an agreement—unspoken, of course. I speak like an imbecile, and they give up correcting me. One sentence, a phrase, sometimes a word—*con*—and they understand it's fruitless.

In many places of the world, I'd be the crazy uncle in the attic and avoided—but in Plobien, Loscoat, and Brittany, I'm a curiosity. People come to my house to visit. They stop me in the village to speak. People *want* to know more about me. Unfortunately, I can't tell them very much—so their desire to know more increases. Thesis. Antithesis. Synthesis. It's a wonderful dialectical circle. The dumber and quieter I am, the more interesting. All I can figure is what I say is so inane people must either correct it in their own minds, thereby making it interesting or profound to themselves, or they turn it into metaphor and search for hidden meaning, like Jerzy Kosinski's Chauncey Gardner and his dumb-ass garden. Instead of being the incomprehensible, boring, illiterate dumb guy, I'm the writer/artist/ professor/ homeowner whom no one can understand. I have my own argot and patois. I'm the *Brother from Another Planet*, the Noam Chomsky of Plobien, L'Enfant Sauvage . . .

Somehow, I've joined the pantheon of untamed Americans who French people—with their zillions of rules and social constraints—appreciate for being unconstrained, natural, and free. People like Buffalo Bill Cody, Annie Oakley, Sitting Bull, Jerry Lewis, Lucky Lindy, Harpo, Charlie Parker, James Dean, the Three Stooges, Clyde and Bonnie, and me . . .

10 Things I've Learned about Speaking French

1. Now that Brexit has been voted in and England will be separating itself further from the European Union, more and more French people are speaking English. In some circles, it's even the cool and classy thing to do. Someday, perhaps, French people—like many Europeans—will be bi-, tri-, and English-lingual. Until then, When in France, speak French. When speaking with a French person, speak French. When in a French-speaking country or region, speak French. If a person speaks to you in English, speak French, as the odds you'll misunderstand are greater than the odds you won't.

2. Think like a three-year-old, or the parent or grandparent of a three-year-old: When asking for something, say please: *s'il vous plaît*. After getting what I asked for, or any reasonable facsimile of what I asked for, or after any serious effort to get what someone else thinks I asked for, say thank you: *merci*. When meeting anyone, a dear friend or a stranger, and when entering any shop, business, office, enterprise, or agency, including the post office and bank, say hello: *bonjour*. When leaving any of the above, say goodbye: *au revoir*. Anything more is gravy, so ladle it on. Bad French—at least for a foreigner, *especially* an English-speaking foreigner—is better than no French. *C'est vrai*.

3. Nouns are more important than verbs, and pointing is often clearer than speech.

4. There's no way to know how to pronounce the words weight, knack, like, and cease just by looking at them. It's the same with a lot more words in French. The best way to learn how to speak French is to listen to French and repeat what you

hear. If I look at the word, I have to figure out how and when to pronounce the last letter, which syllable to accentuate, and what to do with the all but impossible to pronounce *ou* and *r*. The downside is if I *don't* look at the word, I won't know how to spell, read, or write it—which doesn't matter when I'm speaking, but is hell when writing or reading a note.

5. Familiar words are the most dangerous. In American English, mercantile means commercial. In French, it means money-grabbing. In American English, I go to an art exhibit. In France, I go to an exposition. In American English, the word expose has the smell of sex. In France, exhibit does. You don't want to say, "Je vais a l'exhibition," unless, of course, you did, *and* you want everyone to know.

6. Americans speak in positives and superlatives; it's wonderful! Great! Terrific! Incredible! Amazing! French people say *bon*—everything is good: *bonjour, bonne journée, bon dimanche, bon shopping, bonne lecture, bien mangé, bonnes vacances, bonne fête*—or *merde*. Ask an American how he or she is feeling and you're likely to hear great—terrific, perfect, wonderful, couldn't be better. Ask a French person, and it's *ça va*, it's going—and it's said in a way that tells you they don't expect it to be going too long. French people do speak of grandeur, magnificence, and the incredible, but they tend to reserve those words for lofty things like food, art, history, statecraft, and football—the first four of which most Americans pooh-pooh. American superlatives are reserved for themselves and Michael Jackson, especially now that he's dead. To French people, if you're always happy and everything is wonderful, you're a liar, a jerk, or American, none of which is a compliment . . . Unlike the U.S, criticism is what counts in France, not agreement.

7. French people don't casually sneer, which is probably why there's no world-class French rock and roll. They excel at love, loss, pain, malaise, romance, nostalgia, melancholy, outrage, ennui, passion, ridicule, fatalism, and mockery. For in your face, up your ass, drop dead, eat shit, go to hell, fuck you, motherfucker, they rely on Americans and Brits, and seldom are disappointed.

8. Americans make fun of themselves. Self-deprecation and personal foolishness are a huge part of American humor. French people are uncomfortable with both and don't want to be subjected to either. They appreciate and enjoy Jerry Lewis, the Marx Brothers, Abbott and Costello, and the Three Stooges precisely because these horrible things are *not* happening to them, but to someone else, like Americans or Belgians, who deserve them.

9. French people speak with great authority. No matter how circuitous the conversation or how much or little a person knows, she or he says it with great weight and command. English, at least American English—see that at least—is spoken with many qualifiers and qualifications, and the more a person knows, the more he or she *tends* to qualify. In France, the more a person knows, the more absolute he or she is—and tells you so.

10. French people always want to know if I'm English or American. I tell them, and I'm happy and thankful that after I say, "Je suis américain," less is expected of me than from any other people on Earth. Knowing that sets me free, allowing me to try, and fail, and try, and fail, again, and again, and again . . .

Afterword

What began as a trip has become a journey. I've learned a lot about France and Brittany over the years, and also a lot about me.

When I bought my house, I thought I was being bold, brave, a pioneer, an explorer. Even now, twenty years later, I'm amazed I did it—and even more amazed it has worked out for the best. At least, I think it's for the best. About France and things French, I'm much more forgiving and optimistic. In France, my glass is half full. In the U.S., where I know and expect so much more, it's half empty. In the U.S., the less I know, the harsher my judgments. In France, the less I know (and I know a *lot* less), the more accepting and accommodating I am, as I always assume *I'm* wrong. In the U.S., I assume it's the other person. In the U.S., everyone else is the problem. In France, it's me. In the U.S., I engage, question, doubt, and dissent. In France, I'm the yes-man, "Ah, oui, oui, oui." I've become bipolar: in France, I'm egoless; in the U.S., ego—super and regular—are the way I usually go.

When I bought my house, I could do little and say less. I relied on more than a bit of help from my friends. I still do.

Sure, I can say and do a lot more now, but I continue to get it wrong about a third of the time. Given my language skills, that's not surprising—but this is: never in my life could I have imagined that I'd fail so much and so often and be so accepting of it.

In the U.S., I plan things and most of the time most of them happen, even though I worry that they won't. In France, I also plan things and worry that they won't happen, and most of the time they don't, at least not in the way I planned them, but then they often turn out better, or at least seem to be better, or my French definition of better is worse, less, diminished, reduced. Whatever it is, I'm happier getting what I get in France than I am when I get what I want, or think I want, in the U.S. In France, I move through the seven stages of grief, from anger and denial to acceptance, very quickly. In the U.S., it's a Richter-scale struggle that more often than not ends short.

In the U.S., I never would have tasted oysters or langoustine or gone alone to Jacques's apartment after I totaled his car, and I'd be shamed and ashamed to be the know-nothing village idiot, but in France, I'm the child Picasso said it takes a lifetime to become. To me and the people who know me, it's an amazing and startling transformation. In the U.S., fear of foolishness deters my action. In France, foolishness is my only choice, and I make it every day.

One step forward, two steps back. Two steps forward, one step back. That's how it's been learning new rules, customs, and traditions . . . It *is* like being a child again: the good part is (as Picasso meant) it is freeing; the bad part (he didn't mention) is I'm dependent and inept. And because I'm not a child, it's even more difficult—a slower and more humbling process— learning and attempting to speak a new language. There, it's one step forward every summer, half a step back the other nine months, so every year I start over, unevenly making progress, relearning the same words and phrases, still unable to properly say "déliceux" or "Thierry".

I can't have an easy, flowing conversation with anyone, read a French newspaper with anything more than rudimentary understanding, or comprehend French packaging, instruction booklets, road signs, my electric bill, or any other official notice I receive in the mail, or worse, by phone, but I can drive, shop, bank, eat properly, cook, and get medical assistance with a tenable rate of success, and I have friends I care about, who care about me. It's not quite mastering the art of French living, but it's something, and certainly more than I, and probably everyone else, thought possible when I bought the house.

The biggest step is the first step, and it may actually lead to a leap, though to my greatest surprise and chagrin, I've discovered I'm not a leaper. I bought the house in France, and I married Donna. Those are the two great leaps in my life—and every time I enter a plane. The rest of my steps have been baby steps. In that way, I progress slowly, deliberately, inexorably, looking backward as much as forward, feeling happy and lucky to have the bolstering of my family's, friends', and Donna's words and hands, sometimes even believing I'm in control of my life, and knowing—ontologically—that I'm not.

It's a scary and exciting journey: flying blind, mapless, relying on instruments, occasionally breaking through the fog and the clouds into the clear blue sky and the light. If you're lucky, as I've been, you'll discover one or two glorious unforgettables that make and change your life for better, forever. *Quel surprise!*

Acknowledgements

Sometimes it takes a village to complete the task. In my case, for this book, it took four countries and a couple of continents. I want to thank the following people:

In the U.S.: Readers, helpers, commentators, kibitzers, schmoozers, and fixers; Timmie Chandler, Lucha Corpi, Bob and Loni Dantzler, Peggy De Coursey, Anne Fox, Roy Glassberg, Dorothy Greenside, Bob Grill, E. Sherman Hayman (Mur), Bruce Jacobs, Gerald and Sheryl Kramer, Marshall and Danuta Krantz, Leslie Meredith, Paula Panich, Janice and Warren Poland, Fred Setterberg, Bill and Helen Shyvers, Joanna Smith, Phillip Spitzer, Donna Umeki, Kate Vergeer, Le Roy Votto, George and Marion Wallach, Eric Weiss, and Kim Wu.

In France: Sharon Ahearn, Gilles Goulard, Bruno Lamezec, Sophie Picon, and Jean Rival for reading, editing, correcting, informing, supporting, and, to my great dismay, lamenting.

Also in France, for opening their hearts and homes and lives to me: Yvonne, Joe, Patrice, and Thierry Bastard, Eric

Behar, Nicole and Jo Bellec, Val and Alan Bennett, Xavier and Martine Bourrier, Charles Castan, Eric and Marcel Claude, Ella and Richard Cole, Michelle Cooper, Judy Datesman, Yvon Derrien, Christiane Dupuis, Christian Foix, Yvonne and George Goulard, Claude and Annie Jourdren, Dominique Kermoal, Françoise Lamezec, Christine Le Bellec, Bob and Christiane Le Lionnais, Jean-Pierre, Joëlle, and Gaëlle Le Meitour, Marie and David Le Meitour-Le Carrer, Jacky Link, Tatjana Lomic, Manu Maho, Noé and Yann Rival, Catherine and Olivier Roche, Gerard and Marie-Thérèse and Michel and Francine Tricoire, Fred and Muriel Vasseur, and Beatrice Vierne.

In Poland: Anna Augustynczyk, Magdalena Hildebrand, and Malgorzata Maruszkin, my editor, translator, agent, and friend.

In Hungary: Norbert Uzseka took me under his wing and brought me back to the U.S. by introducing me to his American colleague, Taryn Fagerness.

Back in the U.S.: Taryn took me under her wing and introduced me to her colleague, Deborah Ritchken, who read the manuscript, loved it, improved it, and became my agent extraordinaire, who brought the book to Skyhorse Publishing and my editors, Joe Sverchek, who made everything easier, and Marie Lambert, who saw possibilities I didn't see and made the book a better book.

And here we all are.

Voila!